W9-AZW-480

Jim Murray: An Autobiography

Jim Murray:
An Autobiography

···

JIM MURRAY

MACMILLAN PUBLISHING COMPANY • *New York*

MAXWELL MACMILLAN CANADA • *Toronto*

MAXWELL MACMILLAN INTERNATIONAL • *New York* • *Oxford* • *Singapore* • *Sydney*

Copyright © 1993 by Jim Murray

All rights reserved. No part of this book may be reproduced or transmitted in
any form or by any means, electronic or mechanical, including photocopying,
recording, or by any information storage and retrieval system, without permission in writing from the Publisher.

Macmillan Publishing Company   Maxwell Macmillan Canada, Inc.
    866 Third Avenue   1200 Eglinton Avenue East, Suite 200
    New York, NY 10022   Don Mills, Ontario M3C 3N1

Macmillan Publishing Company is part of the Maxwell Communication
Group of Companies.

Library of Congress Cataloging-in-Publication Data
Murray, Jim,
Jim Murray: an autobiography/Jim Murray.
            p.   cm.
Includes index.
ISBN 0-02-588151-5
1. Murray, Jim, date   . 2. Sportswriters—United States—
Biography. I. Title.
GV742.42.M87.A3 1993   92-30313 CIP
070.4′49796′092—dc20
[B]

Macmillan books are available at special discounts for bulk purchases for
sales promotions, premiums, fund-raising, or educational use.
For details, contact:

Special Sales Director
Macmillan Publishing Company
866 Third Avenue
New York, NY 10022

10 9 8 7 6 5 4 3 2 1

Printed in the United States of America

Acknowledgments

Thanks are due to Tim Hays, the demon literary agent whose idea this book was. Also to Rick Wolff at Macmillan who wet-nursed the project from the start and is a sports author of note himself.

Thanks, too, to Frank McCullough, one of the greatest newspapermen of our time, who made me a sports columnist in the first place, and to Otis Chandler, who, as publisher of the *Times*, okayed the hiring and held fast even when the Soviet Union's track team threatened to take their javelins and hammers and go home over something I had written in jest.

There are too many colleagues to thank individually, but special mention must go to the great Sid James, the first editor of *Sports Illustrated*, who was in my corner all the way, and Bill Dwyre, executive sports editor of the *Times* who never once said, No, we can't do that.

Contents

Jim Murray: An Autobiography

1

. . . .

I Saw Ruth Hit a Home Run

I was a Depression child. With all that connotes.

That means you never trust the system again. You know what can happen to it. That means you go through life never able to fully enjoy it. That means you have an ever-present sense of foreboding. I don't know how it affected other people but I have never been off a payroll in my life. I'm sure I would get the shingles if I didn't know I was getting a paycheck every day. I never quit a job in a huff. I swallowed guff.

I don't recommend it. It's just the way I was. A legacy of hard times, constant fear of the future. I was disgusting. Good Soldier Schweik. That's because the most terrible thing in life to me was to be out of work. I had seen what it did to people. To families. To marriages.

If someone had promised me in 1939 that I would make $32.50 a week for life if I would sign a paper, I wouldn't have hesitated.

I noticed in later life all those people who said money wasn't important to them always had plenty of it. I don't apologize for it but I never quibbled on a contract in my life. I was a terrible businessman. What I was, was a wimp.

But I knew I was a writer. When I arrived in Los Angeles in January 1944 I was the greenest of greenhorns. I had on a rust-colored overcoat you could have worn in the Bering strait (and the temperature outside was in the eighties), wing-tip shoes, button-down collar and maybe a vest. Do you know where City Hall is? glowered the city editor, James H. Richardson. No. Do you know where the FBI is? No. Do you even know where Figueroa Street is, for cryin' out loud? No, sir. Richardson threw his pencil down. Well, can you write?! he wants to know. "Oh, Mr. Richardson!" I cooed. "I can write like a son of a bitch!"

I got the job.

I was raised in Hartford, Connecticut, which is a nice place if you're going to be a literary man. It's not so nice if you're going to ship goods.

Mark Twain lived there. I think he wrote *A Connecticut Yankee in King Arthur's Court* there. My mother's family was from New London. My grandfather had put in all the sidewalks there in the early 1900s. He was a poker-playing buddy of the mayor's. My mother's brother, my uncle Mike, was buying an old New England home on Pequot Avenue one day, a lovely old place with cupolas hanging off it and elm trees all over the yard. He came to one of these hanging attic offices. It was a mess. Papers everywhere with scribblings on them, typewritten passages, notes. Hip-deep in scrap paper. "What's this?" snaps Uncle Mike. "The former own-er's," says the real estate man unhappily. "He was a slob," says Uncle Mike. "What do you want me to do with it?" asks the real estate man. "Burn it!" says Uncle Mike. They did. The home had belonged to Eugene O'Neill. He had written *Ah, Wilderness!* and *Desire Under the Elms* there. Ah, Uncle Mike!

I was raised by my grandparents. My father had been a drug-gist. He had lost his stores, I was told. I was too young to remem-ber. I don't know whether he was a poor druggist or a poor businessman. Either way, my parents got divorced.

Don't ask me how but my grandmother got custody.

I had heard my father had got caught selling liquor without a prescription. Every drugstore in the city in that Prohibition era did. Dad simply paid off the wrong people, I was told.

I knew one of them that sold liquor. My father used to take me to the fights with him. One night, as we changed streetcars, he dropped into a friend's drugstore. In the backroom, he began playing checkers. For money. He was a good checkers player. But, as he played, he kept getting up to go to the water cooler. As he did, his eyes kept getting redder. So did his nose. I kept begging him, let's go to the fights, Dad. When we finally did, his gait was unsteady, his speech slurred. My father was drunk. The water cooler was full of gin. It was my first lesson in the unwork-ability of Prohibition. Every drugstore in the city had a storeplace for gin. They made it in the bathtub. In later years, lots of times when I went to a fight, that image was superimposed on it.

My grandparents' house was full of uncles. I loved them. They were lively, funny, irreverent—and great sports fans. Every boy should have uncles like these. My earliest recollection is of them arguing about Dempsey fights. The first time I saw Jack Dempsey years later, I didn't know whether to curtsy, kiss his ring or genuflect. Or faint. Those sports heroes of those early days were larger than life. Gods. I drove Carl Hubbell to the airport once. I never had any trouble communicating with Pete Rose. But with Hubbell, my mouth was dry all the way.

My uncles—and my father—took me to fights, ballgames. I listened to World Series on crystal set radios. I learned math by computing earned-run averages and batting averages. The nuns in the parochial school I went to never could have provided that incentive. I learned more arithmetic figuring league standings than I ever could from If Farmer A has ten apples and Farmer B gives him four, how many will he have? The logarithms of sport we persevered with, no matter how complex. It took us longer to learn The Apostle's Creed than compound fractions.

If you're going to be president, I recommend you be born in a log cabin. If you're going to be a doctor, get a tolerance for bleeding. But if you're going to be a writer, I recommend a chronic illness.

I had two. The first was Saint Vitus' Dance, otherwise known in that day and age as a "nervous breakdown." I had that at the age of three or four. At the age of ten, I got rheumatic fever. I very nearly died. I had the last rites of the Church. Pleurisy and pneumonia complicated the issue. I hovered between life and death for a long while.

Bed rest is prescribed. And you have nothing to do in bed but read. So, I read.

I read everything. I knew as much about history as Toynbee. I knew about Hitler (from John Gunther's books) before some Germans did and certainly before any Americans. I corresponded with Eamon De Valera, the prime minister of Ireland (my grandparents had come from the county of Sligo sometime before 1880 and I had romantic notions about that poor benighted land).

People always think sportswriters are frustrated athletes, wannabees who weren't good enough. I tried out for my grade school baseball team, I actually got on the freshman team in college. But I never hankered for a career in sports. Anything but. I couldn't imagine anything worse than finding myself in center field in Yankee Stadium and expected to catch a long high drive in the bottom of the ninth of the seventh game of the World Series with my team one run ahead. I knew I could never catch it. I knew the one thing no athlete could have was imagination. If he thought what was at stake he could never catch that ball. I knew I couldn't. I was a choke hitter. Not my bat, my throat.

I didn't want to be a fighter, I wanted to be a promoter. I actually put on fights. Roped off a ring with clothesline, made matches (of neighborhood boys). When someone didn't show up, I would don the gloves and substitute. That is, until one day in Boy Scouts, I had a bout with a scout from another troop. His name was John McMahon. And he almost killed me. The rounds were only two minutes but I can still remember wondering why in hell the bell didn't ring when we had obviously been fighting (in my case, I use the term loosely) for a half-hour. Do you have any idea how long two minutes is when your nose is bleeding, your lip is cut, your knees are rubbery and you're trying hard not to cry? An eternity.

I had a happy childhood, given some reservations. Psychiatrists later asked me if I felt unwanted, dumped on my grandparents at an early age by my parents, but I don't think so. My grandmother, and later my aunts and uncles, loved me. I was spoiled, really.

Psychiatry doesn't know everything. Children accept the roles thrust on them by the world. It's adults who make the mischief. God save me from well-meaning adults. I remember a time when I was maybe happiest, we lived in a house right next to the railroad tracks. Quite literally the wrong side of the tracks (except that across the tracks were Hartford's iron foundries and chainsaw manufacturers).

I thought it was great. You have no idea what fun it is to be living right alongside tracks leading out into the great world of our dreams. Kids don't feel deprived. We thought we were the luckiest guys in the world to be living alongside a railroad track.

Oh, sure, the house shook at night when a fast express went by. But we had the whistles. The lovely whistles. A train whistle on a summer night is the most magical, seductive sound in the world. It sets you dreaming of faraway places, all the places you read about and want to go to. It makes you yearn to see them, to promise yourself you will.

We had more adventures on that railroad track and in the lumber yard next to it than I ever did when we moved to the fancier suburbs of West Hartford where life was easier and more genteel but less fun.

As I look back on it, I was a super-disciplined child. Some psychiatrists have since tried to convince me (not under analysis but just in ordinary conversations) that I must have toed the mark so assiduously because, deep down, I knew I dassn't goof up, dassn't test my position by staying out late, skipping school and so forth. Because I knew deep-down I had no legal right to be where I was. Slip up and I'd be handed over to one of my parents. Interesting, but I rejected it, as I did all psychobabble. I did what I did because that was the way I was. I never *wanted* to goof up. I hated goof-ups. I was boring by nature.

I was never really formed by familial attitudes. Being Irish, we lived in an opinionated atmosphere. But I learned more by observation than by listening. I remember, for instance, that I often have a greater sympathy for slumlords than the general population. This is because I used to accompany my grandfather sometimes to the house he had moved out of and rented out to another generation of immigrants. He used to get calls in the middle of the night to come fix a toilet that had been torn from its piping, or repair a hole that had been kicked through an attic floor.

These—I couldn't help but observe—were always the fault of the tenants, not the landlord. They would get in a fight and rip the toilet—or a light fixture—apart, kick a hole in a ceiling, break a door down to abuse their wives. Also, I knew they didn't pay their rent. But their trash barrels were full of bottles. Grandpa never said a word. But little boys have sharp eyes.

When the Depression came, four families were living in the same tenement. This made the one bathroom a lively place. One of the families that moved in was my own—my father and my two sisters. My sisters had gone with my mother in the breakup of the marriage but now she—like the rest of Hartford—had lost her job and had to move back with *her* family in New London.

That was my Broadway producer phase and I promptly wrote musical plays and pressed my sisters into being the chorus line. I had a show called the *Nevertheless Show*, which I've been meaning to show to Barbra Streisand. All it needed was a hit song.

I soon returned to sports and history. I adored my uncles, particularly my uncle Frank, who owned a big diner and dance hall in town, wore big diamond rings and smoked cigars. To this day, I love the smell of cigar smoke.

Frank was my roommate. We slept in a made-over attic room that was so hot in the summer you could float out of bed in the morning. He instilled his love of fights in me early. In later years, I never wrote a story suggesting it was too cruel a sport to continue to exist without thinking I should call up Frank and ask his forgiveness.

My uncle Ed was my gambling uncle. I always liked the epitaph a character in a checkered suit and phony diamonds gave my sister Eleanor at Ed's funeral. "They was better crapshooters and they was better pool-hustlers. But for one man for two events, I'd have to take Eddie. He was the best."

You remember that *Reader's Digest* series they used to run, "My Most Unforgettable Character"? Well, Ed, he was my most unforgettable character.

Ed was what they used to call the "black sheep of the family." As I look back on it now, I realize there were plenty of them, but Ed was the pioneer black sheep. He was the only one in the family who made night court. He made it regularly.

As I remember it, they were pretty tame arrests. Just Ed and a pair of dice—sometimes both of them loaded.

Ed's philosophy of life he used to express to me lots of times. It was simple and basic. Also, as it happens, misguided. "Work," he said, "is for horses and mules—and they turn their ass to it."

Ed's whole life was dedicated to not working for a living. He got clear to the sixth grade in school before he dropped out to take up crapshooting. He got on his knees behind the trash cans and, in a sense, never got up.

He was a dead ringer for the actor James Cagney. The same curly hair, round face, squashed nose, the same staccato talk, cocky walk, bad temper and restless energy.

He scandalized the family. He would come home drunk from the pool halls and pick fights with his brothers, my uncles and father. Some nights the police would come and my family—my aunts were as prim as nuns—would be mortified. As a kid, I sort of enjoyed it. I was safe. Ed loved me, too.

He had his dark side. He bullied my grandmother for money to bankroll his various cons. I dreamed of getting big enough to knock him downstairs. But I learned to stop fearing him when he stole my shoes once and slept with them under his pillow. (I told you times were hard.) I jerked the shoes back one morning. And, when Ed didn't attack me, I knew I was safe. He would never lay a finger on me. And, even though he made her life miserable at times, I never saw anyone as overcome with grief as Ed was at his mother's funeral.

Grandma always forgave him anyway. She always ascribed his antisocial behavior to a motorcycle accident he had been in as a teenager. It was my first lesson that a mother will forgive a son anything. When that boxer's mother in England climbed in the ring and began beating up the pug who had beaten up her son, I understood perfectly.

Ed cheated, of course. I used to come downstairs in the morning (well, *late* morning, Ed got up at the crack of noon) to find him boiling eggs and dice in the same pan. The eggs he ate. The dice he put in a wooden vise and bent them till they wouldn't come up a six or eight if you rolled them down Wilshire Boulevard all night long. Still, Ed was the first person I ever heard say, "You can't cheat an honest man." W. C. Fields made a movie by that same title years later.

Ed considered the world a "mark." A "mark" was a victim, an unsuspecting dupe who never seemed to know the dice were loaded, the deck was marked.

Ed, of course, was the ultimate "mark." I think he knew it. I remember once I pleaded with him to teach me how to shoot pool. He angrily refused. I was on my way home from a classroom at the time and Ed pointed to the books. "You'll make more money with them than you'll ever make with a pool cue," he told me.

One night, as I was on my way home from a job waiting on

tables (to pay my way through college), Ed came upon me in one of those illegal all-night clandestine clubs—I think it was called the Greek-American Club. I was playing a nickel slot machine. Ed pointed to the machine. "They don't make those for *you*, you know." I got the message.

I got a lot of messages from Uncle Ed. I saw how his lifestyle, as addictive as it was, as free as it seemed, was destructive. Ed knew it. Once, when, like any good businessman, he sought to expand, branch out, the results were catastrophic.

Ed had built up a poke of thousands of dollars, which he kept in a stove at the New Texas Wiener all-night hot dog shop on downtown Main Street. Ed didn't trust banks. Or bankers. He thought they were the ultimate hustlers. Besides, in those Depression years, banks sevened out all over the place.

Ed was almost as elated as Winston Churchill and the British government when Franklin Roosevelt took over the war contracts that the factories around Hartford had been awarded by the French government before it fell. The war plant boom might have built up the RAF but it also meant money in the stove for Uncle Ed.

He had an oilcloth crap apron with crap table markings on it, which he would carry to the places where the war-workers had their lunches. He also had the warped dice. He made almost as much money (relatively) out of the war as Pratt & Whitney.

So, like any good businessman, he looked into new locations. He took his crooked dice to Florida where the big boys waited. He faded them. But the big boys had their own boiled dice. Ed could hold his own with Pittsfield Dick and local guys named "Rocky," but he couldn't handle the major league hustlers like the Nick the Greeks and guys called "Lucky." He came home in a barrel.

Ed had this partner, one Johnny Pachesnik, insensitively known as "Johnny the Polack." (Ed's nickname was "The Gimp" because he had one leg shorter than the other—the family found out about his nickname when my grandmother had a caller looking for him one day and she asked my uncle, "What is it they call you, 'The Goat'?" "The Gimp!" exploded Ed, embarrassed.)

Ed and his partner, Johnny, had a card club (it really was a bookie joint) called the Parkville Young Democratic Club, which was a hoot because nobody in it ever voted and Johnny Pachesnik didn't even know who the governor was, never mind his congressman.

One night, a pal of mine, Jim MacIntyre, and I borrowed Ed

and Johnny's new Chevrolet to go to a prom. We owned an old V-8 but it had ripped upholstery, an uncertain gear shift (you couldn't back up, as I remember it) and a short in the headlights (apart from which it was fine). We left our car with the Parkville Young Democrats—there was a no-limit poker game and two open bottles of rye on the table at the time—and left for the prom.

At one o'clock in the morning, we returned the car. Johnny was passed out on the table at the time. Ed was conscious. But not very. We gave him his keys and left.

The next morning, I was awakened to a frantic phone call. It was Ed. "If anyone calls, you don't know nothin'!" he warned. "Well, that's easy. I don't," I told him. "What's this all about?"

What it was all about was that Ed tried to drive the car home to its parking lot that night and didn't quite make it. He put it into a iron streetcar pole instead.

Since the accident happened not too far from his rooming house, Ed scurried away and left the steaming car wrapped around the pole. He crawled into bed where his partner, Johnny, was already sleeping the sleep of the saturated inebriate.

Ed was wakened by the police barging through the door and shaking him and Johnny awake. "Are you John Pachesnik?" they demanded. "You're under arrest." That was not a new experience for Johnny but this he couldn't account for. "What for?" he asked. "For hit-and-run driving and leaving the scene of an accident."

Johnny, of course, had no idea what they were talking about. Or, rather, he was beginning to have a glimmer of an idea what they were talking about. He was the registered owner of the vehicle (Ed never liked to leave footprints anywhere for authorities). Someone else had wrecked it. Probably his partner's nephew. Off he went to jail.

Later that morning, Ed came downtown to bail him out. Pachesnik was livid. "You know what that lousy nephew of yours did?!" he demanded. "He wrecked our car last night! Wrapped it around a pole in Whitman Court!" "Shhh!" Ed told him. "He didn't wreck it. I did. I'll show you the bloody shirt when we get home."

The moral of the story is, if Johnny Pachesnik hadn't adhered to the code, had been indignant enough to rat on me, thinking I was at fault, there is no telling what calamitous consequences might have befallen our hero here. True to their code, neither he nor Ed ever told the police anything.

Justice never triumphed in this case. Johnny was able to persuade the police the car must have been stolen out of the parking lot and the thief wrecked it. The insurance companies were not fooled. They paid up. Then they canceled the policies—and any future policies Johnny might apply for.

Ed never married. I think he knew he'd make a lousy husband and father. He'd take himself periodically to a house of ill-repute he knew in New York City. I know. Because he took me there with him when he felt I was old enough. I lost my virginity to a girl called Rosa. She chewed gum the whole time.

My uncles formed me as much as anybody. We are a product of all the influences in our lives but I think a love of sports came from my father's brothers.

Ed showed me a sporting world I would not otherwise have known existed. He proved to me that fights were fixed, points were shaved, larceny was part of the human condition and skepticism is a useful if unworthy emotional response.

He left me with some words to live by which I have chronicled before:

Never bet on a dead horse or a live woman . . .

Never take money from an amateur—unless he insists . . .

Never play a house game whether it is a racetrack, a roulette wheel, or just a tired guy cutting a small pot . . .

Never play cards with a man with dark glasses or his own deck . . .

Never make change for a guy on a train . . .

Never play a man who's better than you . . .

Never buck a slot machine—they don't make them for *you* . . .

Never play a guy named "Lucky"—at anything . . .

Take your time chalking your cue—they'll wait.

He didn't live long—fifty-one years. He drank himself to death. I think he did it on purpose. He kept escaping from hospitals. What they call "rehab units" today. Ed didn't want to be rehabbed.

Maybe you saw the movie *The Hustler?* Paul Newman played the role of Fast Eddie? Well, that was my uncle Ed.

Jackie Gleason played the role of Minnesota Fats. Years later,

I met the real Minnesota Fats. Only he was really "New York Fats." His real name was Rudolf Wanderone. I met him when I was back in Illinois for the Du Quoin Hambletonian.

Fatty, as everyone called him, was living in Dowell, Illinois, at the time. He said he was "outta stroke" and was living with twenty-two cats and this voluptuous wife whom he shadowed all over the St. Nicholas Hotel. Fatty didn't trust his wife. Looking at her and looking at him, you could see why.

He made a beeline for me when he heard I was from L.A. Fatty had a gripe. "Them Hollywood bastids!" he would begin. "Im'na sue 'em! Every one of 'em! They stole my life story and din give me a penny! They changed my name to Minnesota but that don't cover 'em. I got my lawyer!"

I sighed. "Fatty," I told him, "Twentieth Century-Fox has 250 lawyers at last count—all of them Clarence Darrow. You sue them, they'll wind up owning your cats. Why don't you get in on the publicity? That's the way to go. Cop out. Say, Hey! I'm Minnesota Fats! Have-pool-cue-will-travel."

No way, Fatty told me. He was going to sue.

We dissolve a year. I'm back in Du Quoin at the St. Nicholas Hotel. The first day, this big, block-long Cadillac pulls up. It's Fatty. He has two-toned shoes, a hula shirt and Panama hat. He calls to me, "Hey, Murray, look here!" He opens the trunk. He has tearsheets with his picture on them. "Come see an exhibition by the original Minnesota Fats!"

He has taken my advice. He has become a television celebrity. He has gotten rich.

I was sad for Uncle Ed. He was born thirty years too soon.

Growing up in Hartford gave you a split personality. You were midway between Boston and New York, geographically and emotionally.

The pull of New York was that the glamor teams were there. It was the glamor center of the universe so far as sports were concerned. The real heavyweight champion was the one recognized by New York State. The WBA was just a bunch of farmers.

And the glamor players were in New York. The Yankees, Giants and Dodgers were there. Babe Ruth was there.

I'm happy to say I saw Ruth. In his last season with the Yankees. I actually saw Babe Ruth hit a home run. One of the last he would ever hit.

I can still remember the awe I felt walking down the hill from the Grand Concourse for my first sight of Yankee Stadium. Lancelot couldn't have been more overcome if he suddenly saw the Holy Grail glimmering in the distance. I remember details about that September day. The crooner Russ Columbo had died and the tabloid headlines were full of it.

You had to painstakingly save up for a trip to New York in those days. The excursion fare on the train was only two dollars round trip. You could stay at a YMCA for twenty-five cents a night. You could buy a T-bone steak for fifty cents.

But that was big money in the Depression. And a box seat was $1.65 (surprisingly, baseball prices have gone up over the years less than any sports ticket I know of).

The Yankees were playing a doubleheader against the hated Philadelphia Athletics that Labor Day. So, it was a double-dip for me. I got to see not only Ruth but my *other* favorite ballplayer, Jimmie Foxx, of the A's. Old Double X, the newspapers called him, he of the bulging biceps and powerful thirst.

My companion, Alvar Kraft, and I were barely settled in our seats when it began to rain. This was highly unsettling when Babe Ruth came to bat—I think it was in the third inning—and hit one out. On looking back, I think it must have been about his seven hundredth career home run but we didn't pay attention to those things to the extent we do today. After all, every time Ruth came to bat he would probably break the all-time home run record. He broke it—what?—six hundred times? He broke it every couple of days for twenty years.

I remember feeling it was somehow anticlimactic. An uneasy feeling. I remember Red Kraft turning to me and saying something like, "Is that all there is?" I don't know whether we expected to break out in hives or faint or get transported into a wave of ecstasy or what, but there was Ruth trotting in that mincing way of his around the bases, tipping his cap—the crowd was modest—and disappearing into the dugout. And no doves flew out of our ears.

It was, looking back on it, my first lesson that the event itself had to be dramatized. We were there, in a sense, because we had been lured there by years of purple prose. The home run itself was hardly a cataclysmic event. But Grantland Rice made you think it was.

But then another terrible fear erupted. Suppose the game got rained out?! The home run wouldn't count! Horrors! It was only the third inning when the Babe hit it out and the rain was coming down in steady sheets.

We got very depressed. We would never be able to say we saw Babe Ruth hit an "official" home run. Our life would be in ruins.

We needn't have worried. Baseball teams in the Great Depression were not about to have future gates sullied by rainchecks. They would have played the doubleheader in an ark if they had to.

We got thoroughly soaked. They played a full eighteen-inning doubleheader in conditions where they should have taken canoes on the basepaths. But we saw Babe Ruth hit a home run. At the time, I thought they should have put it on my epitaph.

The next year, we went down to see the Giants play. The Polo Grounds was no less a shrine to us than Yankee Stadium. After all, the year before, hadn't the Giants' Carl Hubbell struck out Ruth, Gehrig, Foxx, Simmons and Cronin in a row?

We never got to see Hub pitch. It rained. This time, the Labor Day doubleheader was wiped out.

If New York was where it was happening, Boston was where the heart was. The Red Sox owned New England. Their games were broadcast all over New England. New York had the Yankees but the real Yankees preferred the Sawks.

Like the rest of baseball, they were hardly economically competitive with the Yankees. But they had a millionaire owner, Tom Yawkey, who tried to keep up. But he never got championships. He got rosters full of spoiled brats, alcoholics, malingerers, goof-offs. In 1941, the curmudgeonly columnist Dave Egan was to write, "On the other hand, Master [Ted] Williams was carrying on his slim, young shoulders a lot of tired veterans, pleasant yes-men and family retainers. The Red Sox are not a baseball team. They are a country club."

The label stuck. Decades later, the public image of the Red Sox was still that of dilettantes, playboys, pampered pets. The truth of the matter was, Yawkey couldn't match the Yankees' cash flow. The Yankees had all the chips, market superiority with concomitant broadcast and ad revenues. I began to perceive the Yanks as an economic hegemony, not athletic. That formed me. Some years later, I was to write a piece for *Life* magazine titled "I Hate the Yankees" in which I conclusively proved my point: The Yankees outhit everybody in the counting room before they could do it on the field. A rueful outgrowth of that was to see the line "rooting for the Yankees is like rooting for U.S. Steel" for evermore ascribed to Red Smith. Red didn't say it. I did. In the *Life* piece. I lived with it. Because I have since had many things I never said ascribed to me. I call it "the Dorothy Parker syndrome." Journalism is, at best, an imprecise science.

I went to the minor league Hartford ballpark every chance I got. I was always struck by how few of the hopefuls ever made it to the big leagues. There were only two hundred players in the big leagues in those days and there was a proliferation of minor leagues. I can remember only one local favorite who made it up there, Sibby (for Sebastian) Sisti, a journeyman infielder with the Braves and a utility player. He had been a big star, a can't-miss, for Hartford. But he hit only .244 in an undistinguished big league career. It was another lesson. Many are called but few are chosen.

My father took me to my first World Series game in 1938. We saw Game Four of that Series between the Chicago Cubs and the Yankees. It was a disappointment. I had begun to hate the Yankees by that point and on this day, so did the paying customers—even though it was Yankee Stadium. They littered the field with torn papers in the late innings to show their annoyance. The Yankees, typically, were winning in four straight and by lopsided margins. I think the score was 4–3 for the Yankees when, in the bottom of the eighth, they blew it open with a four-run explosion. The fans had come to see Dizzy Dean try to stave off the vaunted Yankees but Diz was a pathetic shadow of himself in those days. He had broken a toe in an All-Star game a year before and his unnatural motion had destroyed all his stuff. It didn't endear the Yankees to me. None of us knew that would be Lou Gehrig's last year. We should have known when he batted only .286 (he had batted .529 in a World Series in 1932). I always feared Lou Gehrig. He was a relentless batsman. You knew if the pitcher somehow got him out three times in a row, the fourth time he

was going to hit the ball off the loudspeakers in center field. He
was Roy Hobbs incarnate.

Actually, my disenchantment with the Yankees had started
in 1932. I was a rabid Yankee fan that year, looking forward to
the World Series with relish. When the Yanks won the first game,
12–6—the game was over by the sixth inning—I felt a bit disappointed. I almost began to hope the Cubs could creep back into
it. They couldn't. They lost the fourth (and final) game, 13–6. I
was vaguely dissatisfied.

But when the Yankees won a World Series game 18–4 a few
years later, that was it. I put them permanently on my enemies
list. It took years (and George Steinbrenner's mishandling of their
proud tradition) to bring me to tolerate the Yankees again. I always regarded Steinbrenner as Heaven's punishment visited on
the arrogant Yankees for their sins of pride.

Football in that benighted era consisted solely of the Ivy League,
Notre Dame and West Point. Pro football was nothing. Bunch of
fat has-beens taking a day off from their trucks to make fifty
dollars a game.

Like every red-blooded Irish Catholic kid in the country, I
was an unregenerate Notre Dame fan. I listened to Harvard-Yale
on the radio but Notre Dame–Army was The Big Game in our
little world. The Sidewalk alumni, the sporting press called us.

They weren't really known as the Fighting Irish in those
days. I don't really remember when that epithet came into vogue.
They were called the "Ramblers" in Knute Rockne's era because
of their proclivity for playing all over the map of the United
States. They played everywhere, against anybody. They played
Yale, Princeton, Penn. They were the first team to travel all the
way out to the West Coast to that strange new metropolis where
they made a new art form called motion pictures.

I thought everybody loved Notre Dame. Particularly after the
Hollywood picture starring Ronald Reagan as George Gipp and
Pat O'Brien as Knute Rockne. I was to get disabused one day
seated near a group of business types clustered around a portable
radio who stormed and cussed whenever Notre Dame scored a
touchdown. Catholic-bashing was alive and well in America at that

time. Some people thought Catholics should be drowned at birth. Even if they became the Four Horsemen.

People will always find things to divide them. You despair of humanity when you think of it. When I was growing up, my best friend was Joey Patrissi. Joey's parents were from Sicily. My forebears, as you know, were from Ireland.

But guess what set Joey and me apart. The fact that he was a lefthander and I was a righthander! We had lively arguments. Lefthanders were better ballplayers, particularly batters, he argued. No. Righthanders were, I countered.

Then an extraordinary thing happened. The greatest batter in the American League was suddenly righthanded. He was also Italian. He was Joe DiMaggio. Joey was torn. Then, in a few years, the best batter in the league was lefthanded. He was part-Irish. He was Ted Williams.

It was hard for Joey and me to keep up the charade. Joe D. was righthanded, a despised orthodoxy to Joey. But he was also a goombah. Ted Williams was a cockamamie southpaw, the characteristic of my enemy. But, hey! He was a goombah, too. Of mine.

Joey and I switched idolatries. After all, blood is thicker than batting position.

Actually, we all came to love Joe D. anyway. He had more dignity, more class than any great ballplayer I ever knew. In 1951, the *Life* magazine editor, Sid James, promised the New York Giants' publicist, one Clay Felker, a job on the magazine if he could get a World Series scouting report on the Yankees. Felker did. In that report was the telltale intelligence on the great DiMaggio: "Can't get around on the fastball anymore—throw it to him inside and he'll pop it up, won't get it out of the infield."

That slur went all over the country. Joe DiMaggio read it. And was mortified. He quit the game.

He knew he could hang on a year or two more, collect the money, play out the string. Not Joe DiMaggio's style. He walked. He took his strike zone with him. Joey Patrissi would have been proud.

I don't think it was then—we had no troubles in interacting or discussing any subject from girls to gyms with each other—but some time later I made a remarkable discovery: Sports is not only a universal language like music, but it's a nice, safe topic of conversation. You don't have to reveal much of yourself if you stick to sports—unless, of course, it happened to be the Jackie Robinson era when two kinds of people loved the Dodgers—baseball purists who loved him for his skills and political liberals who loved him for his color and his symbolism.

But you can walk into a room of strangers and have a long, even heated discussion about baseball, or football, or basketball and the other person will have no more insight into you (other than your opinion of the infield-fly rule) than he had when you entered. This is not reassuring to those who want to argue religion or politics. But for the rest of us, it is a lovely way to spend an evening. Once, when I was in the newsmagazine business, I went to an important screening. It was the Alan Ladd picture *Shane*. The director was the great George Stevens. We had dinner at a restaurant near the theater. George appeared bored with the movie talk. Then his eyes brightened when I chanced to make some baseball allusion. Soon, he was raptly describing for me his all-time, all-star team. "On first base, Columbia Lou! On second, the Fordham Flash!" He was ecstatic when he found out I knew exactly whom he meant—Lou Gehrig and Frankie Frisch. I was his friend for life.

We are a numerous breed, we sports fans. But we are a happy breed.

I took away from my childhood that love of sports and never lost it. I am amused when I read of the advent of the "Rotisserie" Leagues, the imaginative games people play with imaginary ties to real athletes. We did that even to the extent of inventing our own leagues, players and franchises. I devised a baseball game using a standard deck of cards. A picture card would be a hit—a jack was a single, a queen, a double, king, a triple, and ace, a home run. I tinkered with that until I thought it approximated the real life probabilities.

I remember when I was vexed with it because the averages came out notches below what the real cycle of probabilities was. I had whole clumps of people batting .249 to .261.

Life has imitated art. I like to think the cards knew more than I did. It wasn't long before the real game of baseball found itself barnacled, too, with .240 hitters. The .300 hitters all but disappeared. Team batting averages that looked frustratingly low to me and my game proved to be prophetic.

I suppose I never grew up. That's all right with me. That's the nice thing about sports. You can be Peter Pan.

2

• •

I Go Hollywood

I didn't set out to be a sportswriter. I was going to be Eugene O'Neill. Hemingway. Hell, Tolstoi. I was going to stand Broadway, Hollywood, the Old Vic on their ear.

I got to be a sportswriter in my journalistic dotage—which is just the right time for it.

Harry Luce, of all people, made me a sportswriter. Harry Luce, the publishing giant of *Time* and *Life* magazines, the block-buster journals of their time. Harry knew everything there was to know about world politics, the domestic economy, Hollywood, Foggy Bottom, Whitehall and Park Avenue. But he didn't know any more about sports than Mother Teresa.

Harry, who was not a patient man, was constantly coming up against the sports syndrome in his trips around the world. Dinner conversation upon dinner conversation would find the subject switching around to sports—the World Cup, Wimbledon, a heavy-weight title fight. Harry got annoyed. He wanted to discuss casus bellis, European Economic Communities, the Middle East and related inconsequentialities.

He conveyed his annoyance to his aide—it may have been Emmett Hughes. Legend has it, the conversation started, "Who in the world is Rocky Marciano?" Harry was exasperated. "Why does every conversation switch around to sports?" he demanded. "Well, Harry," Emmett told him, "because sports, like music, is a universal language. Everyone speaks it."

"Well," sniffed Luce characteristically, "why don't we have a sports magazine then?"

On that chance remark, *Sports Illustrated* came into being.

I didn't know it at the time but because of that chance remark I was to become a sportswriter.

You wouldn't think a power decision arrived at in Belgium (Luce was there at the time of the Hughes colloquy) would affect someone eight thousand miles away. But I guess I wouldn't be writing this if it hadn't taken place.

I was, as it happened, the cinema correspondent for *Time* magazine at the time. This was a highly prized assignment in the company that was about as movie-struck as a high school sorority. You couldn't walk the corridors of Time, Inc., at the time without tripping over ten people who were sure they were going to be the next great film directors.

My job was to keep the cinema section apprised of the movements of the film industry and to pick out three or four cover stories a year—that is, pick a movie star, hopefully female, to put on the magazine's cover and break up the monotony of the series of grim-visaged secretaries of state and military men who ordinarily glowered off its page and sold precious few copies on the newsstands.

It was a heady job for a young man. The considerable prestige of the magazine—together with the fear it inspired via its reviews and its mordant interest in Tinseltown gossip—might find me having lunch with Cary Grant or dinner with Marilyn Monroe, receiving aisle seats for the Oscars and getting invited to the major premieres. It was pretty hard to keep your feet on the ground in that rarefied atmosphere and I'm not sure I did.

Old Hollywood was in its setting-sun stage at the time. A terrible new rival had appeared over the horizon, home television. The movies panicked. No one told them this had merely multiplied the number of theater screens by a few million and that product would be more needful than ever. Hollywood simply got its paws up in the air and rolled over.

It doomed the "little" picture, the B movie, the program picture. Hollywood felt it had to make blockbuster films to lure the customers away from the (then) twelve-inch (black-and-white) screens. TV stars like Milton Berle could darken every theater in the East with his weekly telecasts—and often did.

Hollywood not only made the movies bigger, they made the screens bigger. CinemaScope projected onto a wide screen that seemed to put the moviegoer in the middle of, rather than in front of, the action. They even distributed polaroid glasses to create the illusion of three-dimensional filming. "A lion in your lap!" screamed the tearsheets.

Hollywood had a lion in its lap, all right. That damnable little box that was wired to the world.

I did my best to supply the editors with the longed-for love goddesses for their cover. It wasn't easy. It was a period of male dominance of the silver screen. The teenage girls who made up the bulk of the movie audience paid to see people like William Holden, Kirk Douglas, Marlon Brando. Paul Newman was coming along.

I struggled manfully. We put Betty Hutton on the cover *(Annie Get Your Gun)*, Ava Gardner *(Showboat)*, Rosemary Clooney, Katharine Hepburn, Lucille Ball.

It was how I happened to be taking Marilyn Monroe to dinner. Marilyn was a strange creature even for Hollywood. A onetime Valley girl and wife of an L.A. cop, Marilyn had drifted into show business via an old, well-traveled route. She was by way of being Joe Schenck's mistress, one of the girls he kept around from time to time to decorate his swimming pool parties. The first time I ever laid eyes on her, I was in the company of a sportswriter friend, the late Vincent X. Flaherty.

Vince was sitting next to Joe Schenck, who was chairman of the board of 20th Century–Fox Film Corporation at the time. Marilyn chanced to walk by.

Now, Marilyn in a tight white bathing suit was a sight to behold. Five feet six inches of whipped cream, a sweet little-girl smile. Vincent let out a whistle. "You want her?" asked Schenck. "I'll call her over. You can take her upstairs."

Hollywood lore has it, the director Joe Mankiewicz put her in his movie *All About Eve* as a practical joke on the boss. All Marilyn had to do in that film was sit on a staircase and look— well, Marilynish.

She stole the scene. Right away from Bette Davis and Anne Baxter, no less. The preview cards made her a star. "Who was that blonde sitting on the stairs in the party scene?" the public wanted to know.

And a star was born.

I pitched a story on Marilyn to the magazine. They agreed. The studio saw a *Time* magazine story as an entree to a bigger, picture story in the big-brother *Life* magazine, one of the most highly prized publicity plugs a film or film star could get.

I researched Marilyn's life story. It was not a pretty one. I went down to City Hall and purchased her birth certificate. (You could do that in those days.) I found out she was illegitimate, that her mother was of Mexican descent (and at the time in a mental institution in Pacoima) and her father was a fry cook named Lee Mortensen, whereabouts unknown at the time of her birth. (Many years later, when Mortensen died, there were stories in the paper speculating on whether his claims to be Marilyn Monroe's father were true—I had every reason to believe they were.)

Marilyn had been in and out of foster homes. She used her mother's name in those days and was Norma Jean Baker. She was a stunningly beautiful, vulnerable girl, whose life was a succession of abuses by her foster parents. Marilyn never really felt she belonged anywhere.

My assignment was to do a story on her and explore her as a cover possibility later on. I took her to dinner on the Sunset Strip, to one of those mob-owned restaurants (Alan Dale, I believe, ran it) along the boulevard, after picking her up at her residential hotel on Olympic Boulevard.

Waiting for Marilyn to get dressed and ready for a night out was always a trip. She could never leave her mirror. She was as insecure about her appearance as Quasimodo even though she was one of the world's great beauties.

The trick with Marilyn was to tell her the dinner was for seven o'clock. Then you would call the restaurant, making the reservation for 8:30. With luck, you could get her there by quarter to nine. You brought magazines to read while waiting for her to get every hair in place and change her dress four to seven times.

As we dined and talked, out of the corner of my eye, I saw a famous former athlete come into the restaurant by a side door. He was escorted to a private dining area by the owner and a screen was placed around his table.

I knew the great Joe DiMaggio when I saw him and, later in the evening, when Marilyn leaned over and breathed, "Do you mind if you don't take me home but I go home with a friend of mine?" I was ready. "Only if you introduce me to Joe DiMaggio first!"

Hollywood was a good crucible for the later coverage of sports. Unlike professional athletes, Hollywood performers knew they needed publicity. Or that, if they didn't, their pictures did.

Some athletes, on the other hand, never did get the message they were in show business and that they—and their sport— needed the enormous attention lavished on them by the national media for them to be getting those swollen salaries. It was always frustrating to try to explain to younger players that you were a necessary evil to their careers. It was easier in the days when salaries were nominal and the athlete was motivated to open a bar or related business to capitalize on his notoriety. When .260 hitters started to get $3 million a year, you became less important to them.

Hollywood had no such ambiguity. It courted the press. Even a standard Hollywood house party would invite a half-dozen press or TV types so as to be able to write the party off on their taxes as a business expense.

However, as hard as I looked, it was not easy to come up with a female star of cover-story dimensions in that male-dominated era.

One of the toughest sells I had was John Wayne. It's hard to remember or believe it now, but in the late forties and early fifties, John Wayne was not perceived as a star but, in the Hollywood pecking order, was taken to be just a program-picture (that is, B picture) maker, just a step above a singing cowboy (which he had been), making pictures for the "Poverty Row" studios, Monogram and Republic.

I knew Wayne had become bigger than that, had, in fact, become Big Box Office because part of my job was keeping tabs on the nation's film exhibitors and what their needs and preferences were. Their newsletters often offered more real insights into what the moviegoing public wanted than any other kind of survey ever taken. I remember once reading a comment from an exhibitor, fed up with Hollywood costume dramas: "My folks don't like it when they start writing with that feather!"

They knew what they liked in what *Variety* used to refer to as the "sticks." ("Sticks Nix Hicks Pix" was one famous headline arguing that the boondocks were rejecting bucolic Judy Canova offerings in favor of more sophisticated fare, albeit not pictures in which they wrote with a feather.)

One player the sticks exhibitors loved was John Wayne. They kept warning Hollywood it didn't make enough John Wayne movies. His pictures sold out from Broadway to Prairie Junction. One exhibitor once offered to trade two Cornel Wilde sword-wielding dramas for one John Wayne with a Remington rifle.

Like the exhibitors, I kept sending teletypes to the home office telling them that Duke Wayne was the biggest star in Hollywood.

But no one in the New York office had ever seen a John Wayne movie. They didn't hit the carriage trade. Nobody up in Rye or Mamaroneck or Old Greenwich ever went to one.

It was a hard sell. The editors wanted to put Kate Hepburn or Claire Bloom on the cover, somebody they wouldn't have to apologize for at the Harvard Club. We put Kate on the cover for *African Queen* but my notion was, they should have put her costar, Bogart, on there.

The editors couldn't ignore John Wayne and pretend to cover Hollywood. They finally relented and put him on the precious cover for *The Quiet Man,* a bit of John Ford blarney about a pugilist who had killed a man in the ring in America and retired to Ireland to forget. And, then, he meets Maureen O'Hara and gets in a fight with her brother (Victor McLaglen), which takes in the whole map of Ireland before it's through.

The public adored it. The editors capitulated. Wayne went on the cover.

John Wayne lived in a man's world on and off the screen and a lot of my interviewing was spent sitting around a poker table with his cronies or riding down to Baja for a pigeon shoot.

Duke was a massive man with wrists like wagon tongues and fists to match but I always thought his macho posing was in part due to his real first name—Marion. He was really an intellectual in some respects, an A student in high school. He always liked to say that movies taught him to say "ain't." It was not otherwise allowed in the Morrison household.

Wayne had been a football player at USC. Not for long. He broke his leg in practice. He went to work in the movies—but with a broom, not a horse. The irascible, cantankerous, sadistic

John Ford made him an actor (and ever afterward said he hoped Heaven and the ghost of Edwin Booth would forgive him). It was typical of Hollywood of the time to hire football stars off the USC campus. It helped immeasurably with the recruiting and some became stars and others cutters and producers.

Ford treated Wayne typically. He called his flunkies about him, then invited the ex-footballer Wayne to show him exactly how he got down in a three-point stance. When Wayne obliged, Ford quickly kicked his arms out from underneath him and Wayne went crashing, chin-first, to the floor.

Ford was that way. I interviewed him once on the subject of filming *The Quiet Man* in Ireland and I alluded to the Irish—reasonably enough, I thought—as "natives." Ford bristled. He allowed as how he resented that superior attitude on the part of my magazine and held that he didn't care for *Time* magazine or its representatives. I was fed up. He had bullied me throughout the interview. "That's OK," I told him. "I didn't much care for *She Wore a Yellow Ribbon*, either." Instead of getting mad, Ford hooted with laughter. A very complex man, John Ford, a Maine-iac with an attitude.

Wayne was about what you would expect. Patriotic to the core. A simple, uncomplicated man's man who kept marrying Latin-American women and who spent his holidays in Mexico.

He was as right-wing as Bank of America. And he (along with the columnist Hedda Hopper) was instrumental in founding the ultraconservative, rightist Motion Picture Society for the Preservation of American Ideals, which he saw as a bulwark against what he conceived to be a rising tide of Communist propaganda in Hollywood.

If any Communist propaganda found its way into Hollywood films, it never did in Wayne's. His pictures were formula. *Sands of Iwo Jima, She Wore a Yellow Ribbon, Rio Grande* and *Hondo* were as American as a pumpkin pie and as patriotic as a Sousa march. Wayne carried the flag wherever he went. He was as Republican as the Taft family.

If he were alive today, he would probably see the dissolution of the Soviet empire as a lousy Communist trick—but he was not without his sense of humor. He did not really take himself seriously. He used to say he was the only guy in the world who played football in 1930 and became an All-American in 1960. He was chosen, he said, not by the Grantland Rice board but by the Hollywood Publicists' Guild. He liked to joke that he had won the war, retaken the Burma Road, won the West—and then the wimps gave it all back at the peace table. When the *Harvard Lampoon* poked fun at him, and gave him a mocking award, he came back for the celebration riding on top of a tank.

He was careful to people his pictures with players as big or bigger than he was. He wanted the public to root for him, not some runt opponent. He departed from the formula only once— in a film called *Red River*—to fistfight Montgomery Clift, who played his adopted son. Sticks exhibs didn't like that scene. Wayne went back to fighting Ward Bond on film.

The Hollywood stars of the day were as approachable as insurance salesman. They had a symbiotic relationship with the press, which they recognized and dealt with. Hollywood gossip columnists were stars in their own right.

Bogart was Bogart. The sardonic, wisecracking cynic of the screen played the role off-screen, as well. But it was a little phony. Bogey liked to pretend he was a dead-end kid, a product of the slums, the streets. In reality, he was the son of a Park Avenue doctor and a high society mother. He grew up playing golf and tennis and sailing on Long Island Sound. He came out of, not Sing Sing, but Philips Andover Academy. He was about as tough as a ballroom dancer.

Many of us in the press knew him before he became Bogart. When he was married to his third wife, the tempestuous Mayo Methot, it was not unusual for the city desk to get a call from some Figueroa Street wine joint that an actor named Bogart and his wife were having a chair-swinging, ashtray-throwing, alcoholic fight and that the cops had been called. In fact, I first met Bogart in the Georgia Street Receiving Hospital where he had been taken for repair for a head cut caused by a bar stool bounced off his head by his wife.

Bogey was playing bad guys in those days. *Casablanca* made him a big star but it is my recollection it took about two years or so before Hollywood thought of him as leading man material.

They were so used to him in "Drop the gun, Louie!" roles that it was hard for studio heads to think of him as anything but a racketeer.

He played tough guys but he was anything but. Alcohol fueled his role playing in that regard. "After two drinks, he thinks he's Bogart," the restaurateur Mike Romanoff, who knew Bogey about as well as anyone, used to sneer.

Romanoff was a major player on the Hollywood scene. Officially branded an impostor, this self-styled last of the Romanoffs had nevertheless posed for years as a member of the Russian royal family who had somehow escaped the Bolshevik firing squads.

Born Harry Gerguson in central Illinois, according to one version, or in Vilna, Lithuania, of peasant stock, according to another, Mike always held he was the czar's nephew or third cousin or illegitimate son and his story was unshakable, even when he was confronted with contradictory facts.

Facts bored Mike. Mike was a glorious pretender. Hollywood loved him because he treated it and everyone in it with the contempt it probably deserved. Mike couldn't abide common people but his restaurant was the most popular in town. He had been bankrolled into it by a committee of Hollywoodians who included Charlie Chaplin, no less, as a kind of practical joke they wanted to play on the town's premier restaurateur, Dave Chasen. Romanoff used to hang around the bar at Chasen's cadging drinks from the mighty but when he opened his own restaurant, he surprised everyone by working night and day till it was the most prestigious in town. If you didn't get a good table at Romanoff's, you were nobody.

Dave Chasen was not amused. He promptly socked Mike Romanoff in his rather substantial nose, which already resembled nothing so much as a large baked potato.

Mike closed his business because he couldn't abide serving anybody not wearing a tie. He was a snob to the last. He hated to live in a world without manners. He would have made a perfect czar.

He also had the last laugh. After the immigration department spent a decade trying to deport him ("How can you deport anybody born in Cairo, Illinois?" the wags used to ask, "where do you send him to—Hoboken?"), he was made a citizen by a special bill signed into law by President Dwight Eisenhower.

Mike was great preparation for covering Al Davis. Hollywood

was great preparation for covering that other great show business world of the twentieth century—sports.

Marlon Brando was a trip. Marlon was the earliest of the Method actors who parlayed a brief stage triumph into a memorable movie career. But Marlon was the first of the anti-establishment rebels. He mumbled his lines, frustrated directors at every turn— but once he got on screen, the public was awed. Brando was in charge once the film screened. He had that animal magnetism the great ones have, male or female, and he didn't play the game. He took Hollywood on *his* terms, not theirs.

One anecdote will suffice: In the summer of 1953, Brando was already hot box office. He had starred in the role he made famous on Broadway, the loutish brother-in-law, Stanley Kowalski, in Tennessee Williams's *A Streetcar Named Desire,* and he had made a top independent flick, *The Men,* in which he played a paraplegic injured in the war.

Twentieth Century–Fox had signed him to do a film called *The Egyptian* in which he was to play the character of Sinuhe, a doctor in the ancient land of the Pharaohs. Brando walked out on the picture. He did that a lot.

Marlon rubbed Hollywood's nose in it whenever he could. The studio went ahead and recast the character of Sinuhe, giving the role to a then-popular English actor, Edmund Purdom.

I was having lunch with Brando in the Fox commissary one day when the producer of *The Egyptian,* Julian Blaustein, dropped by our table. Not above a spot of gamesmanship, Julian began extolling the merits of his film. "The part of Sinuhe is working marvelously with Edmund," he crowed. "He is making a perfect Sinuhe." Brando looked at him wide-eyed. "Who," he asked, twisting the knife, "is Sinuhe?" Bear in mind, this was a part he had assiduously studied all winter before deciding not to do it.

Blaustein had been one-upped.

I had almost as much trouble with Marlon as Hollywood did. One afternoon, he made an appointment with me for two o'clock at a small house he was renting up in one of the canyons behind the Beverly Hills hotel. I showed up, naturally, at the appointed hour. I knocked on the door, I rang the bell, I shouted. I sat on the steps for a half-hour. I went back, tried the bell again, peered in the windows. I sat on the steps again.

Finally, I decided to leave. I was in the act of pinning a note on the door when it flew open. And there was Brando, laughing. He had sat inside enjoying my discomfiture and frustration for over an hour.

I would listen while he answered the phone in the sing-song dialect of an Oriental houseboy, promising to give their messages to "Mr. Blando."

Marlon's father was a dignified man with an Old World brush mustache, bench-made shoes, the correct tie, and I never saw him in anything but a suit and tie. Lewis Stone would have played him in a movie, not his son. He had the vaguely harried look of Judge Hardy and he found son Marlon (whom he called by the family name "Bud") as hard to fathom as the rest of the world did. Brando marched to music no one else could hear.

If he had a pattern, it was that he preferred Asian women. He was dating Movita when I was doing the cover story on him. He later married an Asiatic whose real name proved to be Callahan. He finally moved to an atoll in the Pacific as far from Hollywood as he always insisted he wanted to be.

When he began to play roles parodying himself, some of us thought back to the time when John Barrymore did the same thing. Booze killed Barrymore. But Brando became psychologically destroyed when his son, Christian, shot and killed his brother-in-law, the husband of Marlon's daughter. His last role was that of a broken-hearted, beaten-down father. For once, Brando wasn't acting.

Brando was a lifelong boxing fan. I always thought he would like to have been a top middleweight boxer. He often said he despised acting, which, he complained, locked you in eternal childhood. But Brando's dubious gift to the world was that he was the first to show a generation of the young that you could misbehave, dress sloppily and mock and scorn convention—so long as American Business wanted you badly enough. He was the original rebel without a cause. He had a contempt for institutions.

The only part I've every known him to really want to play was the Godfather. Brando went after that role. To give you an idea of his usual mockery of Hollywood, when his dropout from the role in *The Egyptian* resulted in 20th Century–Fox winning a suit against him, Brando settled by agreeing to do another film for them. He played Napoleon in a disaster called *Desiree*. He walked through the picture doing an imitation of Claude Rains. He was the first guy in history to make Napoleon funny.

Brando was not Tinseltown's only fight fan. Or sports fan. It would not be too much of an exaggeration to describe Hollywood as a sports-mad community. In the old Hollywood, the moguls were often off-the-wall betting maniacs. Their background, often, was gambling. Hollywood was often the biggest gamble of them all. Harry Cohn, the irascible, czarist head of Columbia Pictures in its heyday, used to keep the bookmakers hopping. Cohn was a dedicated horseplayer and self-styled pro football expert. It was nothing to find Harry on the phone to a sportswriter trying to figure the spread on a Rams-Bears game in the middle of a story conference on a Kim Novak or Burt Lancaster picture.

The USC Trojans were the darlings of the industry in the early days. Producers like Ben Hibbs and Aaron Rosenberg stepped right off a Rose Bowl lineup and into a producer's chair. A Cotton Warburton became an esteemed film cutter.

When the Dodgers came West, Dodger Stadium had more stars on the club level and in the locker room than the backlot at MGM. Jack Benny loved Steve Garvey. Georgie Jessel used to be abroad in the seats in his brigadier general military jacket and a field marshal's baton telling everyone who would listen how he had been the batboy for the John McGraw Giants and how misunderstood Ty Cobb was. Nat (King) Cole never missed a Dodger game when he was in town. Jim Garner sat on the Raider sideline at the Super Bowl games.

I met Cary Grant in an elevator at Dodger Stadium. The English-born Cary was a dedicated baseball fan. His other love was horseracing. Basically a shy man, Grant was unlike most show business personalities who wanted to be the center of the action. Tommy Lasorda's locker room looked on some nights like curtain call at a Vegas showroom: Frank Sinatra might be on hand, Don Rickles, Danny Kaye, crooners, old vaudevillians, sitcom stars.

It all changed when the Pittsburgh Pirates' drug scandal surfaced. This was Baseball's least fine hour, wherein drug dealers were found to have wormed their way into the locker room swarm at Three Rivers Stadium to dispense their wares, which, among other things, included cocaine and amphetamines. Baseball cracked down and locker rooms—and the manager's office—were open only to accredited journalists and members of the ballclub and trainers.

The interaction between sports and show business was always a fascination. Perhaps it was a recognition that both were in the entertainment industry—one made its living in song or dance or drama, the other in athletics—but in both the idea was to sell tickets or air time, or both.

Baseball was the sport of choice of the older show biz troupe but basketball came with a rush in the late sixties and early seventies. As with baseball, the expansion to the West Coast made the sport more visible to the movie types. Also more accessible.

It was the wit Bob Goldstein, a film producer, who first took the climatic boast of Californians, "No matter how hot it gets in California in the daytime, it still is cool at night," and modified it to read, "No matter how hot it gets in the daytime, there's still nothing to do at night."

It was largely true. Hollywood was not a nightlife town, à la New York. The Industry's idea of a good time was dinner at an actor's or producer's house, followed by a screening of the latest picture.

The move West of professional sports teams changed all that. Dodger Stadium and the Forum in Inglewood became places to be seen at night. Sports figures became social lions.

Early Hollywood chafed under the perceived ignominy of having no major league sports to draw from and feed on. The sound stages were always awash with dyed-in-the-wool fans, from top directors to top stars to grips, electricians.

Moguls were quick to cash in on athletic notoriety. Babe Ruth made pictures—disastrous ones. So did Red Grange, Jack Dempsey, Max Baer, who appeared in a bit of fluff titled *The Prizefighter and the Lady*. Bobby Jones appeared in a series of useful instructional short subjects.

Hollywood liked to rub elbows with the sports great and the feeling was mutual; a visit to a sound stage by a reigning athletic idol was treated as a visit from royalty.

The movies they made were less successful. Sports movies were, by and large, poison at the box office. Not until director Sam Wood made the Lou Gehrig story, *Pride of the Yankees*, did a baseball picture so much as break even. And it was not so much a baseball picture as a tragic love story. Camille in cleats. A superb young athlete dying young was surefire box office. Hollywood tried to repeat the formula with the Monte Stratton story, the chronicle of the young pitcher who had lost his leg in a hunting accident and tried to make a comeback on the mound. The picture, with Jimmy Stewart in the title role, was not a disaster. But neither was it an Oscar winner. It wasn't even *Pride of the Yankees*. Cracked Hollywood wit Bob Goldstein, "Stratton lost a leg but Gehrig lost his life. You went from a four-handkerchief picture to a Kleenex."

Boxing films were more lucrative. They were formula: poor but honest kid from the wrong side of the tracks fights his way out of poverty with his fists only to run afoul of the mobsters who want him to fix the big fight. He has a hometown sweetheart trying to save his soul and a big city moll who is trying to ruin it. The sock finish, to coin a phrase, has him triumphing over a contender and corruption in the bloody windup. It couldn't miss.

Sylvester Stallone got rich on a variation of this theme with his Rocky pictures. Stallone perceived a backlash of public opinion to the flashy, arrogant, taunting behavior of the reigning heavyweight champ, Muhammad Ali, whom he transposed into an on-screen titleholder named Apollo Creed who had all the gaudy trappings of the real heavyweight champ.

Ali admitted at the time he had borrowed his shtick from the wrestler Gorgeous George, who had proved that villainy sells in the prize ring far more than heroism. Ali set out to fill seats with a public who would pay good money to see him get a drubbing. Perversely, the public grew to adore Ali, who was personally more attractive than the brutes the promoters fed him.

Stallone's Rocky was a poor slob from the slums who was hardly Frank Merriwell. He made a living busting heads as a collector of usurious loans for waterfront mobsters.

The plot was as juvenile as a comic book, but Stallone struck a nerve and the Rocky films were probably the most successful sports films ever and four sequels were made before Rocky, so to speak, finally threw in the towel. They became the longest-running series in cinema sports annals.

Hollywood has otherwise never been able to cope successfully with sports pictures. Its football flicks ran heavily to the Toby

Wing musicals, which featured Toby as the cheerleader and Richard Arlen as the star halfback who would beat Harvard (or Army) in the last minute of play, win the girl and glory for dear old alma mater. There was a great deal of tap-dancing and very little football. An exception was *Knute Rockne—All American*, in which Pat O'Brien played the immortal Notre Dame coach and Ronald Reagan played his star halfback, George Gipp. The picture rode the rails of success because it told the American saga of two men superbly skilled at what they do who both died young at the height of their prowess.

The studios could never come to grips with baseball. They had to put angels in the outfield or ring in the supernatural to sell the product. A picture in which a baseball player had not sold his soul to the devil or had a magic bat sawn out of an Excalibur-like tree was beyond Hollywood's ken.

The filmmakers tried a golf picture with the Ben Hogan story, *Follow the Sun*, which endeavored to tell of the great golfer's near-miraculous comeback from a catastrophic bus accident in the winter of 1949.

It was a tough sell. Glenn Ford struggled courageously with the role. It was a triple bogey. The screenwriters had no feel for golf, the director, Sidney Lanfield, had no feel for anything. The picture bombed.

Some years later, the producer Tom Laughlin (who wrote and starred in the Billy Jack pictures) approached me to join him in a remake of the Hogan story, "This time with some golf in it." I turned him down. "Hogan wants you," he told me.

That was different. Tom Laughlin, I could turn down. Ben Hogan, I could not.

The trouble with writing a screenplay, I would find, is that it consumes you. The only real way to do it is to lock yourself in a closet with a typewriter and a biography and eat, sleep and breathe the story for weeks.

This I couldn't do. I had a column to write. Daily. It consumes you. I would pen twenty pages of the Ben Hogan story, then put it aside while I went to a World Series or a Muhammad Ali fight or even a golf or tennis tournament. I would return to the Hogan story. But each day I had a column to dismiss first.

It was more than I could handle. I finally wrote to Ben with a sick heart. Of all the people in the world I would dislike to let down, Hogan would be in the top three. But I told him that this was like his trying to get ready to play in a U.S. Open while he had a club job in Keokuk and a night job as a timekeeper in a tire plant. I couldn't do justice to it.

Neither, as it turned out, could anyone else. The Hogan story was rich in human drama, heartache and even a love story (Valerie Hogan was one of the great wives in all of sports or show business). But that story never got told.

The Hollywood years were instructional. Show business is slightly mad. It's like living in a permanent, never-ending fairy tale. A psychiatrist on Libido Row (Bedford Drive in Beverly Hills) once told me that actors could be great actors because they had no well-defined personalities of their own, that they could then take on the characteristics of everyone from Napoleon to a pope to a psychopathic killer. But I found great actors who had perfectly well-defined, even overpowering personalities of their own—James Cagney, Jimmy Stewart. Did John Wayne ever play anybody but John Wayne?

Jimmy Stewart was the same guy off-screen that he was on. Kind of bumbling, sentimental, kindly, considerate. He lives by a code others only talk about. He's as middle-American as the Mississippi River. I don't care how many years he went to Princeton. He should have been president.

Irving Berlin knew it. There's no business like show business, they laugh when they are sad. A comedian to be great has to be loved. A movie star has to be adored. You can't fool the public. They either like what they see in that emulsion. Or they reject it. I have found over the years that the successful movie stars were, basically, lovable. Cary Grant was Cary Grant. Cagney was Cagney. Jimmy Stewart was Mr. Smith going to Washington. The proof is, did you ever see any of them play a villain? When Cagney played a public enemy, you rooted for him. When Bogart was a beleaguered gangster, you felt sorry for him. No one was ever foolish enough to cast Stewart or Gary Cooper or Cary Grant as a bad guy. Who would believe him?

3

. . . .

I Could of Been Secretary of State

I've forgotten what I was doing that July day in 1953 when the phone in the kitchen rang. Probably nothing. Having a Coke, perhaps.

"It's someone named Ernie Havemann from *Life* in New York," my wife told me.

I was mildly surprised. Intrigued. Ernie was one of the top *Life* magazine writers, a highly respected journalist.

I was the movie correspondent for the companion magazine, *Time*, at the time and I thought Ernie was probably coming out for a *Life* profile on an actor or actress and wanted my input.

"How would you like to come back and work on a top-secret project? We're thinking of getting out a weekly sports magazine," Havemann asked me, without preamble.

Fatal words. I couldn't know it at the time but that call, those words, were to rearrange my whole life, make Jim Murray a whole other person from what he had been or thought he would be.

I was, initially, just intrigued. Only weeks before, I had received a call from another company editor, a Willi Schlamm, who wanted to know if I would be interested in coming back to work on a projected culture magazine. But my interest in culture was minimal to nonexistent. I declined.

Sports was something else again. Sports had been an abiding interest all my life. In fact, I knew why I was being tapped for this signal honor.

I was one of the few persons in the company who knew anything about sports. In a company where nearly everyone wanted to cover the State Department or be a correspondent in the capitals of Europe, I had frequently been called upon to do many of the sports pieces that the magazine felt constrained from time to time to do.

In this way, it had fallen on me to do major parts of the Ben Hogan cover, as well as the cover on Olympic sprinter Mel Patton. The Olympic team was always composed in major part of Californians and I had done the cover story on the record-holding shotputter, Parry O'Brien, and chunks of the research on decathlete Bob Mathias. I had done cover stories on Notre Dame footballer Johnny Lattner, and Detroit Lions quarterback Bobby Layne. I knew the field.

It's strange how a ringing telephone can change your whole life. It's possible to reflect on what might have happened had I not been home at the time. I was on vacation, as I recall it, and might well have been out of town for a few weeks. Would Havemann have gone to another company resource? If so, would I have become a sportswriter? I find it highly unlikely.

I took the train to New York the next week. Our project was known in the company by the code name "Muscles," and I soon learned why. This was a derisive term. Most of the occupants of the executive suites thought it was just a passing fancy of Harry's (Henry Luce always insisted on being called "Harry" by staffers even though some of us found it smacked of calling Queen Elizabeth "Betty"). They responded by dumping every company expense, like junkets to the Bahamas, onto Harry's new little project in the confident belief it would die in its crib (and take those expenses with it).

This practice of the thirty-second floor was to give rise to the canard that the start-up costs of the magazine were in the high millions (twenty to thirty to forty). This was simply not true. My salary was somewhere in the neighborhood of fifteen thousand, and of the eight or so co-workers we had in the start-up roster, I could think of only one or two who made more. We never rented any airplanes for our assignments. We took the subway. How much could you spend interviewing Sal Maglie at Ebbets Field?

How did I get to this eminent position, being asked to mid-wife new company projects?

Well, I had worked in the vineyards of L.A. for the magazine for five years at this point, mostly on movie coverage. But I had done other things.

In 1949, for instance, a new phenomenon had hit Los Angeles—a downtown revival meeting, sawdust trail, big tent and all. Someone called Billy Graham had opened up shop to save the world.

The William Randolph Hearst press embraced him with all stops pulled. The old man was still alive then and he instructed his editors to lend their full-throated, roaring, unstinting support.

The result was, Billy Graham was all over the front pages. At *Time* magazine, we were always disdainful of the Hearst press. So we took a skeptical, not to say scornful position vis-à-vis the Reverend Dr. Graham.

At that time, we had a young trainee, an Englishman named Eldon Griffiths, in the bureau. Eldon was a gung-ho liberal at the time, a young reporter who had been an RAF flyer in the war. His quondam liberalism is interesting because Eldon would later return to his native England and become the most conservative of Tories in the British Parliament. In fact, he came within a whisker of becoming prime minister, I'm told. He is now *Sir* Eldon Griffiths, if you please.

But in 1949, he and another colleague had tried manfully to get Billy Graham's crusade in the magazine.

They satirized it. They were sure it was Elmer Gantry revisited, a shuck, a fleecing of the public. They pitched their stories to the national affairs section of *Time* with that point of view. They proposed to mock. We had a *Life* photographer who had been the cameraman for one of these revival shows—by an itinerant charlatan preacher—and he was derisive of the whole olio when he went down to watch the penitents on the sawdust.

The editors kept rejecting the story. Editors are that way. Editors would have rejected John the Baptist.

But I thought I saw a way to put the Reverend Billy Graham in the book where I thought he deserved to be. Believe me, he was a phenomenon as a speaker.

I bet Eldon Griffiths—and colleague Eddie Rees—twenty dollars I could get Dr. Graham in the book.

Now, if you knew *Time* magazine, you knew one thing: Harry Luce was religious. He had been born in China of missionary parents.

I knew that, if I pitched my story to the religion section and

if I coated the suggestion with the scents and sounds of candlelight and organ music, I could get it in the magazine.

The editors bit. I am happy to say I spent two solid weeks
meeting with Billy Graham—and his associate Cliff Barrows. I
found out all monies were being scrutinized and books kept by a
council of Baptist bishops and ministers. I was allowed to pore
over the books.

Billy Graham was not Elmer Gantry. Or Jimmy Swaggart.

I got a full-page story on him in the religion section. He was
later to say it was the most important breakthrough in his career.
Luce became fascinated with him. So did succeeding presidents
of the United States. Dr. Graham later was to make the cover of
Time. This made him an international celebrity.

Me? I got my twenty bucks.

In 1952, I took a break from Hollywood. It was a presidential
election year and the editors wanted someone to cover a West
Coast campaign trip by the vice-presidential candidate, a young
congressman named Richard Nixon.

It was to be a whistlestop train trip and it sounded like fun.

The day before we took off, I contacted a fellow reporter in
town, Ernie Brashear, who had just done a two-part series on
Nixon in *The Nation*. Naturally, Nixon didn't get any of the best
of it. I phoned Ernie to ask what would be in the third part of
the takeout. Ernie was embarrassed. "I have asked Frieda Kirchway
[the editor of *The Nation*] to take my name off it. They say some
things about Nixon I didn't find to be true and I don't want my
name on fabricated news."

I was titillated. "Hey, that's what *The Nation* accuses us of
doing at *Time*," I told him. "That's a good press story." Ernie
demurred. "Well, I'd appreciate it if you'd drop it. Because we're
doing a big scandal story on Nixon tomorrow. It'll break simultaneously in our paper [*L.A. Daily News*], the *New York Post* and
Frontier magazine." He started to tell me what it was. I stopped
him. "I'll be on that train with Nixon's people tonight. I may
have a bourbon or two and spill the beans," I warned him.

That night, I did brace Nixon's men—Bill Rogers, who was
later to become attorney general and secretary of state, and Jim

Bassett, who was to turn down White House press secretary. I asked them what about the scandal that was about to break. "Oh, we know all about it! It's going to backfire," they assured me.

They underestimated it. The next day, the story broke. Nixon had a secret slush fund put up by a bunch of Rotary Club types (what you would now call "yuppies") in Pasadena who couldn't keep their mouths shut about it.

It didn't backfire. It mushroomed. By the end of the first day, *The Washington Post* and *The New York Times* were out with editorials urging Eisenhower to kick Nixon off the ticket.

I kept pleading with Bill Rogers to meet the contretemps head-on. He kept predicting it would blow over.

It didn't. The trainside crowds started to heckle the candidate. Eisenhower kept sending mixed signals. Nixon kept telling the crowds about how his wife and mother wore "good Republican cloth coats," how they owed big money on the family grocery store, how they had to practice thrift to make ends meet.

It didn't work. The trip was supposed to end in Seattle but, at two o'clock in the morning at the Benson Hotel in Portland, Nixon came downstairs to the press room to tell us he was breaking off the campaign trail to fly to Los Angeles and take to the airwaves to explain himself. He had just come from a meeting with the senator from Washington, James Cain, where he had angrily advised Eisenhower to "shit or get off the pot." He was bitter with Ike.

We were to fly back the next morning, a Monday. The speech was to be Tuesday night.

At five o'clock Monday morning I got awakened by a phone call from the national affairs editor, Max Ways, a very forbidding character, one of the lions of the company. His wants were simple. To him. The magazine was going to press Monday night, but wouldn't be in the stands till Thursday, two days after the Nixon speech. They had to know what he was going to say on Tuesday night. Was he taking himself off the ticket? Was he going to fight? Was he going on?

"How am I supposed to find that out?" I screamed. Max was unmoved. "Just do it," he warned.

*   *   *

The plane ride down to L.A. that day was a nightmare. My little vacation trip had turned into a haunted house.

Nixon was boxed off from the press on the plane. His TV producer, Ted Rogers, sat on one side. Pat Nixon and Bill Rogers protected him from the rear.

I gambled he would have to go to the lavatory before the trip was over. I positioned myself outside its door.

Sure enough, he showed up midway in the trip. As he came out, I grabbed his hand. "Dick," I pleaded (remember, he was just a junior senator at the time), "the magazine wants me to find out what you're going to do tomorrow night." I explained our deadline problem lamely.

Nixon thought awhile. Then he said, "check with Jim Bassett before we get off the plane."

I waited. About an hour later, Jim Bassett came up the aisle, knelt by my seat. "What would you do," he asked, "if your family had obligations, debts to pay, but you never took any bribes and struggled along, if your wife and your mother wore cloth coats, and you had a big mortgage?" He went on like that. Suddenly, it dawned on me. "He's giving me the speech! He's going to give the speech he's been giving from the back of the train!"

When I arrived in L.A., I flew to the phone. I laid out that whole speech. I assured the editors Nixon was not going to take himself off the ticket.

I hung up, feeling good about myself. The whole troupe was staying at the Ambassador Hotel that night. I repaired to the Press Club to celebrate.

While I was on my first libation, the head of the United Press in L.A., Bill Best, came over to me. "Jim," he said, "I think you ought to know we're coming out with a 'rocket' tonight saying Nixon is getting off the ticket."

My world reeled. Here I'd just assured what our ad guys liked to call "America's most important magazine," that the opposite was going to take place. Millions of copies were rolling off the presses at that very moment.

I would be ruined. I would lose my job, my career ended. I was Fred Merkle.

I flew to the phone. I got Nixon's suite. Bill Rogers answered the ring. Desperately, I laid out my predicament. Rogers listened. "Just a minute, I'll check with the candidate," he told me.

The longest four minutes of my life ensued. I had visions of driving a cab for a living. Selling hamburgers.

Bill Rogers came back on the line. He sounded annoyed. "The candidate says, quote, Murray's got the story, what's he worried about?"

Those might have been the sweetest words I have ever heard. "I love you" pales by comparison. "Congratulations! You have just won the lottery" doesn't begin to compare.

Meanwhile, I had aged five years because a young UP reporter had been told by a man who was in charge of the baggage for the Nixon trip that the candidate had to be withdrawing because the luggage had not been checked on the train.

Well, of course it hadn't. The trip was going on to Great Falls by plane the next night. The baggage smasher, one Beck Beckley, had been on loan from the Senate press gallery for the trip and chose the wrong moment, and the wrong bar, to get self-important.

We did fly on to Montana right after the broadcast. We had a few drinks on board. All of us. Then Dick Nixon broke down. He began weeping on the shoulder of my colleague Frank Kuest of the Copley papers. He turned on me. "I know you—you're a stinking intellectual!" he accused. Me, Dick?! Hell, I haven't even read Proust!

As we flew into Washington on the last leg of the trip, after Nixon and Ike had their reconciliation in Wheeling, Bill Rogers and Nixon called us all together on the airplane and announced Dick was forming "The Order of the Hound's Tooth." That was because Eisenhower had told him to "come clean as a hound's tooth or get off the ticket."

I still have the hound's tooth key ring but I've lost the card with the picture of Checkers on it. But Bill Rogers did tell the assemblage, "When we got to Fresno, Jim Murray was telling me we were being unrealistic and this thing wouldn't go away. We should have listened to him."

That was my little victory and I basked in it. I didn't tell them that I felt that way because that's what New York was telling me on the phone every day.

I have a terrible confession to make. In 1960, I flew all the way back from a Hawaiian vacation to vote for Dick Nixon for president. I loved John Kennedy. But I felt I owed the other man.

But all this was before *SI*.

When I arrived back in New York in the summer of 1953, we set about to put together the sports magazine. Ernie Havemann was to be the top editor. But it wasn't long before the rest of us realized our peerless leader had cut out on us. Ernie Havemann had, first, been detached to write the titillating story on the Kinsey Report (Sex in America) for *Life* and, unbeknownst to any of us, he had simultaneously penned a twenty-six-page memo to Luce detailing why a sports magazine would never work.

Luce was in Italy at the time, where his wife (Clare Boothe Luce) was ambassadress (Mrs. Luce was not popular in the company, where her nickname was "Clare Wilkes Booth," and where, when the story emerged about her facing arsenic poisoning from the dripping of a painting from a Roman ceiling, the incident was known as "arsenic and Old Luce").

Luce, fortunately, was not dissuaded by the Havemann memo. He turned the reins over to Sidney L. James, the assistant editor of *Life* at the time and a man who never let a negative image get on-screen in his life. As he came walking through the door, startling me, his first day on the job, I asked, "Sid? What are you doing here?" He pointed a finger at me. "Do you believe in this magazine?" he demanded. At the time, I was not too sure but, thank Heaven, I blurted out, "Oh, you bet, Sid!" If I had slid into my more accustomed equivocation—well, I might never have met Pete Rose. Sid only dealt in unbridled optimism. He was the perfect man to get *SI* off the ground.

I don't know what my contribution to *SI* was, but I do know we worked hard for several months and put together the first three advertisers' dummies (sample copies of what the magazine would look like ultimately) to be distributed to Madison Avenue to lure ad contracts. One of my most prized possessions is a letter from Harry Luce written the day after Christmas that year, thanking me for my many contributions and assuring me that we had, indeed, a magazine in the works.

We all worked on all phases of publication—reporting, editing, photography, makeup. Even the name came up for discussion in our little group. I wanted the company to buy the title *Fame* for the new magazine. It was a title easily purchasable and owned by an organization called Quigley Publication, which used it for a once-a-year movie exhibitors' annual that was more or less a shakedown of the studios and I also knew the title would go for a song. I liked the idea of the family of publications being *Time, Life, Fame* and *Fortune.* It was the second time I had urged this on the editors.

Sometime earlier, the company president, Roy Larsen, casting about for new magazines, had sent out a flyer to employees asking for suggestions. I recommended they take the unused parts of a weekly backgrounder I sent called the "Cinema Letter," add to it unused parts of the "Washington Memo" (from the nation's capital bureau, full of lively gossip) and the backgrounder from the European bureaus and the overset from the "People" section of *Time* and bring out a new publication on celebrities and call it *Fame*, buying the title from Quigley. Larsen wrote me back, thanking me for the suggestion, but saying the board voted it down. If I may say immodestly, *People* magazine today is exactly what I suggested in the early fifties. You know of its success.

I am grateful to Time, Inc., for many things. For making me a sportswriter. (Frank McCulloch made me a sports columnist.) But, also, I think I learned a valuable journalistic lesson from my fourteen years on their masthead. I learned that people are interested in people. People are not interested in things. I remember once I was sitting in as a pro tem bureau chief and we had an aerospace writer who kept coming in with a complicated story on a new kind of fuselage. It was important but dull. "John, can't you take this back and find some funny little old German professor with a music hall accent and dandruff on his collar who invented this thing one day looking at a bird or something? Get people in the tent by being interested in him, then bring in your bloody valves and rivets and aerodynamics. Right now, this story belongs in the pipefitters manual."

My colleague's answer was unprintable but I believe my years at *Time* taught me the essence of journalism is high-level gossip. I am never surprised at the success of the supermarket tabloids or the TV programs like *Entertainment Tonight* or *Hard Copy. The New York Times* is the only publication in the country that can get by with being stodgy.

In all the years I covered him, I never once had anyone c..
up to me and ask me how Sandy Koufax gripped his curveball—
or how many fingers were showing on the seam of his fastball.
But I have had hundreds who came up and said, "What is Sandy
Koufax really like?" I doubt people really know—or care—that
Jack Nicklaus uses the interlocking grip. But everybody knows
how he was a little fat kid who came up and wrested the game
of golf away from Arnold Palmer and whoever else thought they
had it.

In the early, prepublication days of *Sports Illustrated*, we had
a vice-president named Dick Neale with whom I disagreed re-
spectfully. Dick thought you could buy a magazines success. You
bought subscription lists from other established magazines, you
gave out hockey pucks with subscriptions. They all helped, I felt,
but ultimately the success of a magazine would depend on the
writing. The only thing magazines can give you that TV can't is
a good read. You don't buy a magazine to find out who won. You
buy it to find out why he won.

But, basically, you buy it to be entertained. There's no other
reason for sports's existence in the first place. It's an extension of
the opera stage, the traveling troubadours, the acrobats, trapeze
artists. The only difference is, you keep score. The sports fan
knows the score. He wants to know what's behind it. I'm proud
of what we did, and they did, at *Sports Illustrated*. It played its
role in the explosion of sports. So did I.

4

·······································

The Curveball You Can't Hit Anyway!

Whoever invented baseball either got lucky or he was a genius. (General Abner Doubleday never really fit either description so I have to conclude his claim is spurious, at best.)

The bases are ninety feet apart, which is ingenious because any ground ball hit to an infielder requires precisely 3.2 seconds to be scooped up and fired to first base. Not even an ocelot can beat that out. The fastest that a man has ever been clocked going down to first base is about 3.4 or 3.5 seconds. He will be out by a step if everything goes right.

A stealing runner can get down to second from first in less time but that's because he has a lead, he's not running ninety feet. He's not running eighty-five or even eighty if he's daring enough.

Not even artificial surfaces, which probably add a tenth of a second or more to the baserunner's speed, can upset this delicate geometry. That's because the ball gets there faster on this surface, too.

The distance of the pitcher's mound, sixty feet, six inches, from home plate, has also withstood the test of time even though the race is getting so big, the fear was abroad that a skyscraper of a flinger would one day be found who could *hand* the ball to the catcher and bypass the batter altogether.

Baseball is the most leisurely of games that men play and for that reason it more or less constantly flirted with extinction in the frenzied seventies and eighties when our society became addicted to violence and action—accompanied by an ear-splitting noise, which assaulted the ears and sounded like nothing so much as a river of oil drums falling down steel stairs in a thunderstorm, but they called it "music."

The intellectuals loved baseball. Roger Angell wrote about it in *The New Yorker* as if it was High Mass and crack Washington journalist George Will took time out from advising presidents how to run the world to write an adoring chapter about a baseball manager, Tony LaRussa, whom he equated with the great figures of history because he had the good sense not to tell Jose Canseco to bunt.

Baseball players were a sportswriter's delight. They hadn't changed much since Ring Lardner's day and the Alibi Ikes and You Know Me Als were all over the place. The Oakland A's had a pitcher, Jim Nash, one year and, after a sweaty workout, the manager, Hank Bauer, ordered him to go in and change. "And get on another jockstrap," he commanded. "Why," asked Nash, "I ain't got but one cock."

Players in other sports had a veneer of education. Baseball players seldom did. They were the only people I knew who had a vocabulary that seemed to consist solely of four-letter words. Once, when I showed up unexpectedly in a Bradenton hotel where the Dodgers were briefly staying, pitcher Don Drysdale asked me what on earth I thought I was doing there. "I got homesick for the words *fuck* and *shit*," I told him. "I haven't heard them since the World Series."

Putting ballplayers into English for a family newspaper was always a challenge. If old Slugs hit a home run, "I put the hurt on that fucker" was hardly suitable for the little old ladies from Pasadena to read with their morning coffee. Even if he struck out, his reaction, "I was guessing fastball and that pussy threw me the deuce [curve]," leaves something to be written around.

But the ballplayers were honest. None of this "I'm just trying to live up to my potential" garbage that the more tactful of the athletes in other sports favored.

Other sports considered us a necessary evil. Ballplayers considered us an unnecessary evil. By the time they grasped the essentiality of the press to their game, they were mature individuals on their way out. Frank Graham of the old *New York Journal American* put it in perspective when he said of a ballplayer who had been particularly aggravating to the media all his career but suddenly mellowed. "He's learning to say 'Hello' when it's time to say 'Goodbye.' "

Baseball historically had the sports page all to itself. It was, to all intents and purposes, the only game in town for most of the year.

It took television to downgrade it. The rectangular sport of football was perfect for the rectangular screen of television. Also, the ball was big. Television all but ruined hockey. Golf it didn't affect too much because the story was ultimately told with white ball on the dark backdrop of the green.

Baseball was in between. You couldn't always follow that white ball but TV found a way to put you in the perspective of the pitcher. The sophisticated camera shot from center field had the effect of putting you on the mound with a dangerous batsman to be gotten rid of. If the ball was struck, the camera had to frantically search for the cognizant outfielder and trace its progress by his reactions.

Baseball never was a team game. What it was, was a series of solo performances. The pitcher did his solo. When he released the ball, the spotlight switched to the batter. He did his solo.

If he hit it, the spotlight would switch to the infielder or outfielder and he would go into his aria. If he picked up the ball and fired it to home plate, the catcher and the baserunner would do their solos.

It didn't require teamwork. The most storied double-play combination in history (thanks to their being deified in the press by a poem by Franklin P. Adams), Tinker-to-Evers-to-Chance, featured two players—Tinker and Evers—who didn't speak to each other. As chronicled, neither did Ruth and Gehrig.

There were, however, team players. These were usually marginally talented players who made the best of their abilities. Eddie Stanky was the prototype of this breed of overachievers, of whom Leo Durocher once said, "He can't run, he can't hit, he can't field—all he can do is beat you."

My favorite ballplayer was one of these. Jim "Junior" Gilliam was Tonto. Whatever you required, Jim could do for you. He played every position on the ballclub except pitcher and catcher. He was a caretaker they couldn't dislodge. Every year, the club would bring out some phenom who was meant to take over Jim's infield position. Every year, the phenom would fail to meet Jim's standards and would soon be back in the minors and, often, out of the game altogether. When Maury Wills came up and electrified the baseball world by stealing 104 bases, breaking Cobb's record by 12, it was the patient Jim Gilliam batting second, behind Wills, who took pitches all summer to give his teammate a chance to steal. It caused Gilliam's average to slump forty points— he never could swing at the first couple of pitches no matter how good they were—but it helped the team. Also Maury Wills.

Maury Wills was a record-setter but he was, ultimately, a baseball tragedy. First of all, he languished in the minor leagues for nine years until a manager, Bobby Bragan, turned him into a switch-hitter. Maury always had the dazzling speed and the surest instinct on the basepaths of any runner I had ever seen. The Dodgers brought him up in the summer of 1959 and he promptly ran them into a pennant and World Championship. He was the only difference on a team that had finished seventh the year before in its first season in L.A.

The town was his. Wills was the darling of Hollywood. He was more than that to the screen actress Doris Day. Doris, at the time, was almost the biggest comedy star in films. Her pictures with Rock Hudson were box-office smashes. She had started out as a band singer and her records, notably "Que Sera, Sera," were runaway bestsellers.

She was smitten with Maury and began lavishing expensive gifts on him, like color TV sets. The official word was the friendship was platonic but, of course, it wasn't.

What happened to Maury after he left baseball made you want to sob. He descended into a miasma of cocaine addiction and self-destruction that confounded belief.

Maury Wills, the ballplayer, had always been a man in firm control of his life. In all the years I studied him, I never saw Maury do a thing without a purpose, aimlessly. He was as organized a human being as I have ever seen. Other ballplayers would lounge around the locker room in their birthday suits, scratching and spitting, chewing gum and playing cards. Not Maury. He came into a locker room like a company CEO. He checked his mail, made his phone calls, put on his uniform—and went out and practiced precisely the things he knew he would need for that night's game. A curveball specialist going that night? Maury got Tommy Lasorda to feed him a diet of curves.

Maury drove pitchers wild when he got on the basepaths. He was fast—but there were faster. What made Maury the greatest baserunner of his time was not what he did with his feet but what he did with his eyes and his brains. He studied every pitcher who came into the league. He knew their best moves, he knew precisely how big a lead he could take. He knew what their pattern of pitches was. There wasn't a catcher in the league who could throw Maury out on a breaking-ball pitch.

Maury Wills, the addict, was a pathetic sight to behold. Gaunt, gray, in thrall to a thousand raging masters, he tried briefly to manage. He was a disaster, falling asleep on the bench, putting wrong names in a lineup. He never made the Hall of Fame, most likely because voters disapproved of his lifestyle. His numbers supported his election. Wills brought back the stolen base to baseball. Before his return, there were some years when *sixteen* stolen bases (Stan Hack, 1938) led the league. Maury stole sixteen in a week and a half.

When the Dodgers came West, the whole mood of the franchise changed. Laid-back L.A. was a far cry from Ebbets Field. I always noted the differences in the fans from each community could be summed up in the reactions of the two-dollar bettors in the homestretch of a horserace. In New York, they heaped invective on their animal. "Don't die now, ya goddam dog, don't quit on me!" In L.A., they implored, "Just a few more steps, baby, you can do it—just hold on for a few more steps for Daddy!"

Baseball was the same. In Ebbets Field, the bleacherite would scream, "Call yourself a pitcher, Drysdale! You couldn't get my grandmother out, ya choke artist!" In L.A., the cheering was positive. "All right, Big D, we're with you Don, baby! Let him hit it! Willie'll get it!"

Koufax and Drysdale were the most commanding pitching pair I have ever seen. Koufax was very possibly the best left-hander there ever was. Only one pitcher ever made the Hall of Fame with fewer lifetime victories.

The definitive story on Koufax came from the first man I ever heard swear on radio. That was Jim Davenport, the San Francisco third baseman, who sometimes seemed to hit Koufax better than the registered superstars. One night, after he had rapped a hit that beat Koufax, he was on the postgame show and the interrogater asked him, "Jim, with Koufax, do you look for the fastball?" "Oh, shit, yeah," shot back Davenport. "The curveball you can't hit anyway!"

As good as he was, Koufax was never comfortable in the spotlight. He could be almost reclusive. When he retired—too soon, in the belief of most of us—he didn't get a penthouse in Palm Beach or a condo in Palm Springs, Sandy moved to Ellsworth, Maine, where his nearest neighbor was a moose. When he got a job as commentator on ABC, Sandy always seemed embarrassed at intruding on the ballplayer's time. Why, is a mystery. He had the rugged good looks, the intelligence—he was one of the only two ballplayers I ever knew to do *The New York Times* crossword puzzle on road trips, the other was Keith Hernandez of the Mets—and he had a perfect voice with no trace of a regional accent. But, Sandy always seemed to be running from something.

Roberto Clemente might have been as good a player as ever played the game. I remember Hall of Fame broadcaster Vin Scully once told me that, in all the years he'd been covering the game, he never saw Clemente throw to the wrong base or uncork a throw up the line. Even Willie Mays did it on occasion, even Henry Aaron. He never saw Clemente do it.

Clemente appeared to be a cantankerous character on the surface. He smarted at the under-recognition he got. He blamed it on playing in Pittsburgh instead of New York or Los Angeles.

When you interviewed Roberto, you had to withstand the opening salvo of complaint, abuse or scolding. When it passed, you got a good interview.

He usually wanted you to listen to his back. He fancied himself a chiropractor and he would ripple his vertebrae for you at the drop of a "Hi, Roberto." Sometimes, in a fine furious frame of mind when he had just gone 0-for-4 (it didn't happen very often, Roberto never had a slump in his life) against Koufax, Roberto would rage, "He's always claiming his arm hurts, his finger hurts, his elbow hurts! Then, he comes out and pitches a two-hitter!" "Wait a minute, Roberto!" I corrected him once. "You're always telling me your back is killing you, it's all out of whack. Then, you go out and bat .356!"

Another time, I was interviewing catcher Manny Sanguillen. Roberto was curious. "What you say about Manny?" he wanted to know. (After all, Manny wasn't batting .356.) "Oh," I told Roberto, "Manny is smiling all the time, he's happy, he's cheerful." Roberto thought for a moment. "Oh," he said, brightening up. "I'm happy, too. Only my face don't show it."

Well, to my eternal discredit, I suppose, I changed the line only slightly. Not the sense of it, just a consonant or two. I made it, "I'm happy, too, only my face doesn't *know* it!" I'm sure Horace Greeley will forgive me.

Clemente was one of two great hitters who went about it all wrong in the batter's box. Roberto had one foot in the bucket. He looked like a pigeon for an outside curve. (Lefty Gomez used to say of hitters like this that they "had one foot in the American Association.") But you couldn't smuggle an outside pitch past him. (As Don Drysdale used to say of Henry Aaron, "throwing a fastball by Henry was like trying to smuggle a sunrise past a rooster." Ditto a curve past Roberto.)

I was sitting in the press box one night reading a *Sports Illustrated* manual on the correct way to hit a baseball. I am not big on how-to manuals anyway; my credo is that, if they taught sex the way they teach golf, the race would have died out long ago.

I happened to glance down on the field where a batsman was doing everything wrong. He was hitting off the wrong foot, he was coiling in a non-conducive-to-hitting-the-curve way, he held the bat all wrong according to the manual I had in front of me.

The batsman was Stan Musial. The Man. Like Clemente, he was the most dangerous hitter of his time. Like Willie Mays and Ted Williams, he hit home runs almost by accident. But he hit 475 of them. Usually, a guy who bats .331 lifetime hits eleven home runs.

I never saw a man who seemed to get more fun out of playing baseball than Musial. If the pressure ever got to him, he never showed it. He was the exact opposite of Clemente. He was happy and his face knew it. He was as decent a man as I knew in sports. I never met a man who didn't like him.

Steve Garvey was the opposite. The harder he tried to be liked the more hostility he inspired. I don't know why. I think the notion persisted that no one could be that good. I mean, here was a guy who hit .300 every year, got over 200 hits, 25 to 30 home runs and drove in 100 runs. He was unfailingly good-natured, always up. He went to church, drank milk, smiled a lot, almost never questioned an umpire's call. He was the last of the Rover boys, the third Merriwell brother. He was a superstar who acted as if he would do windows.

Someone once said if you opened the average professional athlete's head, you would find a six-pack of beer and a naked woman in there. I always said if you opened Garvey's head you would find a banana split.

Nobody liked him but the fans, the owners, the managers, columnists, the White House and kids with autograph books.

That left his infield. They despised Garvey. Maybe because he used to scoop up so many of their low throws. (You could throw the ball over Garvey—he was only five-eight—but you couldn't throw under him.)

I liked him because he was as available for interview as a guy running for sheriff. He played in more consecutive games than anybody in league history. The last first baseman to set a record like that is lionized today—Lou Gehrig.

Garvey posted the kind of statistics that entitled him, by baseball's code, to overturn pails of water on sportswriters, muscle rookies out of the batting cage, second-guess the manager, criticize the ownership and find fault with the way the country was run. But generally he kept a lower profile than a .220 hitter, some of whom were his severest critics. He was the most underpaid player in the game. He got $300,000 at a time when journeymen were getting three times that much, but Garvey never once mentioned the magic word "renegotiation" at a time when most stars wanted to renegotiate while the ink was still wet on the contact they signed.

His teammates couldn't believe it was all true. They gnashed their teeth and changed the subject when Garvey's name was mentioned. Finally, one day, they unburdened themselves to a female reporter from San Bernardino. The word "hypocrite" came up. A lot.

A big part of the problem, it turned out, was Garvey's wife, Cyndy. A toothsome blonde with show business aspirations, she seemed to have offended other team wives. They complained to

Garvey

husbands who already were resentful of Garvey and his reputation. (Pitcher Don Sutton got in a fistfight with him in a Montreal dressing room.)

Okay, so the dissenters from the Garvey image appeared to be right when "Too-Good" Garvey was said to be spending his time going around the country knocking up girlfriends. You might say Garvey turned into your typical ballplayer *after* he ceased being one.

With any other ballplayer, the news would have been greeted with a shrug. But Garvey was thought of as "Father" Garvey in the Roman-collar sense. This put a whole new spin on the Garvey legend. In point of fact, Garvey did the honorable thing: He acknowledged paternity where it appeared. He got married. He paid child support. But it was further proof if any were needed that a ballplayer's a ballplayer for all of that. And none of them is exempt from what the press likes to call "the temptation of the road."

I liked baseball. It was the right mix of competition, contemplation and calibration for me. A ballpark is still one of the great relaxing venues. It is a great place for the leather-lunged fan to work out his aggressions but there is an undertone of "I'm just kidding" in the baseball fan's torrent of abuse. Actually, he's probably a fan of the man he's jeering. Usually, he's just trying to insulate himself against failure.

Periodically, I would pen a paean to the grand old game:

I like country roads and moonlit nights, homemade fudge and ocean sunsets.

I like songs like "Girl of My Dreams," love stories and happy endings, Norman Rockwell and grand opera.

I like Fenway Park and office pools. I like Opening Day, Bat Night, guest anthem singers and "Take Me Out to the Ball Game."

I like Babe Ruth's bat, Ty Cobb's spikes, Stan the Man, Leo the Lip, the Big Train and ol' Diz, Willie, Mickey and the Duke, Joe D. and the Iron Horse.

I like baseball. I've never been unhappy in a baseball park in my life. Too slow? For whom? I never went to a ballpark in a hurry in my life. I don't plan to start anytime in the near future. As the song says, I don't care if I never get back.

5

· ·

Which Way's Chavez Ravine?

The time is January 1957, the place, Wilshire Boulevard, Los Angeles, a warm, winter day with the sun shining through the windows of the Automobile Club of Southern California as the man pauses at the counter.

This is a pleasant man with a full belly flopping over his out-of-fashion double-breasted suit. He is holding a cigar, which is stuck in a filterless white plastic holder, and an ash flops off onto his carelessly buttoned suit as he stands there.

He is wearing a hat, which stamps him as an outlander in this land of perpetual sunshine. His eyes twinkle behind old-fashioned rimless glasses, without which he would resemble a benign, smiling Buddha.

His voice when he speaks sounds like a rusty file being drawn across a corroded iron pipe and several chins bobble when he opens his tiny quizzical mouth to speak. "Pardon me, young man," rasps Walter O'Malley politely, "but can you tell me where Chavez Ravine is?"

In the little world of baseball, that question has to rank in historical importance as if, say, George Washington were to sidle up to a Hessian guard and innocently inquire how wide the Delaware was at Trenton—or if Abraham Lincoln were heard calling downstairs to ask Mary how to spell "Emancipation." I have often wondered if the clerk who unraveled the auto club map that day knew he was disclosing the future capital of baseball.

Walter O'Malley was the only 240-pound leprechaun I have ever known. He was as devious as they come. He always managed to look as if he had his own marked deck. He was half Irish and half German or, someone once said, "half-oaf, half-elf."

53

He changed the face of Baseball. He might have saved the game. He infused new energy, created new rivalries, brought a new audience, a new dynamism at a time when baseball was the Sick Man of Sport and losing its audiences in droves to pro football.

They have never forgiven O'Malley in New York. A lot of people who moved out of Brooklyn themselves were outraged when O'Malley followed suit. He occupied the same place in the hearts of New York writers as Benedict Arnold. "The Wizard of Ooze," he was called.

He had done what Americans always do when they get prosperous—moved to the suburbs. In his case, the suburbs were three thousand miles away.

He was just following a trend. The population of California was around 8 million when I arrived there in 1944. It was 32 million forty-five years later. That is one of the great migrations in the history of mankind. O'Malley simply joined it. He followed his customers.

He was not forgiven because he had just presided over the most fabulously successful ten-year period any National League team had ever enjoyed. His Dodgers had won six pennants, been in the playoffs two other years. They had drawn over a million customers a year. They had led the major leagues in net profit after taxes, $1,860,744 for the five-year period of 1952 to 1956.

The Dodgers were kind of America's Team. The romance of baseball being what it is, the entire nation took up the fond nickname "The Bums" and took the Brooklyn Dodgers to its heart and reserved for them the special parental indulgence one reserves for foolish but harmless offspring. The fact that the Dodgers had brought up the first black player in the modern history of the major leagues added the vocal political liberals to the mix even though most of them didn't know a squeeze play from a pop fly.

But Branch Rickey had done all of these things. Walter O'Malley was not a baseball man. He was a bottom-line man. He never went into a locker room in his life. He had come to the Dodgers as a caretaker for the company that held the mortgage on the club at the time when the club didn't even meet the interest.

The Dodgers weren't the first major league team to move. That "honor" went to the 1953 Boston Braves, whose owner, Lou

Perini, also didn't stop going till he put two time zones between him and Braves Field. He moved to Milwaukee. Boston belonged to the Red Sox anyway and no one bothered to stop Perini or blamed him very much for trying to better himself.

O'Malley had actually tried to get New York to keep the Dodgers. The locale and character of Ebbets Field, the musty, cracker-box firetrap that had been the home of the Dodgers since 1913, had made going to a ballgame there about on a social level with going to a cockfight.

O'Malley invited the city to condemn the downtown land for him. He would build the ballpark. O'Malley even proposed a domed stadium. He was years ahead of his time.

He only wanted to move a few city blocks. The city and state dragged their feet. They argued over the propriety of condemning land for a purely private enterprise. O'Malley got disgusted. He was a proud man, a stubborn man. When he threatened to move, they smirked. Move the Dodgers! He had to be kidding! He wasn't. He also took the Giants with him.

When O'Malley left, the city of New York fell all over itself to build a park for an expansion team, which turned out to be the Mets.

I first came into O'Malley's world the spring he moved to Los Angeles. I did a cover story on him for *Time* magazine. I spent weeks hanging out with him in Vero Beach, San Francisco and, finally, L.A. He wasn't always pleased with what I wrote but O'Malley had as high a regard for the freedom of the press as Thomas Jefferson. For a different reason. O'Malley always said one of the reasons he abandoned Brooklyn was that "once there were four newspapers in Brooklyn, now there are none. And if you don't think a newspaper isn't important to baseball, you don't know baseball."

O'Malley was not the first to covet Los Angeles. Bill Veeck was. In the early fifties, Veeck owned the St. Louis Browns, a team so feckless John Lardner once wrote that fans were surprised when the team was sold. "They didn't think the Browns could be sold because they didn't think the Browns were owned." Veeck would have taken the team in any direction to escape St. Louis, but he linked up with Los Angeles sportswriter Vincent

X. Flaherty in a bold bid to move the all-but-bankrupt team to L.A. Two things were at work to block the move: 1)The Stone Age owners hated Bill Veeck, they wanted him out of baseball altogether, not prospering in it anywhere; and 2) Del Webb, the owner of the Yankees, wanted L.A. for himself.

They forced Veeck out—and they forced the Browns to move to Baltimore.

O'Malley had no such trouble. O'Malley didn't need the permission of the commissioner of baseball. O'Malley was the commissioner of baseball. In all but name. Come to think of it, he did more for the game than any commissioner who ever ran it.

The O'Malley I knew was the convivial sort who liked to play cards with the boys, drink with cronies. He built two golf courses in Florida and playing with him was a trip because it was understood he could kick the ball out of the rough anytime it was ankle high, any tree was a staked tree (even a hundred-year-old sycamore) and any putt was in the leather so long as it was on the green. O'Malley hit the green, he put the ball in his pocket.

He fancied himself a horticulturalist. He spent hours at a greenhouse bench trying to breed mega-sequoia trees to grow in Florida. Luther Burbank, he was not. They never even made it out of the pot. O'Malley didn't have much of a green thumb.

But he did in the counting house. The Dodgers became the most fabulously successful franchise in the history of the game. They were the first in the league to draw 2 million, the first in the game to draw 3 million.

He never had much congress with his ballplayers. I always thought he regarded them as obstreperous children, fiscally irresponsible, functionally illiterate and as ineducable and temperamental as horses. He trusted his underlings to keep them in line, Fresco Thompson and Emil "Buzzie" Bavasi. Bavasi was a smart, tough negotiator whose ace in the hole was that he knew most players would play for nothing rather than get a day job.

I don't know how O'Malley would have handled the day of the agents. But in 1966, two of the greatest pitchers in the annals of the game, Don Drysdale and Sandy Koufax, linked up to hold out for more money.

They didn't get much. Koufax got $120,000, which is laughable in today's terms. Drysdale got somewhat less. When you think what an agent might get for them today—probably Rhode Island—you marvel at those more innocent times.

O'Malley never made the mistake of degrading or downgrading his players in public. He always knew he would shortly want to be selling them to the public as the second coming of Walter Johnson. Or Ty Cobb. He kept the infighting in.

But O'Malley always kept the image of the proper Dodger player in his mind. A Dodger player, in the O'Malley view, always came out looking like a Republican candidate for the Senate. He wore a tie, took his hat off in elevators and, if possible, went to Mass on Sundays. Other teams put up with rowdies, sociopaths, renegades and scofflaws if they had talent enough. O'Malley's Dodgers never did. O'Malley's Dodgers got rid of players like that. No matter how high they batted, if they missed team buses, scuffled with the law or disobeyed the manager, they were gone. Not our sort. Not Dodgers.

The Dodgers had a few dipsos in their ranks over the years. O'Malley seemed to have more tolerance for that. Perhaps because he liked a glass or two himself on occasion. Bill Veeck once said that, whenever you smelled the odor of a good cigar and a glass of Irish in the air, O'Malley couldn't be far behind. I saw O'Malley tipsy at a few St. Patrick's parties but never saw him what you might call drunk. Walter O'Malley was always in control of Walter O'Malley. And everything else.

He even had exactly the kind of son he would want. Peter O'Malley did everything Dad wanted him to do—prep schools, Wharton School of Finance, a move into the family business. Peter O'Malley is the son everyone would want, a pillar of respectability, one of the most controlled individuals we will ever see. It has been said he was a clone of the old man but the father had more of the pixie in him than the son. Peter made the society pages more than the sports pages. Like his father, he was a very moral man with a high respect for respectability. He never played poker with the sportswriters. But you never wrote that Peter was a living extension of his father that you didn't get a letter from him saying that was the best compliment you could pay him. Peter is still trying to live up to his father's high expectations. He now runs the Dodgers as capably as his father ever did. The periodic rumors he will sell the club and opt for a life of polo and bridge at the California Club meet with polite denials.

The city of L.A. gave the O'Malleys four hundred acres of downtown real estate. But the O'Malleys have proven reliable caretakers. Amid rumors he would build a papier-mâché ballpark and tear it down within a few years and construct some lucrative high rises, O'Malley remained true to his pledges. Chavez Ravine is still a ballpark thirty-five years after that auto club clerk rolled out the map. The lights from a night game dominate the cityscape and provide a reassuring sight to succeeding generations. Dodger Stadium is as neat and clean today as the day it opened. The floors gleam, the walls are not coated with grime. The seats are not filled with alcoholic rowdies. Dodger Stadium is a place you can bring your granddaughter.

O'Malley came close to not building it. When he arrived in L.A. opposition to his move closed ranks. They got a referendum put on the ballot to negate the city's deal; in California you can get enough signatures for an initiative or referendum to bar freckle faces from movie theaters if you pay for them. We have had dozens of initiatives and referendums passed that were later judged unconstitutional.

O'Malley won the referendum issue, but just barely—twenty-five thousand to twenty-three thousand.

O'Malley had a choice of Wrigley Field or the Coliseum to showcase his team when it arrived. That was no contest. Wrigley Field, which he had purchased along with the franchise rights to L.A. from Phil Wrigley, was a 24,000-seat replica of Chicago's Wrigley Field. The Coliseum had 92,000 seats—from about 28,000 of which you could actually see the game.

O'Malley, who never had any trouble adding, had no trouble opting for the 92,000 seats. The baseball establishment was aghast. I remember the commissioner of all baseball, Ford Frick himself, taking to the airways to deplore what would happen to the grand old game in this monstrosity of a ballpark. Frick, who had been his biographer, always worried what would happen to Babe Ruth's home run records.

To be sure, the Coliseum configuration was a little startling. To squeeze a ballpark in, left field was a bare 250 feet from home plate. So they put up a forty-foot wire-mesh fence. "There goes Babe Ruth's record! Also Roger Maris's!" harrumphed Red Smith. "Willie Mays'll bunt them over that thing."

It was a Pittsburgh pitcher, Bob Friend, who first tipped me to the essential characteristic of the Wall. "You'll get a lot of lazy high flies that will go over. But, you'll get a lot of line drive hits that Willie Mays'll hit that would go out for homers anywhere else in the world—but they'll crash into that fence for a single. It'll even out."

He proved prophetic. The most home runs any Dodger ever hit in a year while they were playing in the Coliseum was twenty-five—Gil Hodges, 1959. A Dodger pitcher, Johnny Podres, also accommodated himself to the geometry of the park. "You just get 'em to hit to right field," he said. "It's 440 to the right-field wall. It's inhuman."

The moral of the story: You can play baseball anywhere. Even indoors, as they were shortly to prove.

When the Dodgers came West, O'Malley's manager was a bucolic, unflappable hayseed named Walter Alston. Walt Alston just reeked decency. What the Jewish people call a "mensch." Walt Alston came from the kind of people who won our wars, plowed our fields, fed our children. He didn't understand what people went in nightclubs for. "You mean you just sit there and drink?!" His idea of a big night was a pool game in the basement and a malted milk at bedtime.

Walt came from a wide spot in the road in southern Ohio (does Ohio have a northern part?) called Darrtown, where the trains only stopped if they hit a cow. Walt was the salt of the earth. Walt didn't have a mean or prejudicial bone in his body. Every time I looked at Walt, I saw a Union soldier.

He was almost the most unexcitable man I've ever known. If he had a flaw it was that he couldn't really understand pressure. He would think nothing of putting a rookie in right field in the late innings of a pennant game, as he did repeatedly. If you made the big leagues, you were a big leaguer, was Walt's uncomplicated view.

He sometimes seemed to be a preacher running a wild animal act. He took defeat better than any manager I ever saw. The year his team lost the pennant game they thought they had won (they were leading the Giants, 4–2, going into the ninth inning), Alston's team locked the clubhouse door and proceeded to get roaring drunk and maudlin. Alston just showered—and went over to the Giants' clubhouse to congratulate the winners.

O'Malley didn't hate Alston. That wouldn't have been possible. He was just bored with him. He never gave him more than a one-year contract. He often seemed almost anxious to have Alston refuse.

Walter hankered for a manager who would make headlines— *any* headlines. O'Malley wanted baseball on page one, not just the sports page.

Alston was no good for this. You don't make page one in church. So O'Malley hired Leo Durocher as "coach." Bavasi didn't want him, Thompson didn't want him, Alston didn't need him. Only O'Malley wanted him. O'Malley wanted his bombast, his flair for the histrionics, his trouble-making.

Leo didn't disappoint. He made page one kicking dirt on umpire Jocko Conlan, he feuded with his own players, with the press. Finally, Durocher did what Durocher always did. He self-destructed. The night after the Dodgers blew the playoff game to the Giants, Leo went on record as saying he would have had Don Drysdale in the game. "I came in the clubhouse in the ninth inning and saw Big D walking around in his long johns and I said, 'What are you doing here?! Why aren't you out in the bullpen? What's he saving you for—spring training?' "

That kind of insubordination couldn't go unchallenged. Leo was gone.

Leo's problem was, as Runyon said of someone else, he always saw life as 8-to-5 against. Only moderately talented, he made his way through bluster, cheek and gall. Where none existed, he manufactured controversy. Branch Rickey once said of him, "Leo Durocher is a mental hoodlum with the infinite capacity for taking a bad situation and immediately making it infinitely worse."

Durocher never completely escaped the rumor that, as a rookie, he stole Babe Ruth's watch. He actually spiked Ty Cobb—which was like biting a lion. He was a back-biting, calculating, manipulative man who would have done anything to become the Dodger manager so close to his show business pals. His epitaph, the heartless line attributed to him by Frank Graham, "Nice guys finish last," summed up his philosophy of life.

Leo was defiant to the last. When he finally died, at the age of eighty-six, in Palm Springs, he went out kicking dirt at the world. The veterans committee had, unfairly, kept him out of the Hall of Fame and Leo wanted it in his will that, if they put him in the Hall posthumously, his heirs were to refuse it. Leo, inevitably, finished last himself.

When Walter Alston came down with a failing heart, Walter O'Malley, who was dying himself by then, finally had the kind of manager he'd hankered for.

Tommy Lasorda was a baseball manager right out of Central Casting. From his bandy legs to his prominent gut to his habit of giving orations, he was perfect for the role. You couldn't have built yourself a more typical baseball manager.

Tommy never talked, he shouted. He always managed to sound as if the building were on fire. He reveled in baseball. There were two men in my journalistic career I could always count on when I ran dry and needed a column. One was Casey Stengel. The other was Lasorda.

Tommy was as American as a carburetor, but he liked to drape himself in an American flag and give you the "Only in America" spiel so favored by professional immigrant sons. The truth of the matter was, Tommy didn't even look Italian. But he was the son of Sabbatino and Carmella Lasorda, the pride of Abruzzi, a province in the calf of the boot of Italy.

Sabbatino drove a cement truck for a living in Norristown, Pennsylvania. Tommy had a chance to go down in the quarry, too, except that he had this tricky curveball. It never was good enough to get major league hitters out but it got Tommy a career in the big leagues beyond his wildest dreams.

I first met Tommy Lasorda in a bar in San Diego twenty-five years ago and we've been friends ever since. Ordinarily, it's not a good idea to become friends with someone you may have to sit in judgment on, as journalists sometimes find out the hard way. But I have always found Lasorda had a better appreciation of the symbiotic relationship between press and sportsmen than almost anyone I know of.

He was only a scout for the Dodgers when I first knew him but you always knew he was destined for better things. Even "company man" wasn't adequate to describe his dedication. The "I bleed Dodger blue" spiels the public became so familiar with had their origin long before Tommy hit the big league dugout.

Tommy knew baseball. And he knew baseball players. He was aggressive but patient.

His seemingly sophomoric enthusiasm for the game played well with the kids and the organization soon put him to work developing young talent in the outer reaches of the farm system—such places as Pocatello and Ogden. Lasorda was in his element. "I used to tell them all they'd be playing in Dodger Stadium someday, even the .200 hitters," Lasorda used to reminisce. "I never let a negative thought in. I told them I liked the attitude of the old-time fighter, Jake LaMotta. Jake used to say he fought Sugar Ray Robinson six times and won all but five of them."

It worked with the eager young kids in Pocatello. But would it play on Broadway?

It played. Lasorda and the Dodgers were perfect for each other.

In a sense, he brought his own team with him, the kids he had been assigned when he became manager at Spokane. He had the complete infield—Steve Garvey, Davey Lopes, Bill Russell and Ron Cey. It was a lineup that was to win him his first three pennants and, finally, his first World Championship.

The Dodgers in their other incarnation in Brooklyn had been pretty much labeled a congress of clowns. Overshadowed by the lordly Yankees and the businesslike Giants, overmatched at the box office, they signed players who stumbled to their own music. The "Daffiness Boys," the press labeled them, the team that might find it had three men on base—the same base.

Their image changed when Branch Rickey shrewdly emptied out the last remaining pool of talent not signed to a chain gang farm system—the Negro Leagues. Ricky had always been held to be the second Great Emancipator but, like the first one, he had a double motive. The first wanted to win a war. The second wanted to win a pennant. The Dodgers of Jackie Robinson, Roy Campanella, Joe Black and Don Newcombe were not funny. They won pennants, all right. Six of them in eleven years. Rickey had achieved parity even with the Yankees overnight.

But when they got to L.A., they took on an entirely different profile. They became a team that won smartly. They beat you with speed and pitching. The holdovers from Ebbets Field quickly faded out—Roy Campanella was tragically crippled, Robinson had retired, and Gil Hodges, Pee Wee Reese and Carl Furillo soon followed suit. Duke Snider could not cope with the vast wasteland that was right field in the Coliseum and opted out.

The new symbols became Sandy Koufax, Don Drysdale and Maury Wills. They brought four pennants in seven years. But ak1they were hardly overpowering. When Don Drysdale was in Washington for a government-sponsored meeting one year and a page brought him the news that his teammate Sandy Koufax had just pitched a no-hitter, Drysdale's reaction was, "Oh, yeah? Who won?" Drysdale was later to recall, "They'd bring you one run by the third inning and they'd say, 'Here, now don't squander it!'"

Lasorda's teams won four pennants and two World Championships in his tenure. Smart, tough, energetic, Lasorda very likely lusted for the general manager's job, where he would have been a natural. But when the GM, Al Campanis, tripped over his tongue on national TV one night, the job went to Peter O'Malley's longtime confidant and personal ally, Fred Claire, an ex-newspaperman. Lasorda, ever the good soldier, swallowed his disappointment. He was actually too valuable where he was. Like a lot of people, he probably thought the job would prove too much for the retired, self-effacing Claire. But Claire surprised a lot of people besides Lasorda.

The unfrocking of Al Campanis was probably the nadir of the Dodger organization. Here was the spokesman for the organization that had broken the color line in baseball going on *Nightline* to tell the world that black people lacked "the necessities" for leadership positions in what is, after all, a child's game. He also said, in one of the great non sequiturs of all time, that black people "lacked the buoyancy" to be able to swim. The show, believe it or not, was meant to honor the fortieth anniversary of Jackie Robinson's entry into baseball.

The interlocutor, Ted Koppel, raised in England, had only a superficial understanding of baseball but he knew bigotry when he heard it. So did the rest of the country.

In a sense, Koppel's question, "Why is there prejudice in the front offices of baseball?" was a little like the age-old unfair question, "When did you stop beating your wife?" Still, Campanis undertook to defend baseball. In doing so, he indicted it. It was hardly baseball's finest hour.

The flippant answer would be, "If blacks want to be in the front offices of baseball, why don't they buy a team?" That would have been bad enough. But Campanis's answers were unconscionable.

Those of us who knew him could not but believe Al had been goaded into an unworthy and controversial position. There had never been a whisper of prejudice in the conversations of this man who, himself, had been born illegitimate, on the island of Kos in the Aegean, and who was hardly your ruling-class WASP. He had been a buddy of Jackie Robinson, who had taken his job. He was an educated man, NYU, a scout on the black sandlots of the Dominican Republic and Puerto Rico, the discoverer of Roberto Clemente.

For whatever reason, he said what he said. He might as well have burned a cross on the memory of Jackie Robinson.

I had lunch with Al to see if there was anything salvageable, if there was an apology he could make. Al seemed bewildered by what he had done. He acted as if he had been a ventriloquist's dummy. My notion was that, as was his postgame wont, he might have put down a few scotches between the time the Dodger game finished that night and the time he went on the air, sitting in a chair in the infield of the darkened Astrodome. Al would not cop out in that way.

Al's dismissal stuck. Peter O'Malley hired a black ex–basketball star (Notre Dame, the L.A. Lakers), Tommy Hawkins, to a front-office job. Harry Edwards, the black activist sociology professor from Cal-Berkeley, engaged Al Campanis in a black awareness program—but the lingering fallout from that episode hung over Dodger Stadium for years and can still be detected on some nights when the talk turns to black presence (still not very visible) in the executive suites of baseball.

Lasorda managed to distance himself from the swirls of controversy around L'Affaire Campanis. He became the one constant in the new setup of the Dodger organization. The economics of baseball being what they became, Tommy no longer had a dugout full of pupils he had nursed through the farm system. In fact, he had no graduates of the farm system to speak of. The new franchise players had been sucked up on the free agent market. In large part, they were grizzled, cynical veterans that the old Dodger blue and Big Dodger in the Sky routines should have had no effect on.

Lasorda had an act to fit every occasion. He knew something the public didn't: Ballplayers are kids at heart. As Roy Campanella had said, "To play baseball well, you have to be a man. But you have to have a lot of little boy in you, too."

Tommy preyed on the little boy in every man. He wasn't above a con. When hard-hitting outfielder Joe Ferguson balked at being turned into a catcher, Lasorda switched tactics. "Joe, you ever heard of Gabby Hartnett? Well, he became one of the great catchers in baseball history. But he was an outfielder! He didn't wanna be a catcher! But he's in the Hall of Fame as a catcher! He even became a great manager because of the great knowledge he acquired in the game as a catcher!" Impressed, Ferguson agreed to become a catcher. After he left the room, the general manager, Campanis, who had heard the pitch, objected, "Tommy, Gabby Hartnett was never an outfielder!" Lasorda sighed. "Chief," he said, "you know that and I know that. But Fergie doesn't know that. Now, do you want a catcher or not?"

Another time, when the team headed into a prolonged losing streak, Tommy was ready. "Hey!" he told a meeting. "The 1927 Yankees were the greatest team in the history of baseball. But they had a ten-game losing streak!" The team was buoyed. A writer, overhearing the pep talk, said, "I didn't know the 1927 Yankees lost ten in a row." "Neither did they," shot back Lasorda. "They didn't. But my guys needed bucking up."

How much of the Lasorda mystique was affected? Probably not any of it. You can keep an act up for nine reels or the run of the play. Lasorda has been Lasorda for the twenty-five years I have known him.

Does he love the Dodgers that much? Well, I have known personally of two clubs that were eager for his services and ready with a blank-check offer. One of them was the Yankees. The Dodgers even gave permission for them to talk to him. Lasorda has felt passed over for the GM job he covets. But he stays. Bleeding Dodger blue.

For all his image as a guy whose nose lights up, whose pants are baggy, whose shoes are size twenty and whose hat has a hole in it, Lasorda is never a man to trifle with. He has a monumental temper and was always quick to use his fists early in his career. He has a strong sense of what is right. He has worked with players I know he detests. Eddie Murray comes to mind.

But he cannot be moved from a strongly felt position. When he went up to the drug and alcoholic rehabilitation center in Wickenberg, Arizona, for the counseling sessions of his pitcher Bob Welch, who had been enrolled there, the staffers went to work on Lasorda. Part of the "therapy" is to lateral blame—on your father, your boss, your pressures. Lasorda wasn't having any. He quarreled with the counselors. Lasorda could not conceive of criticizing a father. Not anyone in the Lasorda family. He walked out.

When his son, Spunky, died of AIDS, Lasorda stubbornly refused to go public. The fund-raisers were upset. Lasorda might have been a powerful spokesman for their cause. Lasorda wasn't having any of that, either. His son was going to rest in peace. It might not be an enlightened view. But it was the Lasorda view.

The Dodgers were an economic and artistic success in L.A. They became part of the warp and woof of the city. If another city might have been embarrassed at having a team whose traditions, lore and very personality had seemed to belong to another town, L.A. wasn't. L.A. was full of people whose family traditions lay elsewhere. This was a city already settled by new arrivals. The Dodgers fit right in with all the rest.

Even their pitfalls added to the aura. Pitching to Jack Clark in the 1985 playoffs with first base open. Blowing the pennant in the top of the ninth in a playoff in 1962. An outfielder dropping three fly balls in what was to prove to be Sandy Koufax's last game.

In a way, the Dodgers were really L.A.'s team. In the beginning, it was the Rams. They were the first big league operation to embrace Los Angeles. And their advent coincided with the spurt of interest in pro football, which, for a time, seemed about to put baseball in the supporting role category.

But the Rams jilted L.A. and left the Dodgers supreme. Not even the Lakers, when they came, nor the Raiders, when they did, could shake the Dodgers' hold.

O'Malley's vision had been twenty-twenty. He not only helped O'Malley, he helped Baseball. The game has never been known for its far-seeing approach but, in spite of the fact he was driven to it by a pack of vacillating, obtuse politicians in New

York, O'Malley made the right historical choice. He bundled up the Giants and his team and followed the rest of the population West.

It was so right, it was surprising no one had ever done it before. It was so right, it was surprising Baseball thought of it at all. Baseball was always loath to enter the twentieth century. Baseball will always be three or more decades behind the rest of society. That's part of its charm.

6

....

A Rose Is a Rose Is a Rose Is . . .

Pete Rose, to me, symbolized Baseball. He was what the game was meant to be—or how we perceived it was meant to be.

In the age of the briefcase ballplayer, the walking conglomerate, Rose was a ballplayer right off the *Saturday Evening Post* cover. Norman Rockwell invented him.

He seemed the eternal fourteen-year-old, cap on backward, socks flopping about his ankles, knickers with a hole in them from sliding. He had these eager, excited little boy's eyes and he always looked to me coming to the ballpark like a kid coming downstairs on a Christmas morning sure there was going to be a pony or a new bicycle under the tree.

Pete was as uncomplicated as a summer day, as instinctive as a hound dog. He was born to hunt, or, in his case, play baseball. He never wanted to do anything else. He never could do anything else.

He didn't have the God-given talent of a Henry Aaron or Willie Mays. He had to work to play the game well. He wasn't fast. He got more hits than anyone else who ever played the game but very few of them were "leg" hits. Pete had to hit them where they ain't.

But, oh, how he loved to play baseball. I never knew anybody who derived the pure joy from the game Pete did. Not Willie Mays, Stan the Man. Not even Ernie ("Let's play two!") Banks.

It was in the middle of the 1975 World Series that Pete got on base, clapped his hands and turned to the great Carl Yastrzemski, who was playing first base that day, and exclaimed, "Isn't this just great?! Aren't we lucky?! Can you think of anything you'd rather be doing?!" Yaz just looked at him in amazement.

A lot of us did. Pete not only played the game, he studied it. Pete knew every hit he ever made and where it fitted in the grand scheme of the grand old game.

I don't know when Pete first began to play the game for the ages—but it was long before any of us suspected it.

There was no false modesty (or any other kind) about Pete. Where another ballplayer might dismiss his accomplishments with a shrug ("You saw it—you write about it!") Pete was not so cavalier. Pete would tell you in all seriousness after a game that the double he hit in the fifth inning "puts me in second [or first] place in lifetime doubles by switch-hitters." Pete hoarded his records like a squirrel with nuts.

He was not otherwise a sentimental man. I go a long way back with Pete. I came up, so to speak, as a columnist in 1961, Pete came up in 1963. I wasn't his Boswell. Bob Hertzel was. But I made him national several times a year and when I had my most serious eye problem in the late seventies, Pete almost took it personally. As if I had let *him* down. As I groped my way into the locker room one night shortly after my eyesight had dwindled down to nearly nothing, Pete surveyed me with some resentment. "How the fuck you gonna write about the game when you can't *see* it?!" he wanted to know.

My first recollections of Pete are of his jumping in the batter's box in spring training and exclaiming, "Every summer you know three things are going to happen—the grass is gonna get green and Pete Rose is gonna bat .300 and get 200 hits." He was usually right. Pete got 200 hits ten times in his career (he got 198 hits on another occasion and 192 on another).

Pete used to pal around with the black players on the club when he first came up. He would tell you earnestly, "I may not be the best hitter on this club but I'm the best *white* hitter!"

Pete was not exactly popular with the other whites on the team at first. It wasn't racial. Pete was simply taking the job away from their buddy, Don Blasingame, who was by no means over-age. He just was no Pete Rose.

Pete was Baseball to a whole generation. Everybody's boyhood dream—the skilled but determined blue-collar guy, the singles hitter, the hustler, the little-boy-in-a-man's-body. God made Willie Mays and Babe Ruth ballplayers. Pete Rose made Pete Rose one.

Pete didn't drink or carouse. He played baseball with the fervor of a kid trying to get his high school letter. Pete *ran* out bases on balls. He *ran* out home runs (to the point where teammate Frank Robinson once pulled him aside after a twelve-second sprint around the bases after a home run and said testily, "Kid, why don't you leave those home runs to those of us who can act them out?").

That was how Pete Rose earned one of the most famous nicknames in the game. He was in spring training once and, just after one ball four, he streaked down to first base. Over in the other dugout, Mickey Mantle, observing this, cracked sarcastically, "Well, if it isn't Charlie Hustle!" Pete, characteristically, took it as a compliment.

Pete was confident without being egotistical. He reveled in all aspects of the game, including the interviews. Pete was the sportswriter's friend. Pete liked his name in the papers. I mean, what is the use of setting all those records if nobody knows about them?

I don't think any of us fully realized how serious Pete was about his ambitions till the World Series of 1975. That was a Series I always held up as one of the greatest ever played (I rate the 1934 Gashouse Gang versus Detroit as second in my lifetime). The Boston Red Sox had Carl Yastrzemski, Freddy Lynn, Cecil Cooper, Jim Rice, Rico Petrocelli, Dwight Evans and Luis Tiant. The Cincinnati Reds had their Big Red Machine—Pete Rose, Johnny Bench, George Foster, Joe Morgan, Tony Perez.

That Series endured a succession of rainouts. Most players huddled in their rooms. I mean, rainouts aren't in their contracts. They don't have to be available to the media. But, Pete being Pete, he was available. He came into Boston and down to the headquarters hotel press conference every day. He gave us something to write about.

That was the first time any of us ever heard the name Ty Cobb surface in Pete's catalogue of goals.

Pete had 2,547 hits at the time. Respectable. Even Hall of Fame. But Pete was thirty-four years old at the time. And a long way from Ty Cobb's 4,192.

When Pete speculated on his chances of catching Cobb, we thought he was just trying to provide us with a headline. Pete wasn't. Pete was dead serious. He always was when it came to his game. He not only knew every hit Pete Rose ever made, he also knew every one Cobb ever did.

The knock against Cobb was, he wasn't a team player. Except for his earliest years, he never played on a pennant winner. Cobb got his hits. The team was on its own.

No such charge could ever be made against Pete Rose. Pete's teams were in six World Series and seven playoffs. He did things for the good of the team, not the good of Pete Rose. He came up as a second baseman but, when the team acquired Joe Morgan, he moved to the outfield. When the team acquired George Foster, he moved to third base.

Like a lot of ballplayers, he had no way of foreseeing the salary explosion. When slugger Ralph Kiner unleashed his opinion that Cadillacs are down at the end of the bat (English translation: "Hit home runs if you want to make big money"), Pete always would say, "I want to become the first hundred-thousand-dollar singles hitter." He became the first $3 million singles hitter.

For all his little boy appeal and seeming innocence, Pete was nowhere near as disciplined a human being off the field as he was on it. Pete was a notorious womanizer, indiscreet to the point of recklessness in his affairs. His indiscretions were known to everyone, including his wives.

Pete liked his women flashy. Just go find the nearest beehive hairdo, the shortest mini, the wad of chewing gum being cracked, and you would find Pete Rose's women. They had probably been cheerleaders in their youth and were pliant and not too intellectual. Pete had one or more in every baseball hamlet in the land—including Cincinnati, where he also had a wife. Locker room scuttlebutt resounded with the exploits of Pete Rose on road sex exhibitions. Pete never hid it.

Nor did he hide his gambling predilections. Pete began to be a headache for baseball long before Bart Giamatti became commissioner. Bowie Kuhn was commissioner from 1969 to 1984 and he barred Mickey Mantle and Willie Mays from the game for being employees of a gambling casino (legal) in Atlantic City. But he never had the stomach to take on Pete Rose.

Everyone knew Pete was a gambler. No one knew the extent. Most thought it began and ended with the occasional trip to the horse or dog track. Peter Ueberroth, when he was commissioner, called Pete in and ordered him to slow down.

Pete couldn't. Pete gambled the way he did everything. All out. Win big.

The evidence is, Pete didn't win big—he just bet big. Associates affirmed it was not uncommon for Pete to drop ten thousand dollars a night on the ponies. After all, he couldn't bet like a peasant. He had to bet like a big boy. He had to bet like Pete Rose. It was a macho thing for Pete. If you hauled out a six-dollar across-the-board bet or a place or show bet, Pete looked at you in distaste. "How the fuck you gonna make money *that* way?" he would want to know.

There's no telling if this predilection would have become so catastrophic to the legend of Pete Rose were it not for the entrance into this drama of A. Bartlett Giamatti, scholar, academician and, by the grace of God, commissioner of all baseball.

Victor Hugo would have loved the Bart Giamatti–Pete Rose epic. It had everything *Les Miserables* had except the bishop's candlesticks. The indefatigable, relentless, implacable upholder of the law on the track of his quarry, the helpless victim of his own addiction, who only happened to be the greatest hitter in the annals of baseball, whom Giamatti was accusing of betraying the game that made him.

We all know who Pete Rose was. The man who got 4,256 hits, 64 more than the only other man in the game who ever got more than 4,000, Tyrus Raymond Cobb.

Bart Giamatti took a bit more explaining. A. Bartlett was one of those professorial types who parted his name on the side. President of Yale. Professor of English Lit. Lifelong baseball fan.

Pete Rose never read anything but a box score and a *Racing Form* in his life. Giamatti taught classes in Spenser's *The Faerie Queene* and was one of the world's foremost authorities on Renaissance poets. He could quote the *Iliad*—or tell you why the Red Sox blew the 1949 pennant with equal expertise and enthusiasm.

Bart Giamatti was, in short, a complex man. He was, on the

whole, a cold man with hard, coal-black eyes and a high but rigid moral standard. He was not your everyday pipe-sucking, patch-elbowed tenured professor lost in musty stacks of antiquity. He had a working knowledge of the streets. He equated Baseball with High Mass. He saw himself as a kind of complicated pope.

When he took over at Yale, he brooked no interference with his rule there, not even by the collection of politically correct antiwar activists. Bart Giamatti was not afraid of his student body nor was he about to knuckle under to Chicago Sevens or other spearheads of campus unrest.

Pete Rose didn't scare him either. It's hard to know what turned him into Pete's sworn enemy. For all his intellectual pre-tensions, Bart Giamatti was a fan and, at fount, a hero-worshiper. He should have idolized Pete Rose. He came to despise him.

The best evidence is, it was not so much Pete's gambling that turned him off as it was his lying. Giamatti couldn't abide lying. He particularly couldn't abide lying when it made him look like a persecutor.

When word reached Giamatti that Pete, by then the manager of the Reds, was betting on baseball, his fury kindled. When Pete denied it, it exploded. Giamatti became personally insulted. An "investigation" turned into a vendetta. Bart Giamatti was going to get Pete Rose if it was the last thing he would ever do.

Ironically, he did. And it was.

You had the undignified spectacle of Giamatti bursting his moorings in a way when he penned a letter to a judge who was sentencing a Pete Rose associate for cocaine trafficking. Giamatti was the last man in the world you'd expect to find in bed with a character of this low appeal, but there he was appealing to the judge (in *writing*!) for leniency on the grounds the dope dealer (and admitted addict) "had given significant and truthful coopera-tion" to Baseball in its investigation of Pete Rose.

That put the commissioner in rather poor company, soliciting mercy for an antisocial outcast of that stripe, but it was a measure of his outrage at Pete Rose.

No one really knows if Pete could have blunted the acrimony or even have headed it off if he had copped to his sins, promised to reform or otherwise mollified his indignant prosecutor. But Pete only exacerbated the relationship by appearing to treat the accusations as a bunch of nonsense. "It's crap!" he insisted.

It wasn't. Pete was always too restless or indifferent to keep friends. Like a lot of celebrities, he seemed drawn to the less respectable element of our society. They seemed to have the same fascination for him that he had for them.

Pete wasn't exactly lunching with John Gotti. But he was close to it.

Investigation showed he was a slow to no payer of his obligations to bookies. Very early in Pete's career, the general manager of the Reds, Dick Wagner, paid attention to this idiosyncrasy of his star player when he observed, "One of these days, Pete will be lucky if he doesn't get his kneecaps broken."

Gambling debts are not legally collectible in most states and Pete knew it. He apparently thought he was too big and too famous to be a victim of mob vengeance. But the floor of the East River has been filled with people who thought that.

It was Pete's stiffing of his bookies and his packet of unpaid markers that ultimately led Giamatti to the smoking gun.

Paul Janszen was one of the unsavory characters who found their way into Pete's life. Pete didn't know who the secretary of state was, but he could identify most of the small-town hood bookmakers in this country by their first name.

Paul Janszen was an odd case, even for Pete. Apparently from a standard middle-class family (the family business was steel barrels), Janszen had opted for the selling of illegal steroids to body-builders, of whom he was one.

He became, somehow, Pete's flunky and gofer. The ranks of sports celebrities abound with these sycophantic satellite types, who live in a kind of reflected glory. Janszen took to running Pete's bets. Then he took to booking them himself. Then he took to selling cocaine.

He needed the money. When the FBI came knocking on his door, he had hardly prospered from his association with America's number-one baseball hero. In fact, Pete, he said, owed him forty thousand dollars.

He had carried Pete's bags, run Pete's bets, been his bodyguard, even "beard" on Pete's dates. But, now, he was to become

Bart Giamatti's star witness. He had an encyclopedic memory. He also had tapes.

The evidence against Rose was damning. But was it conclusive?

Giamatti played hardball. He allowed Rose to get out of baseball with his reputation intact as to whether he bet on baseball. But he made him get out. When Pete accepted banishment from the game, what was the public to think?

Besides, Giamatti immediately told the press that he had no doubt Pete had, indeed, bet on games, in fact, on games involving his own team. Giamatti *kicked* him out the door.

Exhausted, embittered, Giamatti retreated to Martha's Vineyard to lick his wounds, recuperate. A lifelong chain-smoker, an over-eater, overweight, overworked, he was shortly to succumb to a heart attack.

He was a figure of high moral righteousness to some. He was the Creature-That-Ate-Baseball to others. He was The-Man-Who-Destroyed-Everybody's-Kid-Brother, Peter Edward Rose.

And what of Peter Edward? Tarnished, unfrocked, demythologized, Pete stayed Pete. There was never anything enigmatic about Pete. He was a boy miscast as a man, a child miscast as a grownup.

Pete had always had an instinct for being at the right place at the right time. He came into baseball at precisely the right moment. Consider the incident in the ninth inning of the final game of the 1980 World Series. Pete was playing first base for the Phillies, who had a 3–2 lead in games and a 4–1 lead going into the ninth inning of Game Six. But Kansas City had the bases loaded and only one out when their second baseman, Frank White, a first-class hitter, lofted a foul ball near the Phillies' dugout. Catcher Bob Boone made a valiant effort to get under it. But, at the last second, the ball popped out of his glove and headed for the ground. Pete Rose was standing alongside. He dove to the ground, too, and came up with a saving catch just as the ball was about to hit the dugout step.

That was vintage Rose. Pete made game-saving catches his whole career. But he couldn't make one on himself. A Rose was a Rose was a Rose.

Shortly after his expulsion from the game he loved, he went to prison for income tax evasion. He pleaded guilty to failing to report $348,720 in earnings from baseball memorabilia sales.

The craze for baseball memorabilia came along just in time for Pete. It reached crescendo in the late eighties when collectors began paying sums of money for baseball cards, mitts and uniforms that had formerly been paid only for Rembrandts, Degases, Lautrecs and Tintorettos.

Pete sold everything but his family. At last count, there were something like fourteen Mizuno bats in existence that were supposed to be the bat he got hit number 4,192 with.

One of the strangest episodes occurred when he sold his diamond-studded Hickok belt to a curator in Oregon named Derrick Walker.

Walker is one of the oddest characters in the whole Pete Rose saga, a Mormon who operated an offshore bank in the South Pacific, and who owned a sports museum in his home state.

Before the sale of the belt, Pete apparently took the precaution of removing the real diamonds from the belt and replacing them with paste. He kept the real ones for a necklace for his wife, Carol.

Before you feel sorry for Walker, be advised that the certificate of deposit from his Bank of Tonga with which he paid Pete proved to be as phony as the diamonds. It was a standoff. (Except that the necklace was later stolen from Carol's apartment.)

Derrick Walker was later found slain in a Las Vegas apartment. The crime was never solved. He had apparently been suffocated, gangland-style.

What are we to make of Pete Rose? Villain or victim? Athlete or addict?

How serious were his transgressions?

Well, given the absence of proof he ever bet *against* his own team, given the absence of proof he ever maneuvered his team or himself into a position to lose, his behavior falls short of that of the infamous Black Sox of 1919. Those guys were crooks.

Was Pete a crook? A liar, certainly. Gambling addicts usually are. Addicts of all kinds usually are.

Pete enraged the moral sensibilities of Bart Giamatti. Should he have outraged the rest of us?

A hard call. It was always hard for the sporting press to find a sense of malice in Pete Rose. Certainly, he was not the boy-innocent we all made him out to be. But the way large segments of the press turned on Pete following the disclosures in a sort of feeding frenzy like sharks shocked Pete—and Pete's supporters.

There were various reasons. A lot of reporters thought they had a special relationship with Pete. They found out instead that his playing to the press was calculated. They were just another curveball to be hit. Some thought they had book or TV deals with Pete. Others were just miffed when Pete would renege on a personal appearance they thought they had him sewed up for. Whatever Pete did appeared to be for Pete. There were no Babe Ruth–type hospital visits, not many public charity appearances. Pete would drive overnight to sell a uniform or a bat or a glove but was not conspicuously present for community or civic projects.

Pete shed friends like a snake sheds skin. He replaced most of them with questionable characters who shared Pete's love of a high-risk existence. "It's all I'm guilty of—picking my friends stupidly," Pete would insist.

It wasn't all he was guilty of. Pete appeared to think two hundred hits and a .303 lifetime average conferred special status on him, which made him exempt from the normal standards of behavior.

Actually, the opposite would appear to be true. In our society, we are apt to hold candlelight vigils or march in parades for convicted murderers, but if a man is successful or famous, he is held to a standard most of us could not meet. He is turned on, viciously.

Pete cheated on his income tax. Who doesn't? Pete bet too much money at the racetrack. Oh? Pete stiffed the bookies? Aw, too bad!

His family never went hungry. Rose sold his sports mementos unsentimentally. Who saves his work smock? Would a door-to-door salesman sell his sample kit if the public were slavering to buy it?

Pete wasn't his own worst enemy. Not while Bart Giamatti was alive. But, as Richard Nixon said when he was brought low by Watergate, "I gave them the sword." So did Pete. He became an unfrocked hero.

There have been others in baseball's past. Whispers abound that even the legendary Ty Cobb had been all but detected throwing games. But, if he was, Commissioner Kenesaw M. Landis swept it under the rug. If Cobb cheated, who in the game could be trusted?

Baseball's defenders point out that warnings against gambling are posted in every locker room in every ballpark in America. But, in an age of state lotteries, proliferation of racetracks, legal wagering in about nine states and wide-open gambling in Nevada and Atlantic City, the line between what is legal and what is criminal is blurring. Why is a crap game that is as legal as divorce in Nevada punishable by five years in prison twenty miles to the south?

They stopped just short of proving Pete did anything dastardly. They appeared to know whatever evidence they had would probably not be enough for a regular court, a clever lawyer.

On the other hand, fandom's suspicions were aroused at the alacrity, almost meekness, with which Pete accepted his punishment. It was almost as if he feared what further disclosures might do to him if he fought. Pete accepted banishment for life with the proviso that he had the right to appeal after one year. But in fourteen previous such banishments not one reinstatement took place.

The agreement between the commissioner and his unfrocked hero contained one concession: "There is nothing in this agreement which shall be deemed either an admission or a denial by Peter Edward Rose of the allegation he bet on any major league baseball game."

Okay, then why ban him? For betting on basketball games? Cockfights? If he didn't bet on baseball, where's the crime?

Giamatti bluntly told the press, "He has stained the game."

Baseball loves to talk of legendary matchups—Hubbell against Dean, Koufax versus Gibson, Ruth versus Grove, Seaver versus Mays, Whitey Ford versus Jackie Robinson.

There never was a deadlier face-off than Giamatti versus Rose. Nobody won. Baseball lost.

7

. . . .

Golf—Me 'n Hogan 'n Jack 'n Arnie 'n Sam

I loved golf. I loved covering it. It was the healthiest journalist work I did—out in the fresh air and sunshine, smelling the flowers, feeling the grass, hearing the wind in the trees.

For one thing, I had a better appreciation of the degree of difficulty. I played the game. I knew how hard—no, impossible— it was to hit a one-iron. I knew what putting could do to the nerves.

Oh, I knew hitting the curveball might be, as Ted Williams always insisted it was, the hardest single thing to do in sports. I knew how intimidating it must be to have to stand there with a football and try to throw it with Deacon Jones bearing down on you. I could only guess what it must be like to have to absorb a Mike Tyson left hook to the temple.

But golf is the most maddening of games. Putting for a living is my idea of a hard, stressful way to go about it. The bleeding is internal in this sport.

There is this story about the great entertainer Danny Kaye to illustrate the point. Danny was sitting in the clubhouse at Hillcrest Country Club in L.A. having lunch one day. He had never been on a golf course. Someone asked him why. "It's a silly sport," shrugged Kaye. "Hitting that little white ball. What's to it?"

His companions urged him onto the first tee to try it. "Sure," said Kaye. And he went out, picked up a one-wood, went into his naturally rhythmic stance—and hit the ball 250 yards right down the middle. He tossed the club contemptuously to the caddy. "See?" he said.

It was three weeks later. Word of Kaye's feat had spread throughout the club. Another group approached. "We heard you hit the first ball you ever swung at 250. We'd like to see you do it again." "Sure," shrugged Kaye.

He went out, waggled, swung. The ball went straight up in the air over his head—and came down behind him. Kaye frowned. He set up to the ball again. This time it dribbled twenty yards to the right like a burrowing animal. Kaye mugged. He took a mighty swing. He missed the ball altogether.

The finale found Kaye, then, annoyed, proceeding to take the game seriously. He took lessons. He became a scratch golfer in time, but it took three years. Kaye was hooked.

The moral of the story is, golf demands respect. And it obsesses anyone who takes it up. I knew many a tennis star—Lew Hoad, Ken Rosewall, Ivan Lendl—who became more hooked on golf than they ever had on tennis. Ballplayers from Babe Ruth to Johnny Bench chased perfection on the golf course. Joe Louis and Sugar Ray Robinson were on a golf course sometimes when they should have been on the heavy bag. Michael Jordan would rather dunk the golf ball than the basketball. Film producer David Wolper, who staged the 1984 Olympic programs and the Statue of Liberty Centennial, became so obsessed with golf, he bought his own course.

I have a friend who calls golf "the pursuit of infinity." And I'll drink to that. It is a game that leaves the best of them. I have seen Ben Hogan shoot an 83. Around a clubhouse they'll tell you even God has to practice his putting. "In fact," goes the old joke, "even Nicklaus does."

It is, as golf editor Nick Seitz once dubbed it, "the king of games." It humbles, it denies, it punishes pride. Golfers are the least cocky athletes I know.

I not only respect golf, I respect golfers. They are the only athletes who play to play. There is an entry fee to every tournament. Years ago, they were playing almost exclusively for their own money. Now, of course, they have sponsor money, television money, gate receipt money. But they still get only what they demonstrably earn. In no other sport is this so. You get a guaranteed contract in baseball whether you hit .300 or .200. You get paid in football whether or not you make a tackle or throw a touchdown or intercept a pass. You are not alone out there. Golfers are.

Golfers are the last of the rugged individualists. And they are the most honest of sportsmen. A golfer calls a penalty on himself. Sometimes, he's the only one who knows the ball moved. Or that his club slipped and he soled it in a hazard.

In baseball, you pretend to catch a ball you really trapped. You hold it up, hoping to deceive an umpire. In football, you hold a lineman, hoping a ref isn't looking. In basketball, you throw an elbow—and look aggrieved if you get caught at it.

Golf is not a win-at-all-costs or whatever-it-takes sport. Golfers are not exactly the Knights of the Round Table—but they come closer to it than athletes in other sports.

I guess I revered Ben Hogan as much as any athlete I ever knew in any sport. But I wouldn't blame Ben Hogan if, whenever he saw me coming, he called 911. Or crossed the street. Or hid in a closet till I went away.

Ben and I go way back. Ben was my golf idol. The first time I saw him on the golf course, I was fascinated. There was something about it and him. He was grim. He was relentless. It was as if he were stalking the course. As if it were some kind of sociopath, some serial killer, and he was assigned to bring it to justice. You watched Hogan go after a golf course and you shuddered. There was something implacable about it, atavistic, prehistoric. It wasn't a game, it was a hunt.

He was the greatest striker of the ball the game had seen. As Mike Souchak, another premier player of the era, was to put it, "Ben Hogan just knows something about hitting the golf ball the rest of us don't know." Jimmy Thomson, a long hitter of the era, once told me, "Ben Hogan had three fairways—right, center and left. The rest of us were lucky we had one. Hogan always hit a shot with the next shot in mind."

He didn't just power his way round a golf course the way the players do today. He *thought* his way around it. He engineered a round of golf, he didn't just play it. Nicklaus was the longest *straight* driver I ever saw but Hogan was long enough. For Hogan.

He drove people off the golf course. It was unnerving to play with Ben Hogan. First of all, he played in such a protective wall of concentration, it was like playing with an invisible man. Or being invisible yourself. George Fazio played with him in an Open once and Fazio carded an eagle on a par 4. As they were totting up the scorecards later, Hogan paused, blinked, then turned to Fazio. "George," he told him earnestly, "you made a mistake here. You've got a '2' down on the twelfth hole." Fazio was dumbfounded. "Why, you little goat! Don't you remember I pitched in with a seven-iron there?!"

Hogan had no recollection of it. He was the original "what-elephant?" type of on-course concentrator.

The name, of course, helped. "Hogan!" It was a name like "Geronimo!" "Cochise!" or "Jesse James!" It was like smoke signals. When Hogan was in his prime, it was the last sound a competitor wanted to hear ringing through the galleries. It meant doom. It ranked in the world of golf with "Dracula" in his hey-day. To a golfer it inspired dread, it had a hide-the-women-and-children-Hogan-is-coming connotation.

The first time I met Hogan was in January of 1949. I was working for *Time* magazine then and we were putting him on the cover because he had just won the U.S. Open—and nine other tournaments—the year before.

I believe he was the first golfer ever to grace the magazine's cover and the sports editor, Marshall Smith, had gone to a great deal of trouble. He had gone out to live with Hogan at Hogan's house in Fort Worth for a week the previous October. Unfortunately, his notes had gotten cold. The magazine's researchers, loath to put a check mark alongside his faulty memory, had sent me a five-page single-space list of things to check with Hogan. As I recall it, this had everything about him but his birthdate to reconstruct and this was sent within a few hours of the magazine's closing on the printing presses in Chicago. We were at the Riviera Country Club in Los Angeles where Hogan was preparing for the L.A. Open and the start of a new golf season. We were bucking a time difference of three hours. The presses were waiting, and the editors were sweating for Hogan to fill in the gaps.

Hogan being Hogan, he refused to devote any more time to me till he had completed an important practice round (every golf shot he ever hit was important to Hogan). I had to wait in the gloom of the locker room with an open phone line to New York till he reported in. He practice-putted till well into the darkness.

When he finally came in, it was getting on into the night in New York and Chicago. It didn't matter to Hogan. He checked each statement as if it were a ten-foot putt for the championship. We got to a chart showing Hogan's "average" distance for each club. Wrong move for Hogan. He insistently refused to OK an "average" distance. There was no such animal, he protested. His distance for a four-wood, for example, he pointed out, would depend on a whole lot of variables, atmospheric conditions, the time of day, the velocity and direction of the wind, maybe, even, the curvature of the earth.

We compromised. Hogan was not a good compromiser but the presses were waiting—at several thousand dollars a minute in lost time. People were waiting to climb out on the cylinders and chisel in the new, corrected, if not compromised, statistics in the chart. Hogan didn't care. Hogan was meticulous.

Well, we put him on the cover. He joined secretaries of state, prime ministers, generals, scientists. He finished about ninth in the L.A. Open, then went to Pebble Beach where he won the Crosby, came back to Long Beach where he won again, then went to Phoenix where he lost in a playoff to Jimmy Demaret.

Then he headed back to Texas. Where he got hit head-on by a Greyhound bus in the fog just outside the town of Van Horn. Police said evidence had shown Hogan threw himself in front of his wife at impact.

Hogan, they thought, would never play again. They had to remove his vena cava, and for the rest of his life, he had to stand on his head every morning to start the blood flowing in the right direction.

Nevertheless, he returned to action in the 1950 Los Angeles Open. Once again, *Time* magazine was on the spot with a story. I approached Hogan as he was sitting in the club dining room, an apparent victor in the tournament, and thus the hero of the most amazing comeback story in sports to that time. He was sitting with his wife, Valerie, and the film director Sidney Lanfield, who was to make a movie (bad) on his life. Almost as I approached with a copy of the magazine, the news came over the club loudspeakers that Sam Snead had just birdied seventeen and had an eleven-foot putt on eighteen to tie Hogan.

As a roar went up from the gallery on eighteen, signifying Sam had made his putt, I laid the copy of the magazine down at Hogan's side. In an unaccustomed burst of fury, he picked it up and slammed it against the fireplace. His normally impassive face was contorted. "That magazine is the only thing in the world I'm superstitious about!" he raged.

I crept away.

We now dissolve five years. It is 1955, we are at the U.S. Open in San Francisco at the Olympic Club. Ben Hogan has just shot 287 on an Open course so monstrous that only twelve players broke 300 and in high rough so impenetrable that Porky Oliver actually lost a free drop!

Hogan is the apparent winner. Gene Sarazen has just told the American public so on television. There is only one player out on the course with a chance of overtaking him. The Sam Sneads, Tommy Bolts, Julius Boroses are all five to seven shots back. Arnold Palmer has shot 303. Only a nobody named Jack Fleck is still in range but he has five of the most hellish holes in golf to negotiate. He is still two shots behind and the prospect is not good.

So, guess who has collected himself and is sitting next to Hogan in the locker room as the apparent winner is cleaning out his locker preparatory to taking a shower and getting ready for the victory presentation? None other than our hero, the Hogan nemesis, J. Murray, who was last seen at Hogan's side as he was on his way to a bus accident or as Sam Snead came charging down the back nine at Riviera to spoil one of the best stories of the year. I am working for *Sports Illustrated* as this tragedy is unfolding, preparing a sidebar story on how Hogan took his record fifth Open victory.

As we are talking, an announcement sifts over the transom in the locker room window. Someone named Jack Fleck has just birdied seventeen. He needs to birdie eighteen to tie Hogan. Hogan squints. He is preparing to go off to the shower. "I hope," says Hogan, "he makes either a 2 or a 5. I don't want to play a playoff."

He makes 3. Hogan is in a playoff. Hogan does not like playoffs because he gears himself mentally and physically for seventy-two holes, not ninety. He loses playoffs.

He will lose this playoff. I have struck again. To Hogan, I must seem like that character in *L'il Abner* who always went around with a cloud over his head. Only I bring the cloud to Ben Hogan. I rain on his parade.

Look at the record: We put him on the cover—and he gets

hit by a bus. The next time I show up, he gets tied (and beaten in a playoff) by Snead (who is not his favorite pro). The next time I show up, a club pro from Davenport, Iowa, beats him out of the Open.

The Hogan legend is like the Lincoln legend. It grows with the passing years.

But it doesn't need much embellishment. In 1953, Ben Hogan entered seven tournaments. He won five of them. And in these five were the British Open, the U.S. Open, the Masters. He couldn't play in the PGA because his legs could not stand the rigor of the thirty-six holes per day that (match play) tournament required in those days.

Hogan was one of a kind. Purposeful, totally devoid of hype, demanding of respect. He came up a hard, lone way. He had to learn to play as a caddy packing bags for a dime a day. A natural lefthander, he had to learn to switch himself around because nobody made lefthanded clubs for poor kids from Texas in those days.

Even his game didn't come easy to him. He was a hook-fighter all his early career. He took himself off the tour in 1945 and resolved to get rid of the hook or rid of his clubs and his game. Being Hogan, he got rid of the hook. He got so, as Tommy Bolt used to put it, he could fade a ball in on top of an umbrella without breaking it and he could impart so much backspin on a ball, he could stop it on linoleum. On a staircase.

One curious outgrowth of the Hogan bus accident was that it gave birth to the myth of a Time, Inc., cover jinx. *Time* magazine had an infelicitous run. It put Hogan on the cover and he nearly lost his life—and career—to a bus accident. They put the prizefighter Sugar Ray Robinson on the cover—and he was one of about three prizefighters who had ever made it—and he promptly lost the first fight of his professional career. To an Englishman named Randy Turpin.

Unreasonably enough, this translated in the public mind into a jinx label on that other Time, Inc., publication, *Sports Illustrated*. This was nonsense. *Time* magazine put a sports personality on the cover every decade or so. *Sports Illustrated* put one on every week. For a *Time* cover personality to have a catastrophic event on the heels of his appearance on the cover was eerie. For an *SI* cover personality to have one would have been supernatural.

The last time I saw Hogan on a golf course was in 1967 at

Augusta. He was fifty-five years old. I was a daily columnist by then. The nature of my job was such that I had to write a Sunday column on Friday (to accommodate predate issues and out-of-state early editions) and hope it would hold up. I chose to write about Hogan. I only hoped he would make the cut and not embarrass himself. Or me.

I needn't have worried. Hogan went out the next day and shot 66. That was the lowest score anybody posted in that tournament. I shall never forget the sight of Hogan moving laboriously up that eighteenth fairway. He had removed his trademark white cap, the only time I had ever seen him do that on a golf course. He waved it to the crowd. He walked up the center of the fairway (where his ball was, naturally) to wave upon wave of the most thunderous applause I have ever heard from a golf gallery.

I saw Hogan for brief periods after that. I always felt I was in the presence of royalty. He was a man of unassailable integrity. Once, when his manufacturer delivered a whole warehouseful of golf sticks that Hogan considered below his standards, he made the factory junk them. The company executives were aghast. "But, Ben, they're not that bad as clubs go!" they protested. "Not under my name!" grimly shot back Hogan.

I couldn't help thinking back to the night when the "average" distances were not accurate enough for Ben Hogan. Even if it meant holding the presses at great cost at Donnelley Corp. in Chicago.

Hogan despised compromise. He was as rigidly ethical as a monk. He had a total sense of dignity. When industrial engineer George May put on the first hundred-thousand-dollar tournament, he made it a condition that golfers wear numbers on their backs for ease of gallery identification. Hogan wouldn't. Hogan didn't need a number anyway. Golfers today do. They could even do with a brief bio printed on their backs, an address and phone number.

Hogan wouldn't play in the Tournament of Champions when it was in Las Vegas. Rumor has it Ben was a dealer himself in a faro game in his vagabond days during the Depression when you couldn't make a living with a golf bag. If so, it was something Hogan was not proud about and doubtless he resolved never to be put in that demeaning position again.

It's hard to imagine what a Ben Hogan would command on the golf tour now. In 1946, Hogan was the leading money-winner with $42,556.12. To get that, he had to win (count 'em) thirteen tournaments. In 1988, Curtis Strange won $1,147,644. To get that, he had to win one tournament. In 1948, Ben Hogan won the U.S. Open—and got $2,000. In 1991, Payne Stewart won the U.S. Open—and got $235,000.

Arnold Palmer was the best long putter I ever saw, maybe the best anyone ever saw. In his prime, a forty-footer was a tap-in for the great Arnold.

What's more, he *expected* to make those forty-footers. He huddled over the ball in that peculiar, knock-kneed stance of his as if it were a "gimme" at a public course instead of a two-break curler for a U.S. Open or Masters. Once, the golfer Dave Marr was in his threesome. He watched Palmer negotiate forty-footer after forty-footer on his way to a typical Palmer 64 and, when Arnold came to a mere six-footer, he took his putter out of the bag, causing Marr to observe wryly, "Wait a minute, Arnold! You have too much club there!"

Arnold had the most charisma of anyone who ever played the game. That's hardly Stop-the-Press! stuff but I found it out early. My earliest introduction to Arnold was at a tournament in, of all places, Tijuana.

My late wife returned to the motel one night to effuse, "I've just seen the most exciting golfer I have ever seen play! His name is Palmer."

At that time, the most famous Palmer on the tour was a North Carolinian named Johnny Palmer, a journeyman pro with a huge head of black hair like a fur hat. "Oh, sure," I said, "I know the guy. Short. Lotta black hair, dark complexion." My wife frowned. "No, that's not this guy. This guy looks like a caveman."

The next day, I went out, abandoning my pursuit of Dutch Harrison, the eventual winner, to see this specimen.

I got to know Arnold Palmer well over the next two decades. Part of his great appeal was his bold, almost reckless play. Arnold never laid up. He never lagged a putt. He went for the course's

Arnie

jugular. He was Dempsey with his man on the ropes, Ruth with a fastball, Montana with a man open. The crowds exhorted him, "Go for it, Arnie!" and Arnie went for it.

He won some sixty-two tournaments with his go-for-broke approaches but I think Arnold Palmer's major appeal was the fact he was the first golf player the man on the street could identify with. He was a truckdriver's delight. First of all, he looked more like a middleweight fighter than a society dilettante.

The public had never really taken golfers to its bosom before. Bobby Jones, after all, was a rich kid from Atlanta. Even Walter Hagen had a drawing-room aura about him. He showed up on first tees in tuxedos and patent-leather shoes, he hobnobbed with royalty. He was not a man of the people. Arnold was.

Arnold always looked as if he were on his way to a main event at St. Nick's. He was a slugger, an attacker.

He had an uncanny success handling the press. He was largely responsible for bringing into being the lecture hall press conference. Too many people wanted to talk to Palmer to permit the old gather-at-the-locker interview. Palmer held audiences like a pope.

The press liked him, too. Arnold had time for us. Arnold liked the press. Arnold would have a drink with you at the country club bar after a round. Arnold was everybody's buddy.

His patented style of play helped. Arnold's rounds of play were never elegant exhibitions of stylish golf. They were more like Dempsey-Firpo. He's-up! He's-down! Arnold and the course went after each other like sluggers in dark rooms, bulls in china closets.

First of all, his shirt would come out. Then, his hair would come down in his eyes. He'd sweat, smoke. He'd look for all the world like a guy who had just climbed down from a truck or off a tugboat to tee it up. It was like one of those movie fights. You could almost hear the broken barroom mirrors, crashing furniture and staircases collapsing when Palmer and the golf course went at it. It wasn't a game, it was a brawl.

Arnold American, I used to like to call him. He either made a 2 or a 12. Either way, Arnold Palmer on a golf course was a happening.

He almost never coasted to victory. He was like a fighter who gets off the floor. He became noted for mounting a late charge. He came onto the back nine like the cavalry rescuing the fort. The sight and sound of Palmer on the spoor of first money was one of the super-exciting events of sport.

He made golf. Nicklaus was better. Casper was steadier. Almost everybody had a better swing. Arnold's lunge at the ball has been likened to that of a drunk at a midnight driving range. He had the 10-handicapper's swipe at the ball, finishing in the strange overhead power lock of a guy trying to block out the hook. The club looked like a Roman candle.

But the ball went—and went and went. Palmer was long, bold, daring—and strong. They didn't make the rough that could intimidate Palmer's swipe at the ball. He could knock it out of barbed wire with a tuning fork. He exuded strength. He had a low center of gravity, his legs were short, his back broad. You couldn't have built yourself a better golfer.

Even his mishaps were the stuff of legends. He came into the final nine holes of a U.S. Open once (San Francisco, 1966) with a—get this!—seven-shot lead! He blew it.

Now, only an Arnold Palmer could blow seven shots in nine holes. He did it in the usual Palmer way. Conventional play in that situation calls for the golfer to cozy his lead into the clubhouse—go for the fat part of the green, lag the putts safely, choke down on the woods, be safe not silly.

Not Palmer. He played as if he were seven shots behind. He was, as it happens, going after Ben Hogan's Open record of 276. He wanted to birdie his way into the clubhouse when he could have won the tournament if he only parred in.

Billy Casper, playing alongside, had long since resigned himself to second place. Billy wasn't playing recklessly. He was more or less doing what Arnold should have been—protecting his position.

Arnold dared the fates—and lost. I walked with him that entire nine and I felt as if I were watching a complicated suicide. He barely managed to cling to a tie—thanks to a seagoing putt on number seventeen—and, the next day, lost the playoff. Palmer lost three Open playoffs, a record.

It was Arnold who hit a shot out onto an island rock at Pebble Beach one year and waded out to play it. The resultant picture, showing Palmer hitting a shot out of the Pacific Ocean with only a seal for a gallery, made every paper in the world. Palmer made news even when he made bogey.

One day, playing in the L.A. Open, Palmer came to the narrow, tricky, fenced-in ninth hole at Rancho Park. He promptly began hitting shots out of bounds. All at once, he found himself in double figures before he finally got the ball on the green in 10. He made 12 on the hole.

In the press tent later, Arnold painstakingly went over the historic crash and burn. He ended up saying, "Finally, I got to the top of the green. I had a six-footer downhill but it rimmed the cup. So I made 12." Golf scholar Stan Wood and I looked at each other. Clearly, here was a quotation that needed tightening up. So, we rearranged Arnold's words only slightly. "What happened on the ninth hole, Arnold?" "I missed a short putt for an 11."

Sometimes, art needs a little help.

Some people have taken credit for inventing Arnold Palmer, but Palmer invented himself. After all, he won sixty tournaments (only three golfers have won more).

He took golf out of the agate columns (other sports last night) and put it on page one of the sports sheets. More than anyone else, he is responsible for the runaway success of the senior golf tour.

When Arnold joined the senior tour in 1980, it was just a kind of cute but unimportant adjunct to the national sports calendar. The public viewed it with sympathy and minor nostalgia like any other oldtimer's game. The total purse for the "tour," if it could be called that (two events), was $250,000.

Palmer joined it—and within two years the purse had shot up to $1.3 million and the events to eleven. Last year, there were forty-two tournaments for $19,875,000.

Palmer is responsible in large part for the greening of the senior tour, but, if I may say so immodestly, so are we inkstained wretches.

It worked this way: Back in the days when the tour had the Palmers, the Sneads, the Hogans and, later, the Nicklauses and Trevinos, we were ready and eager to make them household names. In a symbiotic relationship with television, we were able to do exactly that. For the first time in decades, if not ever, golf stars were able to compete for prime space and prime time with stars from other sports.

Alas! This disappeared with the decline of the game into anarchy. All of a sudden, no one ruled golf anymore. There was a winner a week. The tour regularly began to have a dozen or more first-time winners each year. It became a No-Name Jive.

When golf tournaments were being won by the Palmers, Nicklauses, Watsons, Trevinos, you had a fighting chance to lead off the eleven o'clock sports news. When they began to be won by Phil Blackmars, Mark Wiebes, and Billy Ray Something-Or-Other, editors lost interest.

So did the public. This seems heartless. We're supposed to be for the underdog in this country. But the underdog became the overdog. "Unknown Leads Open" became a stock headline. As they said on Madison Avenue, this dog wouldn't hunt.

You see, golf needs somebody's ball to play off. In your friendly neighborhood Saturday morning round, you canvas each other's handicaps. You take the lowest—let's say it's a 14. And you play off his ball. If you're an 18, you get four shots a round, if a 20, six shots a round. And so on.

The larger game needed a lead ball even more. The game couldn't take anonymity. You needed a want-to-turn-on-the-television-set-to-see-how-Arnie's-doing. Mark Wiebe didn't cut it.

Golf has always been a sports page anomaly anyway. The truckdrivers played it. But they didn't consider it exactly a sport. Pro football was a sport to them. Boxing. Baseball. Pro basketball. Golf finished somewhere ahead—but not far ahead—of tennis.

This was where Palmer helped enormously. But when he and Nicklaus faded, no one took their place. It was not so bad that unknowns won periodically but they vanished as soon as they appeared. They had no consistent success. They won. And then they missed cuts, played out their eligibility (you were exempt from qualifying for two years after you won a tournament) and then disappeared.

Even great names weighed in with this syndrome. Greg Norman looked like the next Palmer when he first showed up on an American tee. Within a very few years, he not only wasn't winning, he wasn't making cuts. Curtis Strange won two U.S. Opens. And then all but stepped off the planet.

I have a theory. It is a familiar one: money. Money corrupts. Money destroys.

Consider this: Hogan got $2,000 for winning the 1948 Open. Payne Stewart got $235,000 for winning the 1991 Open.

But you got $180,000 for winning any Open. Including something called the Hardee's Golf Classic. You got $225,000 for winning the K Mart Greater Greensboro Open.

Why then would a player with his pockets lined with that kind of money go out the following week and work and concentrate and sweat to do as well again? He wouldn't.

Worse than that, when a player reached "celebrity" status—probably by winning the B.C.-En Joie Open or less—he was in demand for corporate outings, that is, jolly, no-pressure sessions with executive suite America, a few clinics—and a big paycheck. No gotta-make-thises. No sneaking anxious looks at a scoreboard to see who's gaining.

This was ruinous to the competitive edge. Back in the early fifties, a Chicago industrial engineer, George S. May, sponsored the first $100,000 (to the victor) tournament. The catch was, you got $50,000 for winning and $50,000 for giving clinics to George May's customers and clients at $1,000 a crack.

The resultant time off the tour ruined the games of winners Lew Worsham and Bob Toski—and almost wrecked the career of Julius Boros.

You multiply that by fifty to one hundred to get some idea of the devastation this practice has brought to American golf today. May was ahead of his time. The corporate grandchild of his scheme is tampering fatally with the games of dozens of potential superstars. Curtis Strange, for one.

There is also the practice of signing on American stars to make appearances in foreign tournaments for big money, win or lose. Appearance money is outlawed on the American tour. It is thriving, for example, in Japan and Australia. You get money—big money—just for showing up. You don't have to win. You don't even have to try to win.

In Hogan's day, you won a tournament, collected fifteen hundred dollars and don't miss the cut the following week. You had to finish first again—or certainly no worse than ninth or tenth, otherwise you wouldn't be able to stay on the tour. You were back cleaning clubs at Pocatello.

Players are under no such constraint today. Only a handful of players even win so much as a tournament a year anymore. They don't have to. The occasional win, plus the occasional twenty-fifth-place finish, pays the mortgage and bankrolls the IRAs.

Jack Nicklaus was really the last of the super players. Jack was consistent, brilliant. Probably the greatest player the game will ever see.

Jack was the most disciplined athlete I have ever seen. He almost *willed* the ball into the hole.

When Jack first came out on the tour, he was—well, fat is the word you would want. Jack was one of the world's great trenchermen. He looked, in silhouette, like something that should be floating over a Macy's parade. This, of course, did not escape my attention. I suggested, among other things, that he resembled nothing so much as a moving bivouac going down a fairway.

At a dinner that first year given by my paper, Jack was a guest of honor. He spotted me. I must admit I had been at the hors d'oeuvre tables myself that winter. "Why, you!" he exclaimed. "You're fatter than I am!" He thought for a moment, then added grimly: "And, it's going to stay that way."

Jack was as good as his word. And Jack's word you could always take to the bank. That winter, Jack Nicklaus lost over forty pounds. It was daring. Jack was playing the best golf on the planet at the time. He was getting prodigious length off the tee and off the fairway. Bobby Jones himself was moved to observe after seeing him for the first time, "He plays a game with which the rest of us are not familiar."

To tamper with this was a risk. But Nicklaus gave up the lobster, the ice cream, the waffles and the pizza-with-everything. And, so far as anyone could tell, never dropped an inch off his length off the tee.

Nicklaus exuded will power. He just stared down a course; that two-fairway squint of his became a trademark of a bear on the prowl. They called Hogan "The Hawk" because of his small-pupil, far-seeing, predatory look down a fairway or green. Nicklaus became "The Golden Bear." He left nothing to chance on a golf course. Golfers as a class are as meticulous as German housewives. Watch them as they nitpick a green before they putt, almost as if they are finding clots of dust in a stairwell. Nicklaus went them one better. He wanted a golf course like an operating table before he began his surgery with a one-iron.

He once told me he derived his great power "from my ass." Nicklaus did it with his head, too. I don't think he ever hit a golf shot that he didn't think he knew where it was going. I don't think Nicklaus ever said, "Well, I'll just swing at this thing and see what happens." Nicklaus was as controlled a human being as you will ever see. He didn't have a careless bone in his body. Lots of athletes at some time say, "Well, I'll just have a little fun here, relax a little." Not Nicklaus. Jack never did anything in his life without a purpose. No one ever saw Jack Nicklaus throw a club. There's a reason for this. He told it to me once. Seems when Jack was young, ten or eleven or so, he, like most golfers, was prone to tantrums. One day, after missing a putt, he heaved the putter toward the horizon. His father, Charlie, a druggist in Jack's hometown, Columbus, was not amused. "Put your clubs back in the bag, pick up that ball and get in the car. We're going home," his father sternly told him. On the way home, the father told his son, "If you ever do that again, you will have played your last golf game." Says Jack: "I never threw a club from that day to this."

Nicklaus and Sam Snead were the only two golfers I ever saw to whom the game seemed to come easy. But with Snead, it was only from tee to green. Sam had this gorgeous swing but his putting stroke was pure spasm. Nicklaus could do it all. I never saw a man who looked so confident over a golf ball or on a golf course. Anywhere. He took defeat more gracefully than any great player I ever saw. When he lost a playoff—or finished second by a shot—he came graciously to the press tent to congratulate the victor and answer questions with smiles and poise. Other golfers would storm out to the parking lot, throw their clubs angrily in the trunk and be out of town before the cheering died.

Nicklaus had a perfectly astonishing record. He won 71 tour tournaments. But he was second an incredible 58 times and third 36. In majors, his record was awesome. He won 20 and was second 19 times.

He won 6 Masters and was second 4 times. He won 4 U.S. Opens and was second 3 times. He won 3 British Opens but was second 7 times. He won 5 PGAs and was second 4 times.

The interesting part of this was Jack—much if not most of this time—was spending more than half his time nurturing a business as a golf course architect. This prompted Chi Chi Rodriguez to deliver the deathless line, "Jack Nicklaus became a legend in his spare time."

Jack was not confident only with a golf club in his hand. Jack Nicklaus was a confident, self-assured individual off the course. As Johnny Miller once observed, "Nobody ever heard Jack Nicklaus say, 'I don't know.' About anything."

I don't suppose anybody outshone his contemporaries as Jack Nicklaus did. Maybe Babe Ruth. Possibly Muhammad Ali. But there, the book closes. To win seventy tournaments in the era Nicklaus did borders on the fantastic. The game wasn't changing. The numbers were. Sarazen, Hagen, Jones—maybe even Hogan and Snead—had a comparative handful of golfers to outshoot. They were good. But they weren't numerous. There were no qualifying schools in those days.

I don't know who was better—Hogan or Nicklaus. But Nicklaus had the world to outshoot. It was no longer a small club when Jack came along. It was Everyman's game.

Jack was no shrinking violet. Jack never had a self-doubt in his life. But, to give you an idea of Nicklaus's strength of character, Jack was a smoker for years. But the public never knew it. The public never saw him with a cigarette in his mouth. He smoked in secret. He thought it was a bad image for him to appear with a cigarette in public.

Gary Player was the most mechanical great player I ever saw. He was like a windup toy. Turn the key and you activated a sweep at the ball that seemed almost jerky as it went from Point A to Point B to Point C.

It was rigid, unnatural, like a little girl at dancing school learning her moves by rote. You could almost picture Lawrence Welk going "a-one, a-two!" as Gary went into his routine.

But Gary did it by the numbers, he did it exactly the same every time. He had that nirvana of the golf course, the repeating swing, the muscle memory that brought the club down through the ball the same way on the same trajectory every time.

We kept waiting for that stilted, awkward, automatic-looking artificial swing to fly apart into a thousand pieces like a too tightly wound clock. But it never did.

Gary was implacable. It was inevitable he would win his U.S. Open (St. Louis, 1965) and his Masters (he won three) and PGA (he won two). Gary had planned it that way and what Gary planned, Gary usually carried out.

He was a very decent sort, humorless, dedicated, a tower of concentration as every great golfer has to be.

He was in the most awkward of situations—a South African in America at a time when a social conscience about apartheid was beginning to manifest itself. His country got to be an embarrassment to him. Gary got invited to play in the Masters without otherwise having to qualify at a time when no American black had ever trod that course other than to carry someone else's bag.

This explosive inequity went unnoticed at the time but, as racial equality became more and more of an issue in America, protest groups began to harass Player. They rolled balls in his line at a PGA tournament in Akron, they carried placards. At a time when no South African athlete could compete in the Olympics or in major tennis tournaments or World Cup soccer, South Africans were abroad in force on the American golf tour.

Gary, at first, tried apologizing for his homeland. But he gradually sensed the temper of the times. He hired a black caddy (Rabbit). He contributed to junior golf (the entire purse—twenty-five thousand—from his U.S. Open win). He contributed to black golf. And he stopped trying to invite American sportswriters to his home country to see "things were not as bad as portrayed."

The reality was, they *were* just as bad as they were portrayed. And Gary's role was to keep a low profile. Hard to do when you're winning three Masters, two PGAs, a U.S. Open and three British Opens. Gary won over $4 million on the American tour, $1.6 million on the regular tour and the rest on the senior tour. He earned it. But he had to walk a fine line to keep earning it.

Gary was a resolute character. He was one of the earliest of athletes to pump iron, chew nutritional seeds, watch what he ate and drank. If he was a manufactured athlete, he was a good one. Nothing he did seemed to come natural to him but he was one of the greatest of the players. He won twenty-one tournaments, almost as a tourist.

You get a clue to Gary when you know that, owing to his

geographical location, he was on more twenty-three-hour flights than a Pan Am pilot. Gary had a simple routine. He would turn to the passenger next to him and inquire, "Do you want the floor or do you want the seat?" This was for sleeping. The other fellow would, nine times out of ten, answer, "The seat," which was all right with Gary, a short fellow (five feet seven). He had long ago mastered the art of sleeping underneath a seat.

Sam Snead was gorgeous. It would not have been possible to invent a character like Sam Snead. He was one of those athletes—Yogi Berra was another—who cried out to be made into a cartoon creature. Funny, lovable, as instinctive as a hound dog, Sam never really left the hills of Virginia. He came from a long line of hill people who sat around in squirrel hats and hunted and fished the mountains for food for the table and built stills for money. And he was one of them to the last, a combination of cunning and naivete that was a delight to write about. Once, early in his career, Sam won some tournament out West and his agent, Fred Corcoran, proudly brought him a copy of a New York paper with Sam's picture and a story about him in it. Sam was thunderstruck. "How can they have my picture?" he marveled. "I ain't never been to New York!"

Sam's life was dogged by what Aristotle called "undeserved misfortune." This, unfortunately, created a kind of comic overtone to Sam's career, which he didn't wholly deserve. I think it was Lord Bryce who once said of Napoleon's career that "it would be the funniest comedy of modern times if it weren't caked in human blood." In a way that could be said of Sam's career.

Sam was a glorious golfer. Glorious athlete, really. He was double-jointed. He could take his pinky finger and bend it completely back onto the back of his hand without even a care. I saw him stand in a country club dining room once, step back, kick his leg up in the air and touch a chandelier with his foot. I saw him jump over a five-foot chain from a standing start at a tee in Les Vegas. He had been a high jumper, punter, baseball and basketball star in high school. When he took a seven-iron back, photos showed his left arm so straight behind his head it hurt you to look at it.

He had this perfectly thrilling swing. It was a work of art. Watching Snead on a tee was like watching Nureyev in *Swan Lake* or Gene Kelly in the rain.

Nothing could ever go wrong with it. Sam was shooting in the high 60s when he was in the high seventies. I always suspected Sam was one of the greatest athletes I ever looked at. If it weren't for Jackie Robinson—or maybe Muhammad Ali—he might have been the greatest.

Sam won more tournaments—81 on the American tour and over 125 altogether—than any golfer before him or since. But Sam is most famous for something he didn't do—win the U.S. Open.

It became part of the lore of the game. In 1939, Snead came up to the seventy-second and final hole of the Open needing only a bogey 5 to win the tournament and 6 to tie.

The things that happened to him on that hole should happen to Saddam Hussein. Sam went from trap to trap. He failed to hit it out of one trap. He struggled, swiped, sweated and trudged. He threw the tournament to the winds. It was the most ignominious day of his life. He shot an 8. What the pros call "a snowman." The most famous—or infamous—8 in golf history.

In 1947, Snead was in a playoff with Lew Worsham for the Open championship at St. Louis. They came up to eighteen all tied. Sam putted. His ball came to rest a foot and a half from the hole. He stepped up to finish it out with a tap-in. Worsham had marked his ball, which was about a foot and a half from the hole, too. As Sam addressed his ball, Worsham spoke up sharply. "I believe I'm away!" he shouted.

It was gamesmanship at its finest. Sam, shocked, stepped back. "I believe I can continuous putt in any case!" he growled.

No matter. The official, Ike Granger, called for a measurement. The ruler showed Sam *was* away. By two inches.

Unnerved, Sam stepped up to his eighteen-inch putt. And missed it. Worsham tapped his in to win the Open.

To some, it was funny. Lew Worsham always told that story with a chuckle. It became a staple on the banquet circuit. Snead never laughed.

In all, Sam finished second in five Opens. It became part of the mystique of Sam Snead. The golfer with everything but sense. The primitive who never recognized subtleties. The uncharitable stories used to abound. If you could put Hogan's head on Sam's swing, went the cliché, the rest of the world would be playing for second every week. And so on.

It wasn't fair to Sam. Sam couldn't think his way round a

golf course in his early days. But who could? Maybe Nicklaus. But when Nicklaus, playing with Hogan, finished second as a twenty-year-old amateur in the 1960 Open (Palmer won it), Hogan was to say, "I played with a twenty-year-old kid today [Nicklaus], who, if he had a brain in his head, would have won the Open by four shots."

By the time I caught up with Sam Snead, he was as crafty a golfer as anyone out there. The mantle of goof-up has since fallen to the Australian golfer Greg Norman. In a playoff for the British Open once, Norman, on a par-5 hole, busted a tee shot about 310 yards from the tee. Into a bunker. The last place he ever should have been, even if he had to one-iron it off the tee.

Sam could have sympathized. But the Sam Snead I knew *would* have used a one-iron there. It was putting that kept undoing Sam. In the Open at San Francisco in 1955, the eminent golf historian Herbert Warren Wind and I were following Snead along the back nine one day. As Sam would fly the ball with that little clog step of a backspin that was his trademark within three feet of the pin on hole after hole, I would become excited. Herb would fix me with a sour look. "It won't matter," he said sadly. "He can't even make a putt inside the leather." It was true. Sam's putting bordered on the spastic. That was another tournament he had the second-best score—to Hogan and Jack Fleck, who played off for the championship.

Sam, with a club in his hands, was superb. But he never got even a veneer of sophistication. It offended some people. Sam never really trusted the flatlanders. I found it kind of refreshing. Sam wrote a book without ever reading one. Sam was a kind of riverboat gambler. His humor had a high content of scatology. He once told President Eisenhower, an avid golfer, when Ike asked him how to get length to his drives, to "get more ass into it, Mr. President!" Ike did.

It was thrilling to watch Snead play. There was a purity, almost an innocence, to it, a rhythmic joy to the swing. He was Palmer before there was a Palmer. Like Arnold, he conveyed an excitement other golfers couldn't match. Like Arnold, he played a bold game, flirting with catastrophe on every slot but very few— maybe Tommy Bolt—struck the ball with the sense of beauty you found in Snead's game.

*   *   *

They were a colorful lot of brigands, the pro golfers. There was Raymond Floyd, whose eyes got big and round and stared off into something no one else could see when he found himself on the spoor of first money. He was the most uncatchable front-runner I have ever seen. He was such a dogged competitor that Ryder Cup Captain Dave Stockton tapped him for his Cup team when he was forty-nine years old. Raymond's swing wouldn't hang in the Louvre, either, but he knew how to win.

There was Tommy Bolt. Whenever I heard that Tommy Bolt had double-bogeyed the last hole, I would make a beeline for the locker room. There was a sure column there. The Vesuvius of golf would be in fine, furious eruption.

Tommy really hated golf. He was a prisoner of his talent. He was convinced the game was against him, the crowd was against him, the fates were against him. He would rail against the gods of golf. Or any other. He would raise his head, shake his fist at the sky and roar, "Me again, huh, God?!" He could use clubs well. But he could throw them better. The definitive Tommy Bolt story concerns the time he was having an abysmal round and came to a par-3 over water that was 225 yards in length. "What's the shot?" he asked the caddy. "A six-iron," said the caddy without hesitation. "A six-iron!" screamed Bolt. "It's 225 yards! What in the world makes you think it's a six-iron?!" "Because," sighed the caddy, "that's all you have left in the bag, Mr. Bolt. Except for the putter. And it sure ain't a putt."

I ran into Tommy Bolt once on a fairway at Indianapolis. I was hurrying out to interview Art Wall, another golfer. Bolt intercepted me. Smoke was coming out of his ears. "Jim!" he shrieked, "you got to do something about these people. They hate old Tom! They're pulling against me. The papers are turning them against me! You got to do something about the papers here!" I sidled over to the caddy. He confirmed it. "He just made a double bogey," he confided.

I assured Tommy I would meet him coming off the eighteenth tee and we would discuss his problem. But, for now, I had to go talk to Art Wall.

As promised, I was waiting on number eighteen for Tom. Out of the fairway came his second shot on the par-5 hole. It was a gorgeous four-wood, soared up and up—and dropped down two feet from the hole. A sure eagle.

As Tom came up, I came up to his side. "Okay, Tom, I'm ready," I told him. Bolt shushed me. He had an ear-to-ear smile. "Hush, Jim! Listen to all them people cheering! They love old Tom!"

We all loved old Tom. And old Ben. And old Sam. And old Jack. They were as colorful a cast of characters as graced any sports scene. And old Arnold. I'll miss lots of sports one day. But I may miss golf most of all.

Having said all that, I have a confession to make. When it comes to tournament golf, I root for the course. In rodeos, I root for the bulls. And the broncs. In golf, I root for the real estate.

I'm a big fan of double bogeys. I love it when the weather at Pebble Beach is blowing a force ten gale and the flags are bent horizontal in the wind. I love unputtable greens.

When a golfer shoots 59—as my pal Alan Geiberger did, and Chip Beck—I feel personally insulted. I don't want the game to be easy. When I hear on the TV an announcer saying, "He's got 225 to the middle of the green, he's got a four-iron," I want to scream abuse. "Two twenty-five!? That's not a four-iron! That's a four-wood *and* a four-iron!"

The nightmare of the tour types is that someone six feet eleven will come off the basketball court someday and go out and make a mockery of the game. Drive all the par-4s, maybe even drive the par-5s. Hit four-irons three hundred yards. That kind of thing. Nicklaus himself once confided this fear to me.

It'll never happen, Five-eleven is a perfect height for a golfer. Or less. Anything over six-three and you're a poor risk.

Look! That ball is awfully small (4.3 inches in diameter). And it's a long way down there even if you're five-eleven. If you're a foot taller, that ball might as well be in the next county. Too many things can go wrong with even a short golf swing. One that has to come down from seven feet will get into more trouble on the way down than a guy who hits a roller skate at the top of a staircase.

Trust me. No behemoth is going to come along and take over golf. Not even Michael Jordan. He'd better keep his day job.

8

···

What's a "High Post," Daddy?

Pro basketball, like Caesar's Gaul, was divided into three parts—Michael Jordan, Magic Johnson and Larry Bird. Everybody else out there was just somebody to go get the ball for them.

Michael Jordan, "Air" to his compatriots, played a game ten feet off the ground. You needed the RAF to stop him. He only came down periodically to refuel, then he took off again.

Magic Johnson came with a ball attached. Like, every time you saw him, there was the ball mysteriously in his hand like a rabbit coming out of a red handkerchief.

Larry Bird was so white he was invisible. If there hadn't been a Jerry West, he would have been the greatest white player of all time. Of course, the way the game was going, that might have made you no better than 246th overall. But Larry Bird was a superstar in any color.

Basketball was a phenomenon. At the college and high school level, it used to be just something to go through to get to the dance afterward. The pros used to play wherever they could pass the hat and make bus money. Just look at the towns and the teams the pro game went through. Sheboygan, Providence, Moline, Waterloo, Anderson, Fort Wayne, Tri-Cities, Rochester, Syracuse, Cincinnati. They moved around like Bedouins in the night. They played league games wherever they could collect a crowd and collect some money. It was at a league game in Hershey, Pennsylvania (between Pittsburgh and New York), that Wilt Chamberlain threw in one hundred points.

I didn't know much about the pro game when, in 1961, my

last piece for *Sports Illustrated* was a diarylike story ("Ten Tall Men Take a Trip") with the Lakers.

In those days, basketball was so low on the totem pole of American athletics that the NBA Lakers and Knicks played the *preliminary* game in Madison Square Garden. The main event—the attraction—was the Harlem Globetrotters. Gifted black players went to the Globetrotters in those days. Wilt Chamberlain went to the Globetrotters, to give you an idea. So did pitcher Bob Gibson.

I learned two things about the game in that trip: 1) Fans who know basketball are as rabid as football or baseball—or boxing—fans ever were, and 2) basketball players were, quite possibly, the finest athletes of all.

I was one of the few writers west of the Mississippi to find this out.

The Lakers had been moved to L.A. that fall by owner Bob Short after he lost everything but his hotels (and political ambitions) trying to run the Lakers in Minneapolis. His instructions to his general manager in charge of the move, Lou Mohs, were simple and explicit. "Take them out to L.A. and, if they keep losing money there, keep on going and drop them in the Pacific Ocean."

The nickname, Lakers, so appropriate for the state that boasts ten thousand lakes, was completely inappropriate for L.A., which didn't have a single body of fresh water that didn't come out of a pipe.

My own rapport with the Lakers was instant. They were extraordinary athletes—and characters. Elgin Baylor, the most majestic basketball player I have ever seen. Jerry West, with such fantastic peripheral vision, it was said he could see his ears. He was such a bundle of endless energy no one ever saw him in repose. Even his conversation was so high-octane and in such a nonstop, sing-song hillbilly twang that the Lakers called him "Tweety-bird." Jerry always looked as if he just sat down on a hot plate and was hurrying off looking for relief. He was so slat-thin, you could mail him home, but he was a dervish on the floor. He cut so fast and darted so unexpectedly that the man guarding him always looked as if he were trying to catch a feather on a big wave. Jerry West could do everything Michael Jordan could do and his 25,192 career points (sixth-best all-time) prove it.

Elgin Baylor was the magistrate of the team. He was the first to dub Jerry West "Zeke from Cabin Creek" (eventually short-ened to "Zeke"). Jerry was never overly fond of the sobriquet but that, of course, was a matter of indifference to Elgin. If Elgin annoyed you, his enjoyment was doubled.

Hot Rod Hundley was one of a kind. He would have had to slow down just to be considered a playboy. Rod never met a girl he didn't like, and vice versa. His teammate Slick Leonard once said Hundley's car would start up all by itself and begin to pull out for the nearest disco before Rod got into it. Hot Rod never took himself or his game seriously and his performance empha-sized it. When Elgin threw in seventy-one points in New York one night and management struck off some cufflinks for him with "71" on them, Hundley wanted to know why they didn't get a set with "2" on them for him. Hot Rod was night people. Like Joe Namath, he never knew any girls named Mary or Alice. They were all named Desiree or Candy or Cherry. They all chewed gum and kept expecting Rod to take them out for dinner. He never did.

The Lakers were a colorful lot. There was Ray Felix, the Count, a slow-moving, slow-thinking seven-footer, a kindly but suspicious man who, when he returned from a road trip, never had any fewer than four women waiting for him, all colors, sizes and hairdos. They all piled into his beat-up old used Chevrolet and took off to God-knows-where to do God-knows-what, the team coach, Fred Schaus, used to say. On the road I never saw the Count do anything but sleep—and play basketball. He was either on court on in bed. He slept with his head in his arms on a plane. The team went coach but Ray always got the first seat in the cabin and when he stretched out, Elgin Baylor liked to point out that whereas Ray rode coach, his legs always went first class.

The beds in those times were in hotels (in Syracuse and Rochester) that had been built in William Howard Taft's presi-dency, and they were built for the five feet eight people of the times. Basketball players had to kneel to shave in the mirrors, they could never get more than 60 percent of themselves into the bathtubs or beds.

The top salary in the league in those days was the nineteen thousand dollars paid to Jerry West (although Wilt Chamberlain, ever conscious of his image, insisted he got a great deal more—a boast his owner, Eddie Gottlieb, would never back up).

The game was slow to catch on. The good news was, the players were highly accessible. They were eager for ink. They had not yet been made millionaires. Journalistically, I had them all to myself that first year. No other columnists in the city had the jump I had.

The best seats in the house were nine dollars in 1961. They were nine hundred dollars in the Forum last year—provided you didn't have to get them from a scalper for the playoffs. There is a large body of people in America who feel they lose social status if they don't show up at Super Bowls, World Series and NBA Finals. Travel agents depend on them. The first thing a successful travel agent has to get is tickets to these events.

The Lakers drew 151,344 at home that first year. They drew 717,349 in 1988–89 and 712,498 in 1990–91.

The game grew. It became an "in" thing in Los Angeles. Even Doris Day dropped the Dodgers for the Lakers.

Women loved the game anyway. It drew the highest percentage of female patronage of any sport people played. This so upset the eminent footballer Elroy "Crazy Legs" Hirsch when he was general manager of the Rams that he began to snipe at a group of women, one of whom was my wife, at a party one night. They turned out to prefer basketball to football nine-to-zero, which made Elroy livid. "You just like to see men running around in their underwear!" he accused.

I decided to launch a minisurvey as to why women preferred basketball. Underwear had nothing to do with it. Basketball was simple, easy to watch, easy to understand what it was all about. You put the damn ball in that basket. Period. No infield fly rule, no esoteric first-down marches, no icing the puck. Put the ball in the hoop more times than your opponent, you win. Women also cared that it was the most balletic of sports. Nureyev would have been a great basketball player. Also the action was swift and exciting. It was more exciting than seeing a guy armored in fifty pounds of plastic plowing into a line of 290-pound troglodytes on the floor of a field two area codes away. No timeout for measurements, no pitching changes at the mound. You couldn't go out for coffee and miss nothing. You had to *watch*.

No one seemed to mind that the black players took over the game despite the predictions that they would. Most fans considered themselves lucky to see the kind of basketball you would have had to go to a Harlem blacktop to see a generation ago.

As noted, fears of a quota system manifested themselves but quotas were no match for good old American greed. No owner or coach was going to suit up a slow, earthbound, clumsy white kid just because he was white when he could have Isiah Thomas or James Worthy. The quota system, if there ever was one, soon vanished and, by 1992, it took Charles Barkley, no less, to charge "quota!" because there was one—repeat one—white player on his squad. Charles didn't think there should be any.

The first black player in the loop was a long-forgotten player named Chuck Cooper who played briefly for the Celtics. But Jim Crow wasn't at work; here, the problem lay in the fact that basketball, like football, filled its ranks from colleges and blacks were not numerous in college athletics (except notably at UCLA) before World War II.

Seven-footers, we all knew in those benighted days, were all in circuses or sideshows and they had the life expectancy of wire-haired schnauzers who chased cars. They were pituitary freaks, is what they were. Their legs ran clear up into their armpits and they walked in unnatural, articulated strides like men made out of tin. They couldn't jump high enough to get both feet off the ground at the same time.

That was the notion of seven-footers. Then, basketball recruiters began to uncover a new race of men—seven-footers by the busful who were perfectly coordinated, perfectly proportioned big men. They could do all the things little men could do except fit in Volkswagens.

Bill Russell was as agile as a pickpocket. He was six-eleven but he had the moves of a startled zebra. He was imperious—I always thought of him as The Emperor—but he wasn't spectacular. What he did, he did in the dark like a spy. You didn't appreciate him till it was too late. Your wallet was gone, or your country's secrets were stolen, so to speak. You measured what he did by the scoreboard, not the stat sheet.

In my magazine days, when Bill Russell was performing for San Francisco State University, the San Francisco bureau chief, Dick Pollard, and I kept recommending Bill Russell for an *SI* cover. It was an uphill fight. They kept looking in the papers where they would see "Russell—6 pts." and they would immediately put Tom Gola or King Lear on the cover. It was not until San Francisco won back-to-back Final Fours that it began to dawn on everybody. They wouldn't notice that, while Bill Russell scored only a few points, so did the team they were playing.

One guy who did his own homework was the Boston Celtics' Red Auerbach. Red was, hands down, the best pro coach the game has seen. The heist he put on the league to get Russell is the athletic version of the Brinks'. Auerbach outslickered St. Louis owner Ben Kerner by trading him Easy Ed Macauley and Cliff Hagan for the draft rights to Russell. Even then, he had to wait out two prior picks by obtuse other GMs. William Felton Russell produced an endless string of annual championships for Boston. He did it when he was the only black player on the team (1956–57) and he did it when the team was 60 percent black players. When you talk of Celtic tradition and the championship pennants hanging from the Garden ceiling, you are saluting William F. Russell.

Into this idyllic setting in 1959 clumped Goliath. Wilton Norman Chamberlain, all seven feet four inches, 290 pounds of him with the wingspan of a prehistoric bird and the ego of a Harvard professor, which he sure wasn't. Wilt had been with the Globies but he got sick and tired of playing Barnum & Bailey basketball.

Wilt was a little less of the perfectly proportioned athlete than some others were. Wilt, whose parents were normal-sized, even small, sort of clanked when he walked as if propelled by some giant's puppet strings. Still, there is little doubt he would have swallowed the game whole were it not for the presence of William Felton Russell. There is a law of physics that holds that, for every action, there is an equal and opposite reaction, and in the case of Wilt Chamberlain, Bill Russell was it.

Chamberlain scored points by the carload. It was obvious when he came into the league he thought this was going to be easy. They had just put in the three-second rule or Wilt might have put in one hundred points *every* night instead of just the one.

But then Wilt stepped into a minefield—Bill Russell country. Russell treated him as just another guy with the basketball. Wilt never really could beat Bill Russell. Wilt tried everything, from being the scoring leader to being the assist leader, but whenever the smoke cleared, there were the Celtics on top of the heap. It wasn't as if Wilt got shut out. Russell just made sure he came up one basket short.

The thing about Russell was, he made everybody else on the team twice as good. You see, the Celtics could play everybody tight on defense. Because if their man slipped away—well, he was walking into the spider's parlor. When he got to Russell, he wasn't going anywhere. With the ball, that is. Chances were, when Russell got through with him, he didn't have it.

Wilt was an outsized character in more ways than one. When you think about it, going through life seven-four cannot be any box of chocolates. People are always giving you that startled look as if they suddenly saw the Empire State Building walking down Madison Avenue.

Wilt was a pretty cheerful character, all things considered. He was almost the proverbial gentle giant. He never fouled out of a game, for instance. He never punched anyone out. I never saw him even look mad on the floor. He periodically wrote complaining pieces in the magazines ("Nobody Roots for Goliath") and he periodically threatened to turn pugilist. Fortunately for him, he never carried through on it. Wilt was all strike zone.

Wilt never appeared to have any hate in him. When you're seven-four, you're probably different enough so that nuances of color would not have much relevance. Wilt's celebrated boast, that he had sex with twenty thousand women—computing out at 1.3 women a day since he was twelve years old—got him more notoriety than his hundred-point night. The press was more impressed with the fact Wilt must have bought at least twenty thousand condoms—which also set or tied a league record. His partners were all raving beauties, to hear Wilt tell it. At least one of them was. Kim Novak, the film actress, was one of Wilt's slam dunks.

Wilt got mad at me once or twice. Once, I treated his new home on Mulholland Drive—which was built to his outsized specifications right down to the tub size and shower heights—with something less than reverence and awe. Wilt punished me by sneering in one of his books that I had once approached him for an autograph for one of my young sons. I showed him I could take it. Given Wilt's dimensions, it's advisable to.

When I first met Kareem Abdul-Jabbar, he was Lewis Alcindor and a freshman at UCLA. He had been locked off from the press, but he had slipped the cordon of censorship to give an interview to a New York paper and my request was honored one day and we sat on the gym steps at Pauley Pavilion.

The subject never really got round to basketball. Lew Alcindor, who had only recently arrived from New York, spent much of the time chastizing California for having the temerity to select Ronald Reagan governor. "California is playing a game on the rest of the country," I remember his complaining bitterly.

The incongruity of these words from a college freshman, newly arrived from Manhattan, struck me to the extent that I reprinted them in my column. UCLA alums, even Reaganites (if there were any such at UCLA), who were afraid to a man that Alcindor might leave their school, wrote me poison letters. Lew and I got off to an adversarial start.

I am happy to say it was forgotten in time and when Lew Alcindor became Kareem Abdul-Jabbar and got traded to the Lakers we got on through a mutually respectful relationship.

Kareem was no Chamberlain. He was a dour man who never smiled and never appeared to be enjoying himself on or off the basketball court. He appeared, like most athletes who embraced the Moslem religion, to be trying to distance himself as far as possible from white America, for which he held a probably justifiable bitterness.

But his religion was not the questionable demonology of the early *Black Muslim* religion, which held that white people were "blue-eyed devils" and the cause of all the mischief in the world. Kareem's was the faith of the prophet, of which he was a student.

He was a bright man and a very great basketball player. He was no one to clap on the back and he found some of the fawning attention he got to be tiresome and degrading. You approached with caution.

All he ever needed was someone to get him the ball. One year, at Milwaukee, he got an overaged Oscar Robertson. And that was enough. With the Lakers, he got Magic Johnson. That was dynasty.

Magic Johnson brought to the Lakers behind-the-back passes, no-look length-of-the-court assists, ball-handling Bob Cousy might envy and the unselfishness of a nearly Christian martyr on court. But what he brought more priceless than a withering jump shot was a smile.

No one ever played basketball with more verve, élan and little-boy enthusiasm than Magic. It soon became clear he could take a bunch of YMCA pickup players and make them into a championship unit. He was quarterback, coach, motivator and a star all in one. He did all this without raising any hackles. He got one coach fired. But Paul Westhead deserved it. Westhead took one of the most inventive, imaginative, exciting—and success-ful—teams in the game and tried to turn it into a robotic, play-by-the-numbers collection of automatons. It was like making the 1927 Yankees bunt.

Magic was disconsolate. It all but wiped the smile right off his face. This was his team. This was Showtime. He led a revolt. To my eternal regret I upbraided him for it. But he was right. Westhead and I were wrong.

But the things Magic did for the team weren't always appar-ent on the sheet. Just being there, he made the difference. This was a team that, under Jabbar, had just been going through the motions. It wasn't clear whether they even spoke to each other. After the game, they showered quickly and headed into the night. You got your interviews on the run in the parking lot.

Magic changed all that. He added air and water to the mix. And he added championships. He even had Kareem grinning from ear to ear.

No one ever got jealous of Magic. The press loved him. Magic never took an early shower in his life. He would sit there, night after night, luxuriating in the attention Kareem found so burdensome. It got so even coach Pat Riley would ask him to turn out the lights when he left.

He had the town in the palm of his hand. Honk-if-you-love-Magic bumper stickers. The Forum went wild when he walked on court. The press loved him, too. Even his mistakes were sugar-coated. He came back from an injury too soon one year and blew a playoff to Houston. The press sent get-well cards. He threw the ball away in a Celtics-Lakers title game once. Magic was forgiven.

The ultimate accolade was, they left his private life alone. An illegitimate child surfaced one year. Magic took him over. No one bothered to interview the mother. Magic led an active social life. But you found out about it only because the girls bragged. There were some stunning-looking movie-starlet types—highly visible—wearing cowboy hats and low-cut Gucci blouses in front-row seats at the Forum.

When Kareem retired, the challenge for Magic seemed insurmountable. Basketball is a game in which the big man in the pivot is absolutely essential.

Magic put the team in the finals in 1990–91. The suspicion lurked that the team consisted largely of Magic Johnson—and not much else. They finally fell to the Bulls.

The proof came the following season: The Lakers were suddenly, shockingly, without Magic Johnson.

In L.A., the Magic Johnson story was like the Kennedy assassination. Everybody remembered where they were when they heard the news.

It was received with such disbelief that most people thought they had heard wrong. I heard it from a grocery store manager. I had stopped in on my way home from a trip. "Did you hear about Magic Johnson?" he asked. "He has AIDS." I remember standing there with a half-smile on my face waiting for the punchline. I remember thinking, "OK, I'll bite. What's the joke?"

There was no joke. I flew home to check my answering machine. Sure enough, there was a message from the Forum's Bob Steiner. "We're having the saddest press conference we've ever had in our history at three o'clock today."

A nation was stunned. AIDS! Wasn't that something only homosexuals and drug addicts got? A disease passed by, so to speak, a dirty needle—of one kind or another?

How could somebody as indefatigably heterosexual as Magic Johnson encounter it?

The way Magic met the cataclysmic news was heroic. The

temptation to claim a mysterious blood disorder, to disappear from the limelight, to go away and live life in seclusion must have been irresistible. It's been done. Film actor Brad Davis concealed his illness till he was at death's door. So did Rock Hudson.

Magic went out to meet it. The world's most catastrophic and embarrassing disease was just another rebound and Magic went after it.

They said he couldn't live life away from the spotlight. But Magic often had.

He had a powerful message to get across: You could catch the deadly virus heterosexually. It was loose. The genie was out of the bottle. The epidemic was in the streets, in the boudoir, it was not just a nasty little infection of the cruise bars, the crack houses. It touched the rich and famous. It touched the innocent, the victims of the transfusions. It was as powerful an enemy as any we confronted in any world war. The public knew this more forcefully with the Magic Johnson announcement than it would have with the distribution of a year of direct mail leaflets.

No one had the charisma of Magic Johnson. When he and Larry Bird were in their prime, Laker-Celtic confrontations took on the dimensions of Armageddon. It didn't matter who was better. The game mattered. The rivalry mattered. There was nothing quite like it left. Michael Jordan was all alone. He had no challengers. Michael Jordan was too good. He was so good, he was boring.

The game used to belong to the big man in the pivot. First Mikan. Then Russell. Then Chamberlain, Willis Reed, Bob Lanier. The old Lakers used to come up a jumpshot or two short every year because they had no dominating center.

But then the game underwent a change. Somehow, point guards, small forwards and trapping defenses had wiped out the Abominable Snowman in the middle. When Patrick Ewing went to the Knicks in an NBA "lottery" (the press fell down laughing at this swindle—there was no way the league was going to let Ewing go to the Indiana Pacers or Minnesota Timberwolves) most experts thought it would be déjà vu—it would return the Knicks to the glory days when they had Willis Reed dominating the middle.

Patrick Ewing was hardly The Dominator. Neither was the admiral, David Robinson, when he went to San Antonio. The days when you needed only a big center and his caddy were as long gone as the center jump and three-to-make-two.

For some reason, black players in sports today prefer to be addressed by their complete unabridged given names. James Worthy is never "Jim." David Thompson was never "Dave." A Richard is a Richard, never "Dick." Michael Jordan is never "Mickey." Some of us once asked a Ram running back, Lawrence McCutcheon, why he never chose the diminutive "Larry." "Because," said Lawrence, "Larry is my brother."

Charles Barkley is never "Chuck," either. But he's sometimes called by other lesser nicknames. Charles Barkley is the basketball player Indiana coach Bobby Knight once booted off the U.S. Olympic team because he was too fat. Charles answered to the nickname "Round Mound of Rebound" in those days.

Charles is never going to make the world forget Dr. J. or Magic but he does have a way with words. His way is to toss them around carelessly. Charles has fought with the commissioner, criticized his teammates, talked trash to some of the legends of the games, got into bar fights that left his opponents, if that's the word, with broken noses and teeth, complained about his ownership and begged to be traded. But he's most famous for spitting on an eight-year-old girl who had been brought to the game by her father, a doctor in New Jersey.

It's not quite as bad as it sounds. It couldn't be. The Round Mound was actually trying to spit on another fan who had been heckling him unmercifully throughout the game. Barkley spat. And caught eight-year-old Lauren Rose squarely in the cheek.

Not surprisingly, Charles Barkley resists the notion athletes should be role models for youth. So, unfortunately, do most athletes.

Charles Barkley is a cut below superstar. He throws in twenty-seven points a night and he pulled down over a thousand rebounds one year but what makes him so promising to those of us in press row is his tongue. Michael Jordan sticks his out. Charles Barkley wraps his around some of the most outrageous quotations this side of an angry fishwife.

With Magic gone, Bird gone, and Jordan unchallenged, Barkley may be the game's last chance to keep its place on page one. Everything else is getting to be Denver against Sacramento.

Is there anyone to stop Air Jordan from taking the game over, from doing what they feared Chamberlain would do—swallowing it whole?

Well, Michael Jordan found out that, whenever he scored fifty or more points, the team lost. He modified his game.

But he's not fee-fi-fo-fum scary. He doesn't make you want to run and cut down the beanstalk. He's as normal-sized as a headwaiter. He's only a guard. You don't have to change rules to neutralize him. When they do, we'll talk.

9

· ·

The Minute Man

J ack Kent Cooke was like nobody I had ever seen in big league sports before. Brash, assertive, megalomaniacal, Cooke was a man in a hurry. He was as unstoppable as a glacier.

He had started out life as a door-to-door encyclopedia salesman. He was a part-time trumpet player in a band, a voracious reader who somehow came under the aegis of another Canadian go-getter, Roy Thomsen.

They were an odd couple. Thomsen, portly, twinkly eyed, a comfortable, rumpled old party, crafty but smooth. Jack, on the other hand, was dapper, vain, egotistical. He was a ruthless businessman but preferred to think of himself as an intellectual. Roy Thomsen preferred to think of himself as your old uncle bringing lollipops.

But Roy Thomsen was the only man I ever felt had Jack Kent Cooke's wholehearted respect and affection. Not many other people did. They were, apparently, a dynamic pair. Thomsen, a Canadian publishing magnate, somehow cottoned to the daring, gutsy young Cooke and groomed him in his business. Together they bought radio stations, publications and anything in the entertainment sector that was for sale.

Thomsen eventually took his act to England where he bought the sacrosanct London *Times* and in time became a knighted member of the Empire—Lord Thomsen of Fleet (as in street, the hub of newspapering in the heyday of the British Empire).

Jack, for his part, branched out into sports. He bought a minor league baseball team, the Toronto Maple Leafs. But Jack Kent Cooke wasn't a minor league anything. He was the prototypical owner who couldn't stand not to be recognized, respected, deferred to and held to be a power broker wherever he went.

Jack was soon embroiled in the effort to start a third major league, an adventure that put him in league with the William Shea for whom Shea Stadium is named, Branch Rickey and a dozen others of the rich and famous.

Out of that imbroglio was born the New York Mets (and Houston Astros) and, while Jack was not a party to the formation, he got a real taste for big-time ownership himself.

Jack had enough money to retire when he was only in his forties. And he moved to Pebble Beach, California, a stuffy, over-civilized, mist-shrouded section of the country where, if you don't play golf or bridge, there isn't much else to do.

It was perfectly OK with Jack's long-suffering wife, Jeanie, who was sick of the bustle and crash of Jack's life in the pits of finance, but Jack was not the sort to play golf every day and bridge every night and tell himself he was having a good time. Jack demanded more action than that. He yearned for the noise and fury of the marketplace, the phones ringing, deals pending, money risking and boardroom fighting.

Jack closed the Pebble Beach operation and moved down to Bel Air, the posh billionaires' retreat, which is only a short Rolls-Royce ride from the turmoils of Hollywood.

Jack plunged back into the crucible. He bid for newspapers (the Hearst *Herald-Examiner*) and magazines (*Los Angeles* magazine), dabbled in movie deals, got a phone back in his ear.

That was when the Laker basketball team came on the market. It was common knowledge that Laker owner Bob Short thought the success of the franchise was temporary and that, when the novelty had worn off, it would slump as it had in Minneapolis. He had little faith in basketball as a sport and lusted to get into baseball, which he ultimately did, almost losing his shirt on the expansion Washington Senators till he again had the sense to move West—this time to Dallas, where they became the Texas Rangers.

They all laughed when Cooke paid $5,175,000—in cash—for the Lakers in 1965. People were always laughing at Jack Kent Cooke. It bothered him not at all. Jack could always see one horizon beyond his contemporaries.

A perfectly typical Jack Kent Cooke operation was the way

he became an American citizen. When Jack decided it was politically and geographically advantageous for him to do so, he didn't just go down to the federal building and stand in line to fill out an application. Not for Jack was there to be the green card, wait-five-years route to naturalization. Jack got Congressman Francis Walters, who was in charge of the House immigration committee, no less, to sponsor a bill making Jack Kent Cooke a full-fledged American (which he was by nature and instinct anyway) overnight. Jack became the first guy since the Minute Men of Concord and Lexington to become an American citizen in one day. He didn't have to learn the names of the secretaries of state, recite key portions of the Constitution or name the pivotal battles of the Civil War.

I, of course, commented on this phenomenon in print, pretending to be gravely upset because my grandfather had to wait the obligatory five years and learn the presidental succession, the dates of the Hay-Bunau-Varela Treaty and the makeup of the Electoral College to get where Jack got with a phone call to a congressman. I did the only two-part series columns I have ever written and titled them, "Citizen Cooke." Jack didn't think it was funny. But our friendship survived.

When Jack bought the Lakers, it didn't take him long to perceive what was wrong with them. They had no big man in the center. They would never overtake the Celtics till they got one.

Jack went after a center the way he went after citizenship. Jack didn't just go for any big man. He went for *the* big man—Wilt Chamberlain, no less.

Wilt belonged to Philadelphia then. It was his second stint with a Philadelphia franchise. The original Philadelphia Warriors had been transferred to San Francisco in 1962. Wilt played there for two years and then was traded to a *new* Philadelphia franchise (the 76ers, who had moved to Philadelphia from Syracuse).

Although it was his hometown, Wilt had had it with Philadelphia. Seeing that, Cooke persuaded the league that it needed a viable, successful franchise in Los Angeles and recommended that they steer Wilt in that direction. Wilt was only too happy to comply.

Wilt was somewhat less than wildly successful—Bill Russell was still around the first couple of years—but he did lead the L.A. Lakers to their first of six eventual World Championships.

Meanwhile, Cooke had combats of his own going. The Lak-

ers played their home games in the L.A. Sports Arena, a munici-
pally owned facility hard by the L.A. Coliseum and run—or more
accurately misrun—by something called the "Coliseum Commission," a body of Class A screwups, politicians and political ap-
pointees who had about as much savvy about running a sports
facility as about running a rocket program.

Cooke was a man who believed in coddling his good customers or the show biz types who brought notoriety to his franchise
by attending. With a view to that, he wanted to construct a VIP
room, a kind of gathering place for the beautiful people, a place
to make a night at the basketball game attractive to people who
didn't know a high post from a free throw. Jack just figured it
was good business. Lord knows he already charged these good
customers enough for the privilege of attending.

Jack thought it was the function of the Coliseum Commission
to pay for this elite hideaway.

But the Coliseum Commission was already hostile to Citizen
Cooke. They had already, so to speak, thrown down a gauntlet
to Cooke when the hockey franchise came up for awarding to L.A.

L.A. had been awarded an NHL franchise and the Coliseum
Commission took it for granted it would go to Dan Reeves, a
longtime tenant of the Coliseum Commission. Reeves owned the
Rams and, in anticipation of hockey going major league, he had
bought and installed the minor league L.A. Blades. It was taken
for granted, particularly by his friends on the Coliseum Commission,
that he would get the major league franchise.

Reeves never had a chance. Cooke, after all, was an ex-Canadian.
He knew where the bodies were buried, he knew the politics of
hockey—and he was an experienced infighter.

However he did it, he got the franchise. Reeves's years of
bankrolling a minor league operation counted for nothing with
Clarence Campbell and the other Canadians who ran hockey.
Cooke called in all his Canadian markers and did the obligatory
backroom dealing with Campbell.

The Coliseum Commission didn't get the message. Not only
did they throw in their lot with Reeves but, when Reeves lost,
they continued to take it out on the man they considered an
upstart, J. K. Cooke.

When Cooke wanted to build his VIP room, they refused
him. When he built it anyway, they refused to pay for it.

Big mistake. Cooke, outraged, began to play hardball. He threatened to move out of the Sports Arena and build his own facility. The Coliseum Commission laughed.

Big mistake.

Jack Kent Cooke built his arena in neighboring Inglewood with his own money and with money he raised by hypothecating the advertising, radio and TV rights to oil companies, a ploy Walter O'Malley had used to erect Dodger Stadium.

Only a few people were prescient enough to realize what sports were going to mean to Madison Avenue in the age of color television. O'Malley and Cooke were two of them.

Jack was also one of the first to catch on to the importance of cable in the video picture and began buying up cable companies far before the rest of American big business did.

The Sports Arena languished after Cooke left. They had no franchise to draw on until the Clippers moved to L.A. from San Diego in 1984.

Jack Kent Cooke was what you would call a hands-on owner. Not for Jack the remote-control approach. No detail of the running of the franchise was too minute to escape his attention. Sometimes, his staff wished it was.

I never saw Walter O'Malley in a locker room in my life. I never saw his son Peter in there either.

Jack Kent Cooke was in the locker room as often as his point guard. He always spoke, in rather too loud a voice, as if he were addressing a huge throng, a throng of people with somewhat less intelligence than himself. Slightly hard of hearing—"Eh?" was a frequently heard expression from him—he tended to orate rather than speak. Jack didn't *ask* you, Jack *told* you.

His clothes were always perfectly tailored, from the finest London tailors, his shoes were bench-made, his pocket handkerchief matched his tie, he wore cufflinks.

He never hero-worshiped his athletes. Authors were Jack's heroes. I remember one time when I invited him out to my modest house on the ocean at Malibu. Jack, who arrived in a chauffeur-driven Rolls, spent the night delightedly talking to Budd Schulberg, the writer. Jack had read all of Budd's books, beginning with *What Makes Sammy Run?* right through *The Disenchanted* to *On the Waterfront*.

Jack, short in stature himself, read every book on Napoleon,

I think, that was written. His English was meticulous, he was mildly pedantic. He was hard to work for. Jack wanted things done. They told—probably apocryphal—stories about him, of the time when he supposedly took his dog and an employee into a dank cellar under the arena and suddenly turned to the employee and exclaimed, "My goodness, it's cold here!" and asked if he could borrow the employee's coat and, when it was proffered, put it around his dog.

He came into a room full of bombast. He took over the conversation. He was a man of flash and dash but he was never boring.

Oddly, basketball, where he had his greatest successes, was not his sport. Jack prided himself he knew hockey. But when he wangled the hockey property, the Kings, he was never successful.

Basketball, about which he was largely ignorant, he had a sure instinct for. He finagled the league into letting him get Wilt Chamberlain and, seven years later when Wilt was gone, he pulled the strings again to get Kareem Abdul-Jabbar.

There are only two really sensational draft acquisitions in pro basketball history—and Jack Kent Cooke swung one of them when he acquired Magic Johnson. The other was Red Auerbach's acquisition of Larry Bird.

But Arnold Auerbach knew everything there was to know about the round-ball game. Jack didn't know a pick-and-roll from a driving layup.

But he had people who did.

Jack began to pick up stock interests in the Washington Redskins sometime in the sixties, and by the seventies, had become the majority owner.

He unaccustomedly kept it quiet, probably because the football commissioner was weighing league legislation barring cross-over ownership from one sport to another.

Jack, of course, was not going to be frustrated by any silly league rules, but he got rid of the Lakers, Kings and the Forum on his own terms ($68 million) in 1979 in a deal (with Dr. Jerry Buss) that also included thirteen thousand acres of ranchland in Kern County, California.

Jack wasn't burned out. But he was embroiled in an antagonistic divorce suit with his wife of over forty years, Jeanie. He had also suffered a near-fatal heart attack in the Forum club at his arena one night. And he was devoting more and more time to the Redskins.

Jack's divorce suit would have been comical if it weren't so costly. First of all, he moved to Nevada, which had no community property laws, and which otherwise had more favorable divorce settlements than California.

It didn't work. Jeanie Cooke got such a large divorce settlement ($42 million) that it made the *Guinness Book of World Records*. Jack got another bride out of it (Jeanne Williams, a college student), but that marriage was short-lived and was less expensive in dissolution.

Jack took the act to Washington in the 1980s. He began to devote more time to his football team, with the inevitable results: They got better and better.

As usual, Jack came up with a better coach than anyone else—Joe Gibbs. Joe, a sunny, religious man with a face as round and pleasant as an apple pie, began putting his teams in the Super Bowl with such regularity (four times in nine years) that the dreaded word "dynasty" began to make its appearance.

Jack reveled in the Washington scene. His owner's box was awash with secretaries of state, vice-presidents, congressmen, senators, governors. When the Redskins made the Super Bowl in San Diego in 1988, Cooke flew an entire planeload of government dignitaries out for the game.

He bought the Chrysler Building in New York, a venerable horseracing stable, Elmendorf Farms, a newspaper in L.A. (the *Daily News*). He figured in a paternity suit, survived that to marry the fiery Marlena, a somewhat mysterious (but beautiful) émigré from Colombia with a shadowy cocaine arrest in her background and a Latin temper, which frequently sees her hurling her expensive jewelry at Jack in public places.

In 1971, Jack teamed up with Hollywood agent Jerry Perenchio to stage what was the hottest sporting event of its day and the most eagerly sought after since Dempsey-Tunney—Muhammad Ali versus Joe Frazier. It was a landmark in what has come to be known as pay-per-view TV. It grossed unheard-of sums all over the world.

It was done with typical JKC flair. He rented an entire floor at the Waldorf; his ringside section looked like a Who's Who in government and business.

He was an owner's owner. He'd come a long way from the fast-talking encyclopedia salesman to the councils of power in the world seat of power. Jack took it all in stride. They were lucky to know him.

10

· ·

Love and Marriage

G erry was the most beautiful person I have ever known in
my life.

It wasn't her looks, it was her soul. She never did a
mean or injurious thing in her life. She couldn't tell a lie. She was
constitutionally unable to. She was nonjudgmental. She couldn't
understand prejudice. To Gerry, people were people. She was
the most moral person I have ever known.

I didn't tell her this often enough, of course. I had it all
planned that I would tell her all this on my deathbed. I would
rise up and I was going to tell her something I should have long
ago. "It was a privilege just to have known you."

And so it was.

She got cheated, of course. After sixteen years of marriage,
she lost her husband—and gained a columnist.

The column came into my life in 1961. And took it over. A
column is more than a demanding mistress. It is a raging master.
It consumes you. It is insatiable. It becomes more you than you.
You are not a person, you are a publicly owned facility. Available
on demand.

It has a calamitous effect on family relations. It confuses the
kids' identities. It rearranges your priorities—and not for the
better.

Jimmy Cannon had the right idea. He apparently accepted the
fact early that he was wedded to the column. And he lived alone
in a midtown Manhattan hotel and devoted his whole life to it.

I think the only reason it didn't have a ruinous outcome in

my marriage was that Gerry was such a strong individual, a person of such rare character.

The first fifteen years of our married life were right out of *Ladies' Home Journal.* I was a young reporter, she was a receptionist for a doctor (who also owned one of the biggest department stores in the city).

We met in a bar. But thereby hangs a tale. I was in the bar for the usual reasons: a drink and a pickup. Gerry was there for an unusual reason, which had nothing to do with either of those things.

She had been an extraordinary pianist in her home in Michigan, good enough to be featured on a radio show in Ann Arbor (this was 1945, well before television).

When she came West, she couldn't bring her piano with her. So, to keep her hand in, she cast around and found out this little neighborhood bar, the 575 Club (it was at 575 South Fairfax), had a piano. She asked the owner, Cy Miller, if he would mind if she played it evenings.

Mind?! Cy couldn't believe his good luck. Here was this gorgeous-looking, dark-haired girl with this lovely olive skin, huge, luminous dark eyes, bubbly and gay personality, beautiful nose and mouth—and she wanted to play the piano for his customers at night. For nothing. Gerry spurned his offers of a salary. She wanted to play only when the spirit moved her. Everybody fell in love with her.

Including me. But Gerry was no pickup. For anybody. She made it a rule never to leave the bar with anyone but her girlfriend and roommate. My advances were pretty much rebuffed until one night I was downtown at the big, venerable old Paris Inn with a friend and two dates, dental hygienists.

Sometime early in the evening, I wandered to the phone to check the action at the 575. My friend on the phone (he was later to be my best man) was grim. "I've got Gerry Brown here expecting you. I've convinced her you were crazy about her but I can't keep her much longer. She's skeptical."

I never flew out of a nightclub so fast in my life. I dumped money on the table in front of the startled girls, mumbled an explanation to my friend and took off for the parking lot on the dead run.

Before I could get out of the parking lot, my friend, Ed Laurent, was running alongside yelling for me to let him aboard. He climbed in, laughing. "I have just left the two maddest dental hygienists in captivity back at the table," he explained.

Girls, I'm sorry. But it was my life at stake that fateful night. I wasn't interested in anything but getting to the 575 Club and my future. I screamed out of Sixth Street in my eleven-year-old Pierce Arrow, running three boulevard stops and breaking the speed limit by six to twenty miles per hour. I got to the 575 just as the love of my life was leaving. I talked her into returning.

And the rest is history.

Those first few years were idyllic, as I remember them now. The babies came—four of them, three boys and a girl. The jobs got better. I was upwardly mobile, as they say today. But I wasn't affluent, by any means. I made $38.50 a week when we got married. I got raised to $50.00 when I threatened to jump to AP.

In many ways, those were my happiest journalistic years. God, we had fun on the old *L.A. Examiner*. It was a Hearst paper and the literati looked down their noses on it but we pulled all the stops on murders, suicides, public scandals and, particularly, on Hollywood stories. L.A. was exciting. The world was in flames. We told it all in dripping red headlines.

The city editor, Jim Richardson, was a one-eyed, iron-lunged, prototypical Hearst city editor, a tyrant of the city room. But he liked the way I wrote and for a time I was the youngest rewrite man in the whole Hearst chain, a fact of life that so irritated another rewrite man, Reggie Taverner (who had been Aimee Semple McPherson's press agent), that he quit. And loudly consigned Richardson to his "bobo" (me). Earlier, before he got too angry at me, I remember Reggie telling me one of the secrets of Aimee's ministry was that she was a practicing nymphomaniac.

I can tell you all you need to know about Jim Richardson with one anecdote: In the Black Dahlia murder, in which a young army camp follower, Elizabeth Short, was found slain and cut in half on an empty lot in L.A., the *Examiner* was able to score a scoop in identifying her by means of wirephotoing (a fairly new process at the time) her fingerprints to the FBI in Washington.

Armed with her identity, Richardson instructed a reporter, Wain Sutton, to telephone her mother in Massachusetts. "Don't r what happened," he instructed, "tell her that her daughter's just won a beauty contest at Camp Roberts. Then get all the information on her."

Sutton did as instructed. The mother happily confided her daughter's life history. Then Sutton put his hand over the mouthpiece. "Now what do I do?" he wondered. Richardson looked at him wickedly. "Now tell her," he purred. Sutton looked at him. "You miserable son of a bitch!" he said. Richardson just smiled.

I wrote that Richardson was such an unholy combination of Attila the Hun and a literary light that another rewrite man, Hank Sutherland, once dubbed Richardson Half-Oaf, Half-Elf.

We had sob sisters, we had sacred cows. But, most of all, we had fun.

After one particularly harrowing day, a colleague, John Reese, variously a City Hall reporter and editorialist, observing my travails with Richardson, was moved to sum up the whole crazy business in a poem titled "The Rewrite Man," which read as follows:

> The rewrite man was writing the death
> Of a miserable skid row whore,
> From the after effects of a drinking bout
> Some two or three weeks before.
> The facts were simple and dull and brief,
> And he had it almost done,
> When suddenly came the raucous voice
> Of James H. Richardson.
> "On that murder case," the Great Man said,
> "You can give it lots of play.
> Go into the mystery angle, too,
> For we're short of news today."
> The rewrite man gave a startled cry
> At the mention of mystery.
> And, round-eyed, turned to the desk and said,
> "Were you addressing *ME?!*"
> "Of course," said the Man, and his voice grew thick,
> "Some merciless sadist slew
> This innocent child of East Fifth Street
> Though he probably loved her, too.
> Get into your lead that a ghostly smile
> Was pitiful on her face
> And in saying how she was slain, hark back

To the Peete and Denton case.
And somewhere high in your story tell
Of the marijuana ring
That made this maid of the seventh grade
A wretched, besotted thing.
Oh, yes, in your opening sentence quote
MacArthur on the Flag,
Ignoring the Coroner calling her
A syphilitic bag.
Write wistfully of the cocktail glass
That broke as her body fell.
The artist will alter the photograph
Of the gallon of muscatel.
Mention a wilted yellow rose
To tincture it with romance.
And refer somewhere to an evening gown
Forgetting she wore no pants.
The barroom bum she was living with
We'll call her mystery man.
And try to mention the Japanese
And the Communists if you can.
Get excited about the drama here
Of passion and crime and greed.
Write a good objective story, and
Get all of this in your lead.
Give me a take as soon as you can
I want to give it a look.
But don't start in till you've got all the facts
Then hold it to half a book."
The rewrite man with a ghastly lear
That the Great Man didn't see
Started again and finished at last
At twenty-five after three.
The climax came the following week.
He was gratified to get
The prize for the finest writing to
Appear in the overset.

MORAL

It served the bastard right, of course,
As philosophers will note,
For being a rewrite man at all
When he could have cut his throat.

I'm sure I know what inspired that burst of poesy on the part of

John Reese. One slow day, Richardson handed me a routine suicide on Skid Row (Fifth and Main streets, in downtown L.A.). A poor old wino had hanged himself in a hotel room.

I wrote it straight. "John Jefferson, 51, was found dead in his room at the Hotel Barclay yesterday. Police dubbed the death as suicide by hanging."

Richardson handed it back to me. "Try to get a little more oomph in it," he ordered. He meant pathos. I rewrote it. He was dissatisfied. I wrote it again. He shook his head. Finally, in desperation, I handed in a lead: "John Jefferson, 51, tired of it all, stepped off a chair into eternity."

Richardson looked at it. He knew he had driven me too far. He dropped the story in the wastebasket. "Why don't you just go get a cup of coffee, kid?" he asked with unaccustomed gentleness.

Looking back, it was the best of times, probably the happiest of my life. Of course, looking back is always done through a prism of roses. What we have lived through and survived takes on an aura of nostalgia and bittersweet memory. We remember only the sunshine.

But, seen through any prism, it was a good time. We had this tiny, sunwashed apartment. We were living in a dream.

The city of L.A., that wacky, sprawling, improbable metropolis that tough men had fashioned out of a quasi-desert, was becoming America's Camelot. Every GI who passed through California couldn't wait to get back. As soon as the war was over, he went back to Omaha, Des Moines or Schenectady, picked up his clothes—and made tracks back to California.

At the newspaper, I danced every dance. The city was serving up a sensation a day.

I remember it in vignettes. On the ludicrous side, I remember a press agent, Milt Stein, coming into the office on D-Day, no less, the day the Allies stormed Hitler's Fortress Europa in what was *really* the mother of all battles—and he was selling the story of Shirley Temple's first screen kiss! I dutifully took it all down, wrote it and it appeared in the paper to our everlasting discredit. Boys were lying on the beaches of France at the time making the world safe for us. And we were offering the scoop that Shirley Temple was going through puberty. On screen, anyway.

I remember going to Las Vegas to cover the trial of an Irish war bride who had been jilted by her husband, a Nevada scion named Cliff Henderson, an air force officer who had married her while he was stationed in Ireland but left her, came home and filed for divorce in Vegas so he could marry a chorus girl. A judge with a conscience instructed that the bride, Bridget Waters, be flown over to have her voice in the proceeding. She did. She shot the guy dead.

What I remember most about the trial (she got eleven months, prompting the notion that murder was only a misdemeanor in Nevada) was that Bugsy Siegel was building his Flamingo Hotel on the Vegas Strip at the time and, because we had a contingent of British press covering the international trial, Bugsy invited all of us to a personally conducted tour of his new hotel. I remember being struck by two things: how handsome Bugsy was—he looked more like the lead in a college musical than a gangster—and how opulent the new casino was.

Bugsy was killed by the Mob the following spring in Virginia Hill's Beverly Hills mansion. My sense always was that Bugsy got a bad rap, that he was betrayed by a new term that crept into the language of construction, "cost overrun." Before the war, if you agreed to build a structure for twenty thousand dollars, you damn well better do it. After the war, labor problems, escalating costs for material and inflation conspired to make the winning bid only an approximation of the ultimate cost. I don't think the Mob caught on right away. They thought Bugsy was knocking down on them.

They resented him anyway. Bugsy had become a darling of Hollywood. The Countess Di Frasso couldn't get enough of him. She used to take him on cruises. Other film beauties had clandestine flings with Bugsy. He began to take himself seriously. He took to protesting to the *Examiner* over the designation "Bugsy," which had been fastened on him in his New York days in honor of his ferocious temper. City editor Jim Richardson was glad to oblige. He thenceforth always referred to him in print as "Benjamin (Don't Call Me Bugsy) Siegel."

I remember the longest lead I ever wrote. It was when the

OPA (Office of Price Administration) was put in place in World War II and put a lid on prices (which only encouraged the black market) and instituted rationing. "The long serpent of moving vehicles that was Connecticut's transportation system writhed in agony and seemed in imminent danger of paralysis today as government shutoff of gasoline dwindled supplies to a trickle." That's still the longest lead I ever wrote. It may be the longest anyone ever wrote.

I remember another lead for another reason. That was sometime in the mid-forties when a young couple in love took their own lives in a suicide pact à la Mayerling. The lead I wrote was, "They tried to tell them they were too young . . ." I don't remember too sharply the rest of it. But around that time a popular song by that title was written. I thought little of it at the time but, as I became wiser to the way things work in show biz—producers, directors, lyricists hawk the papers for story ideas—I came to wonder if I had unconsciously started a song down Tin Pan Alley. Maybe I should have gotten a cut.

I was gone from home a good deal. But I could pursue the holy grail of "success" because my rock—Gerry—was home taking care of the house, the kids, our life.

A little-appreciated fact of life in L.A. is that the postwar era cut off most people from ordinary support groups, that is, long-standing family ties. In other words, you had no grandparents, aunts and uncles, even siblings, to assist in keeping the offspring in line. L.A. was like a perpetual Elks convention. Everyone regarded himself as cut off from the eyeshot and earshot of people he or she cared about. It had a way of doing away with inhibitions. It also had a way of making you raise families on your own. There was no nuclear family to share the upbringing.

I covered the Overell trial for eight months. Most of that time was spent away from my home and family in a hotel in Santa Ana.

This was the trial of two young people, a furniture heiress and her boyfriend, who had blown up the girl's parents on a boat, supposedly because they had objected to the young man as their daughter's suitor.

It was my first introduction to how skewed our justice system has become. There is very little doubt the kids did it. (*Someone* did it, because the boat was dynamited, and the girl's mother had been slain by a pipe to the head before the explosion and so presumably had the father since the autopsy surgeon proved he was dead before the boat hit the water.)

But a clever defense—and sheriff's mistakes—got them acquitted. I became impressed with how fiendishly difficult it is to prove guilt in a capital case ably defended. The lawyers first maneuvered a doltish judge onto the case, then a moronic jury. (One woman juror said later she "couldn't believe any American kids could do such a thing"—which would have been music to Lizzie Borden's ears.)

Life continued to be upwardly mobile for our boy hero. Each home we moved into was bigger and more expensive. The American dream was alive and well.

I was approached by *Time* magazine to be L.A. correspondent in February of 1948. I was one of forty interviewed. Some decided they didn't want the job. Others were unqualified.

It was a bold move for me. I did it for money. Time, Inc., was offering seven thousand a year and unheard-of fringe benefits. But it was a new order of journalism. *Time* didn't linger at what happened. They wanted to know why it happened. They didn't care about hibiscus murders. They wanted the globally significant. And the writing had to be of a high literary order. *Time*, after all, came out once a week. You had to produce in-depth chronicles. The story behind the story.

I think my years at *Time* solidified whatever style I came to use and be known for. *Time* had a unique way of handling the English language ("Backward ran the sentences till reeled the mind," wrote Wolcott Gibbs in a devastating *New Yorker* spoof of the magazine). Unorthodox, staccato, it had been pioneered by one of the cofounders of the magazine, Briton Hadden, an iconoclastic type who reveled in driving down Wall Street and yelling "Babbitts!" at the assembled stockbrokers.

Going from a Hearst paper to *Time* magazine was like going from a honky-tonk to Park Avenue. Where the Hearst identification closed doors, *Time* magazine opened doors. It was well respected as a palladium of democracy—in the future was its overidentification as spokesman for the Republican party. That didn't come till Eisenhower.

The formation of the task force for *Sports Illustrated* in the summer of 1953 was a godsend for me, because I had been besieged with calls from the home office trying to move me.

I dodged them as effectively as I could. I was happy with L.A. I loved every brown hill in it.

One of the moves they wanted me to make was to Boston. I was horrified. I was to be bureau chief, they told me proudly. Concurrently, they would move the Boston bureau chief, one Jeff Wylie, to L.A.

Now, it so happened, Jeff Wylie was more than content with Boston. He had a home on Cape Cod, friends, family, the good life. He was so disenchanted with the notion of the move, he left the company to go to MIT.

I didn't go to Cal Tech. But I didn't go to Boston, either. The chief of correspondents, Bob Elson (a man who used to keep handkerchiefs under his sleeve cuffs), was very annoyed at me. "You can't stay out there in Lotus Land forever!" he warned.

He was wrong. So far, I have.

I didn't change. But Lotus Land did.

Our lives, of course, changed drastically with the advent of the Column (I always think of it as a proper noun).

The Column came about in the complicated way most things come about.

While I was back in New York in the summer of 1953, getting up the dress rehearsals for *Sports Illustrated*, a crack newsman named Frank McCulloch came down from northern California to cover politics for the magazine (*Time*).

Frank was one of the best newsmen I have ever known and it wasn't long before he was the bureau's star. It wasn't long after that he was the bureau chief.

One of the big stories he did was a cover story on the powerful Chandler family and their *Los Angeles Times*. He impressed the Chandlers very much even though the story was very objective. They approached him with an offer to run the *Times*.

Frank couldn't refuse. Even though Harry Luce offered him considerable in return to stay—and, in fact, Luce never stopped trying to entice McCulloch back.

Frank quickly noticed that one of the *Times*'s big lacks was a sprightly sports page.

Although I had the occasional by-line story in *Sports Illustrated*, I was not exactly a household name in L.A. But Frank recommended to management that they hire me. Frank was thoroughly familiar with my work over the years.

I was approached by Otis Chandler, Frank McCulloch and Nick Williams, the editor of the paper at that time.

I took the job. It was daring. The opportunities for falling off a high wire with no net were certainly present. Some years earlier, another paper had hired a sports columnist who had been a UPI editor in Europe. And he fell off the wire. He knew nothing about L.A. sports.

Few in town realized it but I had been living in L.A. for seventeen years when I took the job. I knew the scene. I was no guy fresh off the boat. I had covered California sports for seven years for *SI*.

I became, God help me, a columnist. I came home to Malibu and told Gerry. She was, as usual, supportive. She was also—as was I—a little scared.

The trouble with writing a column is, it's like running a railroad. You have to keep the stock rolling. You can never step back and admire or even take stock of what you've done. Because you're on to the next one. If you write a book, a play, a movie, on opera, ballet or poem, you can bask in reflected glory (if it's good) for a while. With a column, it's around the fish.

I remember going to bed that night thinking, "I hope I've done the right thing."

I still do.

11

· ·

"Gentlemen, Start Your What?"

G entlemen, start your coffins!"
   Most people seem to think that quotation from one of my columns sums up my attitude and relationship with the auto racing industry. Not quite.

I had a love-hate relationship with auto racing. I loved it. It hated me.

Well, not exactly. Our problems arose quite early in the game.

When I first began to write about auto racing, it was a closed fraternity. It wasn't covered by journalists, it was covered by a claque. Automotive writers were just an extension of the pit crew.

When I came on the scene, the first thing that struck me was the danger. I soon found out it was a taboo subject. You never— ever—mentioned the fact that you had a good chance to die driving between concrete walls at speeds up to 240 miles an hour. You didn't point out that cars burned. So did people. The sport was barnacled with the deaths of fine young men in race cars but if you read the accounts, you would have concluded they all had heart attacks or contracted cholera.

I got off on the wrong foot. I arrived at Indianapolis for the 500 in May of 1963. I was syndicated in the local *Indianapolis Times*, a Scripps Howard paper, now defunct. The editor, Irv Liebowitz, tracked me down when I arrived in town and asked if I would pen a Hello-to-Indy note for his paper. It would help my recognition, he suggested.

It sure did. Unwary, I cheerfully complied. Some way, somehow, I alluded to the Indy 500 as "America's Earache." It made the paper, all right. On page one. Not page one of the sports page. Page one of the newspaper.

I was a marked man before I ever set foot on Pit Row or Gasoline Alley.

I didn't see how you could separate the sport from its danger quotient and call yourself a reporter. In those days, something like one out of every three drivers who got into a race car would die in a race car. Some sixty-seven had died at the Speedway alone. Eight of them were spectators.

The machines were low, brutish, temperamental hunks of iron called roadsters. The engines—loud, screaming banshees— were in the front and, when they hit a wall, they fought it. The wall won. Usually, it pushed the engine back through the driver's chest or any other part of his anatomy that got in its way.

The noise at Indy seared right through to your viscera but it was exciting to Americans who, as a class, love noise. If you don't think so, you haven't been listening to their music lately. They even had these 750-horsepower engines called Novis, which made the most unholy roar you ever heard coming out of a combustion engine. They couldn't go very long. They usually had Bobby Unser in them looking for a wall to bang on. Their decibel level was about that of a dawn Luftwaffe takeoff under attack.

When the Speedway types experimented briefly with the turbine engine, which just went around the track with a kind of pale whoosh! the track buffs were unhappy, depressed. Not until the track outlawed these Whispering Smiths and returned the sport to its original grid of thirty-three howling automotive wolfpacks were they mollified.

The drivers were, usually, reckless young cowboys with a lust for speed and a restless, hyperactive nature that made it impossible for them to stand still. They were either in a car or on a motorcycle or on a plane. They wanted to go through life at Mach One. You could see it in their eyes, in their movements. They were impatient, sometimes irritable, anxious to get going.

I didn't know much about the technical aspects of the motor sport when I first came upon it—and I know little more today— but, as usual, my tack was to write about people, not machines. I didn't know the mechanics of the sport, but I knew danger when I saw it. I wrote about that.

You would have thought I had attacked motherhood.

I loved the guys. They were everything I wasn't. I don't think I ever drove a car fast in my life. I had too much imagination

╵ up on a blind curve at eighty miles an hour and the one
╵╵ 1 drove around the Indy 500 oval I think I got lapped by
the track sweeper.

Guys like Johnny Rutherford, the Unsers, A. J. Foyt, Parnelli
Jones and Mario Andretti I had great respect for. I considered
what they did athletic, just as I considered horse jockeys athletes.
They were controlling 750 horsepower of raging runaway engi-
neering just as horse jockeys were trying to control twelve hundred pounds of wilful horseflesh.

A. J. Foyt was as colorful a character as any sport ever saw. Irascible, cantankerous, he was, like all great athletes from Jack
Nicklaus to Ted Williams, a perfectionist. I remember the first
time I approached him (in my naivete) just as he was excoriating
his pit crew over some engine malfeasance or another. "We're at
work here!" he snapped at me, looking at me as if I were a
pothole in turn three. "What do you think I'm doing? You think
I *want* to be here?" I asked him. A.J. almost smiled. I got along
well with him thereafter. I just knew better than to come up and
say, "Well, A.J., how did it go?" just after his car lost a magneto
in lap 190.

When I first showed up at the Speedway, most of the drivers
shunned me. I was widely held to be anti-Establishment, antiracing.

One who didn't was Eddie Sachs. Eddie was the Speedway
pixie, an elf in a flameproof suit. Since he was a Jewish boy raised
in a Catholic family, you would have thought there would be a
war going on in Eddie, but he got along with everybody. He
adored Indy. Eddie could get rhapsodic on the subject of race day
morning when the crowds would pour in off Sixteenth Street, the
engines would fire up, the balloons and the doves would be released, some tenor would sing "Back Home Again in Indiana,"
and the tense words "Gentlemen, start your engines!" would re-
sound through the sycamores, and Eddie would admit he got tears
in his eyes all through the parade and pace lap.

Eddie cried for the last time in the parade lap in 1964.

That was the year they converted to gasoline as a sop to the
manufacturers who wanted the race to most closely mirror ordinary
highway driving and preserve the illusion these were stock block
engines competing at Indy.

The driver was sitting in a bathtub of gasoline and this was the day before the fuel cell came into being. It was also before the forty-gallon limit. The potential for conflagration was high.

Indy had never really had a problem with its older, wiser, veteran drivers. They knew the groove around the track, they knew the flashpoints and they were as interested in their own safety as airline pilots.

The young, wide-eyed, wild-hearted, ambitious rookies were something else. History had shown they were responsible for a disproportionately high percentage of all Indy accidents—and something like 80 percent of the fatal ones.

In the field that fateful year was the rookie Dave MacDonald, anxious to make his mark.

He made it, all right. In the very first lap, striving to move up in spite of traffic, he hit the wall in turn four. His car broached. It broadsided. It blew up.

Eddie Sachs, coming up behind him, had nowhere to go. It is an idiosyncrasy of gasoline that it burns with a black, impenetrable smoke. The traditional Indy fuel, methanol, burns colorlessly, even invisibly. You can see through it.

Sachs could not see through the black smoke. He didn't know which way to go to avoid the accident. He smashed into MacDonald, exploded, died. So did young MacDonald. It was the worst crash in Indy history. For the first time, they stopped the race. For nearly two hours.

I felt as if I had lost a really close friend. I wrote a very emotional column ("Please, God, not Eddie . . . !). I had gotten postcards over the winter from Eddie, one sent from a Catholic retreat he was attending in Detroit.

Two other colorful young drivers I came to know well were to lose their lives in race cars. Jimmy Clark, a fearless young Scot, brought the rear-engined revolution to Indy racing. Actually, it had been brought to the Speedway in 1961 by the doughty Australian Jack Brabham, who took a little, ninety-horsepower, rear-engined machine, so underpowered it couldn't keep up with the mastodons in the straights but blew them off in the corners and impressed racing with a ninth-place finish.

But in 1963, Jimmy Clark and teammate Dan Gurney showed up in competitive rear-engined Fords and, even though Parnelli Jones won in a conventional roadster, most of Indy thought Clark would have won had not the track been turned into an oil slick by Parnelli's leaking oil sump.

Clark was to die in a Formula One car at Hockenheim, Germany.

Peter Revson, like Clark, was a departure from the stereotypical Indy driver, who was usually a refugee from a Torrance or Texas garage or lube rack.

Revson was what the tabloids used to call "a scion" of the well-to-do cosmetic family (Revlon products). Blessed with collarad good looks and a polo-playing background, he was nonetheless highly competitive at Indy. Revson was on the pole and finished second in 1971.

He was a graduate of Cornell, which gave me a bit of fun the year he and Mark Donohue and Bobby Unser were on the front row. Bobby had gotten into a traffic argument with Indianapolis police the night before the race and they had briefly held him at the local lockup. That gave me the opportunity to note that the front row at Indy consisted of a graduate of Cornell (Revson), a graduate of Brown University (Donohue) and a graduate of the Indianapolis City Jail.

Bobby forgave me. Peter was later killed in a race in South Africa. Donohue was killed in Austria.

You couldn't believe the things they did at Indy. In the first place, they had this pit row with the huge multigallon oil drums full of highly volatile fuel sitting up on stilts (tanks were filled by gravity flow) and sitting between Pit Row and several thousand grandstand seats.

I suggested that, to put things in perspective, they should consider putting an apple in the mouths of the spectators seated there. They were flirting with the world's biggest barbecue if one of those machines came into the pits at two hundred miles per hour and airborne.

One year, Mark Donohue's car broke down in turn four on lap sixty-six. He got out of the car, walked to the pits. They left the car there. One hundred and one laps later it was still there when drivers Mike Mosley and Bobby Unser lost control and both plowed into it. Mosley almost lost his life. They all lost about a million dollars' worth of cars.

One year (1967), they stopped the race after nineteen laps

because of rain. Indy cars tend to hydroplane in the rain and come down the track like canoes over a waterfall.

So they parked the cars to await the rain's cessation. It never came. The cars stayed out.

I went out on the pit wall and sat with car owner Andy Granatelli. The rain pelted down. Andy had a five-hundred-thousand-dollar turbine car sitting out in the rain, a flimsy clear plastic covering—with a hole in it—the only protection from the elements. I pointed to it. "It's going to get rusted out," I suggested. "Why don't you get it in out of the rain?" "I can't," explained Granatelli. "It's against the rules."

The next day, that turbine car, leading with only four laps to go, broke a bearing.

In 1973, Indy outdid itself. First of all, a week before the race, the veteran driver Art Pollard got killed when his car got upside-down in the main straight in practice.

Then, someone conceived the idea of the pace car that year being driven by a local automobile dealer.

Now, allowing a local auto dealer to pace the Indy 500 has all the common sense of letting a stockbroker kick off the Super Bowl against the Chicago Bears.

At Indy, a pace car is leading a field of the most highly sophisticated driving machines it is possible to assemble. They stall out if you go less than 120 miles an hour. A pace car has to be driven fast and expertly in front of them.

A pace car is driven before the largest assemblage in American sports in a carnival-like atmosphere. It is a stressful ritual even for the experienced driver. For a civilian, it is a nightmare.

Eldon Palmer hauled off the track after the pace lap like a guy leaving a bank robbery. His out-of-control car, going too fast, roared down Pit Row and plowed into a photographers' stand at the end.

Miraculously, there were no fatalities, although an Argentine doctor, a longtime race fan, suffered a fractured skull.

But no one paid that much attention to the Eldon Palmer debacle because the start of the race quickly became a jumble of mangled metal as a rookie driver, Salt Walther, whose wealthy family owned the car, crashed at the green flag, flew into the air, smashed into the retaining fence and spewed flames into the crowd, then ricocheted back onto the track where he skidded through traffic on fire.

Eleven spectators were burned by the flames of Walther's airborne car. But, as bad as that accident was, it paled before what could have happened if an accident a dozen years earlier hadn't shown the officials what might happen if they didn't cable-stitch that retaining fence.

As late as 1961 that fence was a simple strand of pasture wire separating the customers from the racers when driver Tony Bettenhausen, driving a colleague's car in a practice run, plowed through that flimsy fence in turn four and tore out rows of seats on the grandstand grass.

Bettenhausen got killed and officials turned white when they considered what might have happened if that accident had taken place on race day. They quickly stitched in the heavy steel cable that would keep a race car on the track. If they hadn't, the Salt Walther crash would have been catastrophic, the Indy 500 outlawed.

Nor was that the last of the ill-starred events of 1973.

In the race, on lap fifty-seven, driver Swede Savage's car crashed in turn four, careened off one wall into another across the track and burst into flames. He was to die of his burns.

Meanwhile, back in the pits, a fire truck, rushing to the scene of the accident, started up the *wrong* way through the pits, struck and killed a crewman.

They stopped the race after lap 133 that year before the race began to rack up the casualty list of the Battle of the Bulge.

Racing has inexplicably gotten safer the faster the cars go. For one thing, they moved the engine—and the fire—*behind* the driver. For another, the cars are made of breakaway plastic now. They yield to the wall, which spares the driver.

The Indy 500 was not so much a sporting event as a nonstop party. They would begin to gather out on Sixteenth Street days before the race, a lineup of vans, recreational vehicles, pickup trucks, family sedans and motorcycles. There would be banjos, Jewish harps, accordions and guitars, and country and western music would throb through the night.

In the days when the race was held on the traditional Memorial

Day (May 30), the liquor stores in Indiana were closed by law. So the party animals would have to stock up beforehand. And we all know what that meant. They were overstocked. The night would be punctuated with the sound of popping corks, popping beer cans, the gurgle of whiskey and the aroma of cannabis.

Impromptu dances would break out on the roofs of parked trailers and spur-of-the-moment romances would erupt and be consummated in the flatbed of pickup trucks. Indianapolis would turn into its own Gomorrah by nightfall on the eve of race day.

At daybreak, this whole semi-orgy would surge through the gates and seek its parking spots in the infield where the barbecues would be fired up, the chicken plopped on the grill and fresh liquor supplies broken into, and in no time at all you would have one hundred thousand drunks lighting the sky. Signs would be flashed at passing girls: "Show us your tits!" The occasional inebriate, male or female, would strip down but arrests were few.

They were not, for the most part, racing fans. They were just party-goers. There was one notorious group who called themselves "the Arkansas Boar Hunters" who levied a fine on anyone so much as caught looking at a race car.

Even the infield was a dangerous place to be. Two spectators were killed after being struck by flying wheels. One was decapitated.

Indy's problem always was trying to hold the carnage down to a minimum. They were particularly cognizant of the ever-present danger of fire on the track. You couldn't help but be impressed with the proliferation of fire trucks, ambulances and emergency vehicles that ringed the track. It looked in poor light as if they were expecting the Battle of the Marne, not an auto race. In spite of this, I was moved to observe that, for all their, so to say, firepower, there were still some accidents where all they would need was an ashtray.

The Indy is the only sporting event that has its own hospital right on the grounds. It is the only sporting event that needs one.

It takes a special kind of human to jump into a car, drive five hundred miles at breakneck speed and wind up in the same spot where he started.

In many ways, race drivers get less respect than other athletes. Not everyone can slam dunk a basketball, hit the curveball, trade punches with Mike Tyson, ace John McEnroe, hit a one-iron straight or complete a fifty-yard touchdown pass.

But everyone can drive a car.

You have to be down on a pit wall and hear and feel the throbbing ferocity and downright terror a 230-mile-an-hour race car can generate. It takes a very special kind of human being to get into one and stand on the throttle.

Yet I have never seen any group of sportsmen who love what they do as much as racers. I have known golfers who hate putting for a living, baseball players who always look as if they had swallowed a pickle when they put on their uniforms, football players who are sick of soaking wounded knees, jockeys who hate horses.

A. J. Foyt is still driving a race car at an age when he should be piloting a rocking chair, Johnny Rutherford is returning after four years off the road. They regularly have ninety drivers competing for thirty-three spots in the Indy grid, remarkable in an era when to mount an Indy-car season-long campaign costs in the millions.

Indianapolis's 500 has to be the most concentrated, lucrative revenue producer in the whole fabric of sport. Consider that upward of a quarter of a million people pay amounts up to one hundred dollars just to watch the two-day qualifying (other races fit in their qualifying runs on an afternoon two days before the race, Indy hypes its into a two-day spectacle, two weeks before the main event).

On race day, it has been estimated that four hundred thousand pay to jam this venerable edifice five miles south of Indianapolis, the biggest landlocked metropolis in these here United States.

Anton "Tony" Hulman bought this weed-infested, 433-acre facility for $750,000. Hulman did it largely as a civic gesture, a bet on the future of his beloved Indiana (he was a baking powder heir from Terre Haute).

The price seemed outlandish, the sport was more or less fading—there had been no racing in the war years.

Tony Hulman was a strange sort. A diffident, almost shy man, he was the least pretentious rich man this side of P. K. Wrigley. He never raised his voice or even gave a loud order in his life.

But he made the track work. Ignoring the business associates who told him he had purchased a white elephant with a terminal disease, Hulman devoted the same energy to making it work that he had to his Clabber Girl baking powder business.

He courted the press. He wanted his race to have the same prestige in the minds of Americans that the Kentucky Derby had.

I never had a moment's trouble with Tony Hulman. I had breakfast with him on two occasions, at a time when mechanics, agents, drivers, even broadcasters were condemning me. (George Bignotti: "As far as Jim Murray is concerned, he thrives on writing things to get the public's attention. It could be about a race driver, a football player or anybody. He's just a jerk.")

But Tony Hulman never commented on anything I had written. We conducted our interviews as politely as two secretaries of state. I quite liked the man. And you had to respect what he had done to keep his race in the forefront of the American—not to say world—sports scene. He understood the symbiotic relationship of sport and press (or media) as well as anyone I ever knew this side of Walter O'Malley.

And I could only shake my head at the gold mine the Indianapolis Motor Speedway was for thirty days in May when people by the tens of thousands paid to watch cars *practice*.

The Unser family, leaking down into a second generation on the track, was a study in genealogy. I always imagined Billy the Kid was an early-day Bobby Unser. Brother Al was more like the country sheriff. Once, when a stewardess was telling of having the Unser brothers on one of her flights, she noted, "One of them was up in the galley every two minutes, bothering us, looking for something to drink, or eat, or some cards. The other one got on the plane, put a paper over his face and slept the whole way." Listeners had no trouble identifying which brother was which.

Al won four Indy races driving like the family chauffeur. But Bobby won three, driving like a guy being shot at by a pursuing posse. Bobby hung on more walls than a Dutch Masters painting but, if the car could go fast, Bobby would try to make it go faster.

Mario Andretti came out of a displaced person camp in postwar Italy, a homeless waif with a bleak future in a poverty-stricken, defeated country. He came to America to be the patriarch of the most prestigious racing family in track history.

For Mario Andretti to win only one Indianapolis is as big a

historical injustice as for Arnold Palmer to win only one U.S. Open, for Ted Williams to appear in only one World Series or for Ernie Banks to appear in none.

They are to be saluted, these fearless fellows of the roaring road. There is a sports philosopher who holds that the only true sports are the blood sports—auto racing, prizefighting, bull-fighting. All the others are games.

However you take it, Indianapolis is a Happening. It is unique and uniquely American.

Of the many lines I wrote about it, the deathless one seems to be "Gentlemen, start your coffins." I am not entirely happy with that. Indy-o-philes took it as a cheap shot. It could be construed as such but you have to remember at the time it was written this line pretty much summed up Indy's role in the scheme of things. When you have a race in which scores of spectators are injured, two drivers and a crewman lose their lives and a young driver suffers burns over three-quarters of his body, which he will pay for dearly in later life in kidney trouble and worse, you have to take cognizance of the fact that these guys are dicing with death.

They know it. They just don't talk about it. The race, fortunately, has gotten safer. But it will never be safe. I have never believed, as auto race haters do, that 90 percent of the audience comes to see fatalities or at least spectacular crashes. The majority of them come for the same reasons they come to Disneyland, or Super Bowls or Fourth of July fireworks.

Death takes this holiday. They begin the race with Taps (for the war dead on Memorial Day) and they often end it with Taps. A few of us were sitting around the track one day discussing the peril and I believe it was Pete Waldmeier of the *Detroit News* who said, "They call the Kentucky Derby 'The Run for the Roses.' What's this one? 'The Run for the Lilies'?"

I knew a lot of drivers who knew they might die right there in the corners or main straight of Indy. I don't think they cared.

The 1992 race was vintage Indy. The carnage was deafening. By the end of the race, there was more scrap metal floating around than at the Battle of Jutland. It was virtually "Gentlemen (and Lady), Start Your Crashes!"

First of all, there was the first fatality in ten years. A Philippine driver, Jovy Mercelo, hit the wall in practice and died in the hospital.

Indy, as usual, had been a paradox. There had been seventeen crashes in qualifying and practice. The qualifying speeds for the first time had gone over 230 and cars hit the wall doing 229 and 230. But Mercelo was clocked at a "mere" 172 when he lost his life.

Indy ended the racing career of Nelson Piquet, who had been a Formula One world champion. The Brazilian driver was one of a handful of world star drivers who risked Indy.

The most celebrated of them all, Juan Manuel Fangio, came to Indy in the 1960s, took one look at the track and the speeds, packed his gear and was never heard from again. The sporty car types reacted as if they were called upon to wrestle King Kong. They gave it a wide berth. Even the ones who did tee it up in a race or two—for the money—soon drifted back to the roads of Europe and South America. Indy was not your effete white-scarf-and-goggles, champagne-circuit driving. Indy was a shot and a beer. Not a white scarf, a red bandana.

Piquet paid for his dalliance with Indy. His broken thigh bones and other leg injuries cropped his career to a close.

Of all the European champions who dabbled in Indy, only Emerson Fittipaldi persevered. Jimmy Clark had ceased getting a representative ride at Indy and dropped out. So did 1966 winner and Formula One champion Graham Hill. So did Jackie Stewart.

The carnage on race day 1992 must have convinced them they had done the right thing.

The day dawned cloudy and cold, a raw day with a gelid wind blowing out of the west. Indy can be so hot drivers—and cars—swelter. In 1953, a driver—Carl Scarborough—died of heat prostration.

Cars are supposed to run faster and cleaner in cold weather. The problem is the tires. Cold tires do not grip the road. Indy tires are a foot wide and as bald as Michael Jordan. They cannot even run in the rain. They become surfboards on slippery surfaces. They hydroplane, come down the track spinning like a wipeout at Makaha.

Cold tires also lose traction. And Indy in the wind chill of May 25, 1992, became a miasma of crashing, out-of-control wallbangers. The ambulances were on the track almost as much as the racers.

The experts noted that almost all the crashes occurred at the end of yellow-light running. (At Indy after an accident, they put the pace car back on the track to back the field up and slow it down and keep a caution light on until the debris is cleared and the track is safe for full-bore racing again.)

No sooner would the green light come back on than a car would promptly smack the wall. The experts decided this was because most drivers pitted under the yellow to take on fuel and new tires. The new tires would be like sliding icy rocks, not bonded to the surface and unable to handle a turn at the burst of speed the green light would inspire.

That was all very well. That explained the fourteen race-day crashes. But what about the seventeen prerace crashes?

If it was wild-eyed rookies who were crashing on race day, it would be understandable. But it was the flower of American racing. Former winners like Mario Andretti, Tom Sneva, Rick Mears, Emerson Fittipaldi, Arie Luyendyk. They should have known all about cold-tire racing.

The absence of fatalities probably muted the cry that would otherwise have gone up from the reformers for the abolition of the sport. But the notion persists that race drivers would, so to speak, drive on barges or find secret venues far from the raiding police if their sport were outlawed. It isn't as if these guys are ripping through traffic on I-91. They are in their own little closed circuit. They know the risks. There isn't a one of them who hasn't been in a violent, near-fatal crash.

But you couldn't cut an A. J. Foyt out of a race car. There'll be a third generation of Unsers or Andrettis in one any day now.

Telling them they can't race is like telling Hemingway he can't write, Kelly he can't dance or Sinatra he can't sing.

It's somebody else's job, not mine. Indy is one of America's tribal rites.

You go tell A. J. Foyt he can't drive anymore. I pass.

12

· ·

The Professors Were Always Two-Touchdown Underdogs

F ootball is a coach's medium. That's the trouble with it.
Just as movies are a director's medium. And fascism is a dictator's medium.

I sometimes think the last stand of dictatorship in this world is the college football coach. His word is law, his rule is absolute, his power is unlimited. His legacy is academic chaos.

He has somehow convinced society, or that part of it which lives in his vicinity, that the highest function of a great university is to win the Rose Bowl. Or the AP poll. Or, as Woody Hayes once said when asked what his foreign policy would be, "Beat Michigan!"

It used to be the athletic coach in this country was simply the head of the PE department. His job was to get the cloistered students doing calisthenics, engaging in intramural sports, running 10Ks, working out with the parallel bars, climbing ropes—and then, maybe, on Saturday playing a game of rugby with the nearest neighboring college.

He didn't "recruit"; he accepted quasi-athletes from the student body. He got Frank Merriwells, bona-fide students, not thugs from nearby pool halls.

It's hard to pinpoint when it all changed. Probably with Fielding H. Yost, the old point-a-minute man from Michigan.

But the obsession of football coaching is not hard to comprehend. It's Everyman's dream: the desire to, the opportunity to play God.

Then it became economically rewarding. The football team

became a source of pride to the academic community, then a source of profit. They began to build edifices for the games people played—the Yale Bowl, massive stadiums rose out of the cornfields of the Middle West.

Football became big business. Coaches were no longer genuine faculty members, except in name. They began to separate themselves from the body of the university. Their charter was to win. It began to be an economic necessity to them, too. They didn't have tenure. Their "tenure" was a 7–1 season—or, better yet, an 8–0.

They became dissatisfied with the spindly-legged fraternity boys they had to suit up. They would look longingly at the specimens they saw on the docks, in the coal mines, or baling hay or chopping cane. There began to be a tug-of-war between the academic community and the athletic. When the football teams began to get prideful wealthy alumni to empty out their pockets for dear old alma mater, the athletic always won. The professors were always two-touchdown underdogs.

There were probably others before it, but the first recorded instance of a football coach winking an eye at the off-campus peccadillos and lifestyles of athletes was Knute Rockne with George Gipp. George Gipp was a crapshooter, a class-skipper, a roustabout and a gambler. He was a high school dropout. Football wasn't his game, pool was. Frail, tubercular, taciturn, he had blinding speed. He could dropkick a ball sixty-two yards.

He was hardly your model student. He gambled on the games. And Rockne knew it. Gipp lived in a hotel room so he wouldn't have to play his poker games in the dark. He knew more after-hours joints than Al Capone. He quit the university as regularly as the football season ended. He passed exams without ever taking a lecture note—or, sometimes, attending a class. He was a renegade, an outlaw. But when Gipp got a football under his arms, even Rockne got goosebumps.

So Rockne overlooked his transgressions and set a pattern for football coaches to follow for the rest of the century. If the boy can play, so what if he held up gas stations? Is he an axe-murderer? Everyone makes mistakes when they're young. Look here! He runs the forty in 4.3! Just get him a shyster and make sure we have him for spring practice.

Overdrawn? Sure. But not as much as you might think.

The quality of football players *as* football players went up exponentially. The quality of football players as moral characters went down almost to the vanishing point. You once had a Colorado football team that had something like nine varsity players with police records. The starting quarterback knocked up the coach's daughter, then refused to marry her.

You had a famous pro player who proved to have attended Oklahoma State for four years without learning to read or write. That he didn't learn to read or write was his fault—after all, spending four years in an institution of higher learning (no matter how questionable) without actually learning is like spending a summer in a cornfield and starving to death. But that a player can get *into* an institution of higher learning without being able to read or write is a coach's fault.

Coaches by now had a great deal at stake. Salaries had escalated. Football coaches' rosters looked like the German general staff. They had a coach for everything but feeding the quarterback breakfast.

You began to have starting lineups featuring the type of individuals who would have been on a chain gang in an earlier incarnation. There were ruffians, felons, rapists. They belonged in prisons, not in colleges.

But coaches got multi-million-dollar deals. They got new houses thrown in, weekly television shows to sweeten the pot, shoe and sweatshirt endorsements, speaking fees. To keep this, they had to keep winning. To keep winning, they had to get the guys who could get downfield in ten flat, bench press Volkswagens. You couldn't get these types out of the chem lab. You got them by criss-crossing the country with eager alum flesh-seekers called "birddogs." You got them by offering them money, sex, a general pampering and, finally, a millionaire's life on the Green Bay Packers or Tampa Bay Buccaneers.

In Alabama, the "legendary" Bear Bryant was the first to separate the football team from the rest of the student body. He had a separate dormitory, separate dining facilities, almost a separate university. They were at the University of Alabama but not of it. They were mercenaries, Hessians. I liked Bear Bryant. He was basically an engaging man who knew exactly what he was doing and I don't think he was entirely proud of it. He drank heavily. He spoke in a deep rumble in the twang of his native Arkansas in a pitch that sounded like an underground explosion in a coal mine. I once heard him enunciate his philosophy of coaching: "If you got any milk-drinking, tie-wearing, book-reading, churchgoing young men who are students, you send them to Stanford. But if you got any whiskey-drinking, skirt-chasing, hell-raising young men who are athletes, you send 'em to ol' Bear and we'll kick some ass!"

The coaches left no misperceptions of their intentions. The coach who growled, "I don't want to see this game, I want to *hear* it!" was the prototype of the breed. Red Sanders, the coach at UCLA, once gave me his team's scouting report on an upcoming game against Maryland. But he reached out and expunged one telltale line first. It had to do with the Maryland All-American linebacker Bob Pellegrini. It read: "Pellegrini is their best player. So let's wipe him off the cob right away." On the Bruins, "Wipe him off the cob" meant get him carried off the field.

Coaches knew exactly what they were about. There were no secrets about where the good football players were. Coach Tommy Prothro once got in a wild fistfight with another coach over a prospect in the South. Coaches called these valuable commodities "blue-chippers." UCLA got one once out of Texas who got involved in a drug-related murder in his junior year (it developed he couldn't read or write, either).

Barry Switzer, the Oklahoma coach, finally got fired after his players' dormitory proved to be as well-armed as a Mafia hangout. One or more girls got raped on the premises and the star quarterback got sentenced for dope dealing. Football squads in some communities began to resemble Quantrill's Raiders, but when a local reporter in Oklahoma City once blew the whistle on the outrageous recruiting violations and the nature of the characters they were loosing on the campus coeds, his paper transferred him to a sister paper in Colorado Springs.

Football coaches, like Mafia dons, managed to keep themselves distanced from the chicanery. A favorite ploy was to sic an alum on the prospect's family. NCAA rules could not prevent the boy's mother from being given a cushy, no-pressure job by a wealthy industrialist or banker alum. Who could quibble with a prospect's father getting a low-interest guaranteed loan with payments spread out through the century? Just the American way. None of the NCAA's business. They used to give the kids new convertibles. Bubba Smith used to ride around Lansing in one with his name in gold on the door. That became too visible. Recruiting took a more subtle tack.

The resourceful coach had a line on a few campus "cheerleaders" who liked the boys—any boys. They became key recruitment tools. There is another word for this activity—and it's not "coaching." But the credo of the craft became the oft-repeated Vince Lombardi words-to-live-by, "Winning isn't everything—it's the only thing."

Actually, this was first said by Red Sanders. And perhaps he heard it from the storied General Bob Neyland, the Tennessee coach generally credited with pioneering most of the techniques of modern college coaching and recruiting.

Neyland was the first to term all this corner-cutting and subterfuge as "the program." In football coaches parlance "the program" signified the production of an assembly line of prospects, liaison with the faculty (to keep it from clogging up the assembly line by demanding academic qualifications of the prospects) and the whole seedy business of what had been fun and games but was now simply big business. Football coaches would ban journalists they deemed inimical to "the program"—as if a journalist's business was furthering a social embezzlement.

General Neyland's disciples, and they were legion, spread the tactics throughout the game. At length, Yale and Harvard and other Ivy League schools, which had gone along willingly enough for decades, dropped the charade. They also dropped Division I football. Academia won a mild victory. It's unlikely, though, that the alumni were pleased.

It would not be fair to suggest every football player was a rogue, a thug, an unqualified student. Some seized the opportunity to gain an education, became functioning members of society.

I always remember my first sight of Roger Staubach. Roger had been a marvelous quarterback, an A student, a Heisman Trophy winner and a superb athlete. But he went to the Naval Academy and his toughness was in question. They were kind of semi–Ivy League, they didn't play the kind of bonecrushing football they played in the Big Ten, the Big Eight, the Deep South, Texas or California. Besides, he had to serve his four years in the military on graduation.

The Dallas Cowboys had drafted him on the if-come. I don't think they expected too much of Lieutenant Staubach when he appeared in camp in Thousand Oaks, California, in the summer of whatzis. I know I did a column with Roger and I wrote an upbeat piece (mainly quoting him), but I didn't believe a word of it. All he had to do was beat out Don Meredith, Craig Morton, Jerry Rhome. And he had spent his last years in Vietnam where there weren't too many footballs and even fewer receivers.

Staubach ran them all off. My column on him, to the astonishment of almost everyone, including me, proved to be prophetic. He put the Cowboys in four Super Bowls and even won two of them.

Football otherwise became a brutish sport, far removed from the Ralph Henry Barbour or Burt L. Standish image of the game. Players not only got bigger and faster, they got meaner, nastier. On-field gloating and taunting got so bad, the professional leagues legislated against it.

We had always derived out sporting code from the British. The British view of sports was old-school-tie, stiff-upper-lip, and the policy of the aristocracy who participated was "No gentleman ever plays a game too well." Winning was incidental to the taking part, as a Frenchman, Baron de Coubertin, was to say. Sports were recreational, not apocalyptic.

Americans were having none of this. America was Just win, baby! There was no solace in playing well. You played to win. That was where the money was. A loser was sports's leper. "Show me a good loser and I'll show you a loser," was an oft-heard crack of a southern basketball coach.

Senator Hiram Johnson said that truth is the first casualty of war. Sportsmanship was the first casualty of postwar athletics. The English ideal of the sportsman-athlete disappeared with the first recruit who was lured off the levees not with a promise of an education but with the promise of money under the table and money over the table in the pros.

The situation only got worse. Pro coaches were different from college coaches only in that they were relieved of the hypocrisies of recruitment. They got their players fully refined and finally out-of-the-closet professionals.

This was done at no cost to pro management. Colleges and high schools provided the high-grade ore, shipped it to market, refined it, educated it (or tried to) and then turned over the product to the pros fully developed and trained. Only one other sport enjoyed this kind of preconditioning of its work force—pro basketball. Baseball, historically, did not get its raw material from the college ranks. If a boy stayed in college, he was usually too old to start a career in baseball. Baseball had to create a network of minor leagues to refine its raw material—at considerable expense to management.

The only concession pro football made to this inequitable state of affairs was that it unilaterally agreed not to take a young man until his class had graduated. This was magnanimous of them but it wasn't to last. The whole structure of the pro football draft is as unconstitutional as any other form of slavery and this codicil to the draft a storefront lawyer could break down—and did.

Football players didn't graduate anyway. They saw no pressing need to open the books laid before them or to study the dates of forgotten wars or learn the abstruse equations of economics.

They were shamelessly spoiled. Their whims were catered to. Their way in life was cleared. Most of them came under the aegis of a grade school or high school coach early on. As soon as they showed promise, they were made into a permanent loafer class, kind of like Austrian cavalry officers. People who hoped to profit from their skills opened doors for them, lit cigarettes for their fathers, got jobs for their mothers, carried them around on a chip. They led circumscribed lives in which their bodies were temples of worship. Coaches never said "We need people here," they said "We need bodies here." They were almost inanimate objects. They were one-purpose human beings. They were there to win games. Later on, they were to be used to sell sneakers, beer, Toyotas. If later they became cases of arrested development, well, that's sports business.

I think the most terrible example of this kind of counterproductive cosseting of athletes came in the 1972 Olympics. I was walking into the ABC bungalow preparatory to interviewing Roone Arledge when I almost got bowled over by two frantic young runners and a head-holding, moaning Howard Cosell, who kept groaning that "It's an American tragedy!" They were hustling the sprinters Reynaud Robinson and Eddie Hart over to an Olympic start-line for a heat in their hundred-meter dash races.

They never made it. They had been sitting watching a field line up for a heat in the one hundred when Robinson suddenly sat up straight and shouted, "That looks like my heat!" "Must be a rerun of the morning heat," someone suggested. "No, it isn't! That's it right now!" shouted Robinson, bolting for the door.

This was another case of the American athlete being told everything to do, taking no responsibility even for making his own race on time. The coach, Stan Wright, had obviously misread the international time on the program. A listing of "16:15" came out as six o'clock. It was actually four o'clock.

You had to bear in mind that athletes from Tanzania or the Ivory Coast made their races on time. The sophisticated American runners weren't used to taking that responsibility.

An athlete frequently goes from the control and supervision of a coach to the control and supervision of an agent. As soon as he has demonstrated economic worth, the agent from Century City or the Prudential Building in Boston takes over his care and feeding.

Basketball coaches are as blameworthy as their football brethren. Every time the NCAA and the college presidents try to curtail the recruitment violations and restore some academic dignity to their institutions, a coach cries foul. At Georgetown, the redoubtable John Thompson added a new dimension when he walked off the floor and boycotted games in protest against the NCAA's regulatory Propositions 48 and 42. Prop 48 required that an athlete have graduated from high school and have an SAT score of 700 in order to play sports in college. A student who fails to get those misses his first year of eligibility. Prop 42 eliminated financial aid to athletes who did not meet the Prop 48 requirements.

John Thompson said this legislation was racially motivated, aimed at blocking black athletes with poor grades.

But what of Thompson's motivations? John Thompson is a three-hundred-pound coach whose salary and shoe contracts at Georgetown University bring him in excess of five hundred thousand dollars a year. To keep getting that, you have to have seven-foot basketball players in the pivot who may or may not be able to get 700 scores on the SAT. (It has been pointed out you get 400 just for being able to sign your name.) But would John Thompson be all that interested in smuggling students through those propositions—which are, after all, aimed only at athletes—if the students did not have a good jumpshot? Colleges don't need 4.3 halfbacks or three-point jump-shooters or seven-foot pivots. Colleges need future doctors, scientists, inventors, statesmen.

Some years ago, California instituted something called the "2 percent law." It provided that some 2 percent of the admissions could enter college below the standard requirements. The law was pushed forward to help bright students who had had substandard educations. But history shows us that it was surprising how many of those who got in under the 2 percent law were jump-shooters, quarterbacks, punters, passers and guys who could play the high post.

I must confess I don't like John Thompson. And I will tell you why. In the spring of 1988 when he was named coach of the U.S. Olympic basketball team, I was beseeched to help the team raise funds for the trip by covering a basketball game put on in Las Vegas for that very purpose. I agreed.

I arrived in Las Vegas to request an interview with one or more of the players on the team. The request was refused. John Thompson did not permit the players to talk to anyone. Okay, I relented, grudgingly, how about an interview with John Thompson then? Again, I was refused. John Thompson would talk to the press only for a brief ten-minute period at the *conclusion* of the game. You couldn't talk to players even then.

You can imagine my frame of mind. My paper had shelled out a sizable sum of money for me to go up and cover an event that I was effectively prevented from covering. The game was televised, so they didn't need me to tell them the number of rebounds or the score.

My point was, this was not John Thompson's team to tell what to do. This was America's team, our Olympic team. I have no quarrel with what John Thompson does with his Georgetown University team. That's between him and Georgetown, which is a private institution. My tax money, my contributions to the Olympic movement don't go to Georgetown. But the Olympic team was something else again.

Coaches are people who are happy in their jobs, content to work incredibly long hours. Playing God is addictive. There are places in this country where coaches are high priests. Armed state troopers precede them wherever they go. They are bigger celebrities than the state governor.

But have they served the Republic well? Do we need this emphasis on winning at all costs? Is it healthy? Is it even sane?

The ludricous outcome of this lifetime of questionable values was seen on the evening of December 29, 1979, when, in a relatively minor bowl game, the prototypical football coach, Woody Hayes, burst his moorings when a rival player intercepted one of his team's passes. Hayes actually began to strike the young player who had made the interception. On national television yet. When Hayes's assistants began to drag him off, he attacked them.

Woody, to be sure, had an oar out of the water. I have known coaches who were bright, bon vivant–type companions, lively, funny, interesting. They usually made it their business to be quippy, funny and lovable on the banquet circuit. "You better be funny if you're 2-and-8," Cactus Jack Curtice of Stanford used to say.

But I have never known one who wouldn't suit up Jack the Ripper if he thought he'd get him to the Rose Bowl. And King Kong, they get a new convertible for. And try to get him Fay Wray if they can find her.

13

....

Just Move, Baby!

Al Davis is (choose one) 1) a despicable cad who would do anything to win, or 2) a genius who is light-years ahead of his competition when it came to putting together a victorious combination.

Al Davis is neither of those things. Al Davis is an alley fighter, a gambler, fiercely competitive, impatient with excuses. Al Davis would have been a hit-and-run cavalry officer, maybe general, in a previous incarnation.

He has the sine qua non of leadership—mild paranoia. Davis sees himself always as a guy on his own two-yard-line and the other guys with the ball. Or at least, he professes to see himself that way. It fuels Al to consider all life was a conspiracy against him. He revels in the role of semi-outlaw. He is a risk-taker, but a calculated risk-taker. He considers large sections of the rules we live by to be hypocritical. He rejoices in his enemies. He is no man to cross, as succeeding football commissioners (of which he was one), rival owners, coaches and just plain players were to find out.

He is a worshiper of military thinkers from Clausewitz to Norman Schwarzkopf, and his wide-eyed admiration of the German Wehrmacht was raised as an issue in a court trial to try to embarrass him.

Al Davis does not embarrass easily. The spectacle of a nice young Jewish boy from Erasmus Hall High in Brooklyn admiring Hitler's army, Al did not find incongruous at all. He admired the army, not the philosophy. The German army went deep. So did Davis's Raiders. Blitzkrieg football was a Davis trademark.

He was as nonjudgmental as Mother Teresa, if that analogy is not blasphemous. Al Davis did not care what you did or where you came from if you could run the forty in 4.4, sack the quarterback, catch or throw the bomb, go up the middle.

His team was well-named. They resembled nothing so much as Quantrill's Raiders of Civil War infamy. They were aggressive, ruthless, merciless—to the extent that rival coach Chuck Noll, no Boy Scout leader himself, referred to them in print as the "criminal element" of the National Football League.

Some of Davis's players did look as if he beat the police to them. Some others were frightening specimens. John Matuszak, for instance, had once beaten to a pulp an army officer in a Tampa bar, all but destroying his face in the process. Matuszak was such a terrifying prospect that no one bought his explanation that the man had put his hand on Matuszak's girl's knee. No one short of Mike Tyson would have been that insane. When they turned John Matuszak loose on the football field, the hope was just that he wouldn't eat anyone.

I first ran into Al Davis when he was an assistant coach at the University of Southern California.

Al never really was an assistant anything. He was an aggressive recruiter, so much so that he got the university put on probation for two years over recruitment violations in which he brought in a lineman from Natick, Massachusetts, and a quarterback from Lancaster, Pennsylvania.

He not only got the football team probationized, he got *all* USC teams banned. And that was a year the golf team had one Al Geiberger on it and was a lock for the NCAA title.

Davis was an indefatigable recruiter. The irony was, Southern California was becoming a hotbed of talent in its own right, a breeding ground of All-American football players. The population had exploded and an astonishing number of the new immigrants could run the hundred in 9.9 or so or jar the Empire State Building head-on.

Al didn't need to forage afield for football players. He had coached at The Citadel in South Carolina before coming to Southern California and, when he departed that military institution after lobbying for, and being denied, the head coaching job, he had brought three players with him, Al Bansavage, later an All-Pro linebacker with the Raiders, lineman John Wilkins and the world-class sprinter and running back Angie Coia.

Al would have liked the head coaching job at SC, too, but it went to John McKay, whose jaunty humor and ready charm appealed more to the powers that were than Al Davis's nail-biting intensity.

There was no doubt in anybody's mind that Al Davis was a first-class football intelligence or that he would be a major player in the football world someday. What was suspect was his willingness to play within the rules.

When the new, audacious American Football League was formed by a lot of sons of riches, some of whom had been frustrated in their attempts to buy their way into the existing National Football League, the Los Angeles Chargers were bought by hotel magnate Barron Hilton (and named after his charge-a-card service, Carte Blanche) and turned over to the brilliant football theorist Sid Gillman. Sid in turn hired Al Davis.

It was a marriage made in football heaven. Both doted on the split-the-ends and throw-the-bomb football—for Al, football by von Rundstedt. The Chargers used to roll up six hundred yards a game. "There was no such thing as bad field position for them," sports editor Jack Murphy was to say when the team moved to San Diego.

The Chargers in San Diego were the class of the fledgling league. Davis and Gillman, both good judges of football flesh, put together some of the flashiest teams ever seen on a football field. They were a welcome relief from what someone called the "American Gothic" play of the older established NFL, but the senior league scoffed at what they termed the "volleyball" played by Davis's team and league.

In 1962, the Oakland Raiders were not a team, they were a disaster area. An orphaned franchise that had originally been intended for Minneapolis, they had records of 2–12 in 1961 and 1–13 in 1962.

When the owning general partners, Wayne Valley and Ed McGah, came looking for a head coach to lead them out of this morass, Al Davis was more than ready for them. Al thirsted to be a head coach; he had spent nine years in the assistant-coach category and was tired of it.

This didn't stop him from driving a hard bargain with the two general partners. Although Wayne Valley came bitterly to regret it, he was enchanted when Davis spurned his first two offers—including one for a three-year contract. Davis wanted power, not title. He insisted upon being general manager as well as coach. Al wanted to answer to nobody.

One of his first acts was to convince the league to bolster the Oakland franchise with a special draft of players from other franchises "to provide a more competitive balance."

Davis restored the competitive balance, all right. He took the 1–13 team and put up a record of 10–4.

He was somewhat less than successful in succeeding years but, in 1966, he accepted an even more challenging task—commissioner of the AFL.

Oakland in the meantime had built him a $22.5 million stadium. But its Coliseum authority had neglected to tie the Raiders into a twenty-year contract with options to renew—an oversight that was to cost the community the team fourteen years later.

The league needed a strong commissioner because, without a merger and a common draft, the suicidal draft-signing war was costing each league $25 million and upward a year. Teams were drowning in a sea of red ink. The first five-year television contract (with ABC) was for a measly $1.785 million, which, divided by eight teams, came to about $48,000 a year per team. The league, though, needed the exposure and might have paid the networks that amount. (By 1965, the league had signed with NBC for $36 million for five years.)

Davis was exactly the right guy to make the Establishment league squirm. Al was a brass-knuckle guy from way back when it came to corporate fights—or any other kind.

He thought the best way to bring the NFL to the conference table was to loot its best players. It wasn't long before the stories began to surface about the junior league luring the likes of quarterbacks Roman Gabriel and John Brodie to AFL teams. The NFL knew they were in a shooting war.

The Davis tactics may not have brought about the merger but they hastened it. The NFL took in the AFL (which paid $18 million for the privilege—the NFL threw in the Cleveland Browns, Pittsburgh Steelers and Baltimore Colts, like a guy throwing kids out of a sleigh to the wolves in the deal).

Davis was suddenly a rebel without a cause—or a general without a war. He went back to Oakland. As general manager. By now, the team had a new head coach, John Rauch, and Al came back in the most felicitous position.

Free of the day-to-day pressure of coaching the club, Al could now concentrate on getting to own it.

Al Davis was a complicated man. But the one certainty about him was that he would get what he wanted. And what he wanted on his return from his brief stint at commissionership was complete control of the Oakland Raiders. If Al could spot a weakness in Chuck Noll's Pittsburgh Steelers, spotting one in the so-called managing general partners of the Oakland Raiders was child's play.

Al recognized early that what appeared to be a monolithic band of owners, wise in decision, forthright in action, was a pack of stubborn patsies, suckers for the bomb, so to speak.

Al Davis sensed, sooner than anybody, the decline of respect for authority in this country. It would not be fair to say he encouraged it. But he *understood* it. When a player of his was hauled up on criminal charges—as Warren Wells was on rape charges or George Atkinson on embezzlement charges—Davis did more than pay lip service to their defenses, he spearheaded them.

He reveled in the Raider image as a pack of lawless urban guerrillas, even cutthroats, a swarm of pirates with knives in their teeth and murder in their hearts. It was a Raider defensive man who inflicted the most serious injury at that time—the permanent paralysis of Darryl Stingley—but not even that tragic incident seemed to discourage the thuggery of a Raider game in the trenches. One of the worst places in the world to be was the Raider two-yard-line with the ball. You weren't too safe in the open waiting for a pass—or not waiting. Pittsburgh's Lynn Swann suffered a concussion on a play in which he was not even the receiver and coach Noll's dubbing of the Raider safety men as part of the "criminal element" of society prompted safety man George Atkinson to bring suit against Noll and the Steelers. He lost the suit but silenced the complaining throughout the league.

Davis specialized in getting so many players who seemed malcontents or immersed in controversy where they were that the

Oakland franchise came into focus as a kind of Devil's Island of football. Lyle Alzado had gone through franchises like the wrath of God, striking out at authority wherever he went. He had been a violent street gangster in New York in his youth, who had seemed on his way to Attica until one night in jail he saw a hardened aging criminal point a finger at him and say, "Take a good look at me, kid. In twenty years you're going to be right where I am now."

Alas! Even though Lyle Alzado didn't act out his cellmate's dire prediction, his end was equally tragic and depressing.

Lyle Alzado was a bullish, brutish young man, the son of a Puerto Rican father and a Jewish mother, who went through life with a constant mixture of anger and compassion. He always reminded me of an Old Testament prophet, the bearded look, the angry eyes. You could picture him standing on a hill in biblical times, raging at the sins of his fellow man.

On the football field, he was an archangel, too. An avenging presence, a force for order. He growled, he snarled, he didn't just tackle quarterbacks, he tore into them. He was a violent man in a violent sport. He intimidated. Once, he threw his helmet at a blocker.

He considered himself invincible. Once, he climbed in the ring with Muhammad Ali, no less, and survived an eight-round exhibition. The line of scrimmage was his turf.

Off the field, Lyle was unpredictable. Charming, gracious when he wanted to be, he was no one to approach ten minutes before a game.

He rejoiced in Los Angeles. He had played his whole career in places like Denver and Cleveland. He had been jerked out of a Brooklyn ghetto to become a football player in, of all places, Yankton, South Dakota. He was the only NFL player ever drafted out of that badlands institution.

We never knew it at the time but Lyle's mood swings could be attributed to an illegal substance—body-building steroids. He came along at a time when their use was becoming epidemic. The "in" thing was to bulk up.

Lyle might as well have been swallowing rattlesnakes alive. He enjoyed frenzied years. He got bit parts in movies, which he luxuriated in. He ran with a hep crowd, young show biz types.

He felt he belonged. He was a star-status celebrity on the Hollywood circuit.

He found out what everyone finds out in Tinseltown sooner or later: You're only as good as your last picture. Or your last tackle.

When Lyle retired, he was still a social lion for a period. He still was a staple on the better talk shows around town—he had made the Johnny Carson show in his playing days.

But Hollywood tends to forget you when they pick up the paper on Monday mornings and you're not in there or they turn on Channel 11 and you're not on there.

Lyle was so chagrined, he undertook a "comeback" at age forty-one. He went to the Raider camp in Oxnard in the preseason convinced he still had a pass rush in him.

He didn't. It was embarrassing. He got tossed around like a sack of flour by guys he would have run right through or thrown at the ballcarrier in his heyday six years before.

It was shortly after that Lyle began to notice little things—a slight stumbling in his walk, a dizziness, an awkwardness in the memory.

Lyle had cancer in the brain. Inoperable. Alzado was doomed.

His last year was nightmarish. His hair gone, his limbs withering away, this once avenging prophet was a shadow of his former self. The scourge of the football field was a wasting-away specimen.

They decided to hold a mammoth hotel benefit in his honor. It was embarrassing. Whether through mismanagement or because of public apathy, it never succeeded in attracting the wealthy patrons it had to have. Lyle was history, not news. The people who had cheered him had gone on to the new sensations, a new generation of athletic heroes. The event had to be canceled.

Alzado was crushed. He died a few months later in Oregon. He was forty-three years old.

He had, at least, avoided fulfulling the prophecy of his jailmate all those years before. Or had he?

John Matuszak, six-eight, 280 pounds of hate, had walked out on one team, been thrown off another by a group of sheriffs, been arrested for marijuana use, rushed to a hospital for an overdose of sleeping pills and was famous for pulling frightened motorists who had affronted him out of their cars and beating them. He found a home on the Raiders. So did Ben Davidson, who looked like a one-man motorcycle gang, and Ted Hendricks, who was famous for liquid lunches and played with such reckless abandon he was known on the field as "the Mad Stork."

The Raiders were not exactly a monastery. Even in the headlong, take-no-prisoners violence of the National Football League, these headbusters stood out.

Al's team got in the second Super Bowl ever played and, while on the surface the outcome looked one-sided (Green Bay 33, Oakland 14), the likelihood is the Raiders were overawed by the Packers' reputation. The vaunted Green Bay "attack" included four field goals and an interception returned for a touchdown.

But Al Davis had a Super Bowl of his own. Increasingly, he thought of the Oakland Raiders as his creation. He began, with the unwitting connivance of the principal owner, Wayne Valley, to build up his equity. Valley, to his dismay, woke up one morning in 1973 to find that Al Davis, not Wayne Valley, was the dominant presence on the general partners.

The leadership of the Raiders had been a triumvirate when Valley took the brash young Davis on in 1962—Valley, Ed McGah and the young "genius" they took on and settled some "minor" equity on.

Over the years, Davis wooed McGah away from the irascible Valley until, one day, McGah signed Davis to a ten-year extension of his contract with language that virtually gave him dictatorial control of the team. Valley, outraged, later sued both McGah and Davis, citing the contract as "onerous and unfair," as it would turn the Oakland Raiders over to Davis without Valley's consent. The judge found for Davis. Valley, disillusioned, sold his interest in the team. Davis snapped up additional ownership left on the table. The team was finally his. He moved from general partner to managing general partner to president of the general partners.

Why the move to Los Angeles? Well, it all happened, of course, because the Rams, dazzled by a super-lucrative real estate deal, moved to Anaheim. But instead of leaving a vacuum behind, they left a locked door. The bylaws of pro football provided that no franchise could move into the home territory of another franchise without *unanimous* vote of the twenty-eight owners.

This meant the L.A. Coliseum, which the Rams had to fight to get into in the first place when they moved to L.A. from Cleveland in 1946, would remain locked and empty, a white elephant in the community.

The Coliseum Commission sued the league. The league changed the bylaws (to a three-quarters rather than a unanimous vote) to head off a court showdown. Al Davis abstained.

The Raiders weren't the first to express interest in rushing into the L.A. vacancy. The Minnesota Vikings were. But the community there quickly sweetened the pot, promised a new stadium, kept the team. Robert Irsay, the Baltimore Colts owner, who had been dumb enough to effect a swap deal years before wherein he bought the L.A. Rams, then traded them even-up with Carroll Rosenbloom for the Baltimore Colts, now lusted for a move to L.A.

They were all headed off by a fear of a league turndown, which would have the effect of thwarting the move and alienating the community to which they were rehitched.

None of this intimated Al Davis. Al may not have invented the word "chutzpah," but it was invented for people like him.

Al presented a series of demands on the city of Los Angeles for the move. He presented a series of demands on the city of Oakland to obviate the move.

After all, he had all the cards—the team.

The league disapproval? Al Davis sneered. He could take care of this bunch of bumblers. He always had. When the league voted, 22–0, to block his moving to Los Angeles, Davis slapped the league and commissioner Pete Rozelle with a $160 million lawsuit. He joined the L.A. Coliseum Commission in its suit.

Davis kicked ass when the suit was finally heard. He not only got the right to move, he and the Coliseum Commission collected millions.

There are many explanations of why Al Davis moved his franchise south. One of the sillier ones holds that he hankered to get into the show biz element of Southern California.

Al Davis probably never looked at a movie in his life that didn't have football players in it. The only film star I had ever seen in a Raider locker room was Jim Garner, and he had been a pal of Al's and a number-one Raider fan back in the Oakland days.

No, the thing that brought Al Davis south was not glamor, it was money. He came south for the same reason Walter O'Malley went West.

They both felt their franchises were at a dead end where they were—unless they could get more favorable options. They both felt their teams were disadvantaged in competition unless they were upgraded economically.

Al knew L.A. He had, after all, been coach at USC those early years. He felt that the league could not long leave the L.A. trading area without an NFL team and that the guy who got it would have a big leg up on the rest of the league.

L.A. had long since passed San Francisco as a financial center. It had a population that was growing exponentially.

And Oakland was even in the shadow in the Bay Area. Al wanted luxury boxes, more favorable lease conditions—he wanted monies to pour into his team. Not into Al Davis's coffers. There has never been any indication Al Davis cared more than superficially for money. Power was what he hungered for. He wanted the Raiders to be the New York Yankees of football.

Al was a sentimentalist when it came to sports history. He was a hero-worshiper but his heroes had to be of twenties, forties and early fifties vintage.

He saw to it the old Michigan superstar from the forties, Tom Harmon, ol' 98 to Al, always had a job in the Raiders' broadcast lineup. His old college sprinter, Angie Coia, likewise was kept in the Raider family. If Joe DiMaggio entered a room, Al was awed.

He relished talking of the old Yankee days. He always regretted he never could have met Knute Rockne. He regarded Vince Lombardi as a great man and his veneration of German generals puzzled his coreligionists.

It needn't have. Al Davis respected power—and prowess.

He felt L.A. and the Raiders were a marriage made in football heaven.

It never totally worked from Day One.

The Raiders were the first "carpetbagging" team to come to L.A. and dislodge a local entity. The Rams came into a vacuum. The Dodgers came into a minor league baseball town. The Lakers supplanted nobody.

The Raiders were, in a sense, ousting the Rams—the Rams had only moved thirty miles south.

The makeup of the crowds at the Coliseum changed drastically. Where the Rams were the darlings of the movie crowd and the affluent West Side, the Raiders instantly appealed to the blue-collar types from the working-class East and South sides.

The Raiders attracted a more raucous, not to say lawless, element. The makeup of a Raider crowd was likened to a biker rally—black-jacketed, tattooed ruffians in many cases. Fights broke out in the stands. A police presence, never needed in the heyday of the Rams, was highly necessary at Raider games.

Matters came to a head when a rooter, incautious enough to sport a Pittsburgh Steeler jacket, was kicked into a coma by a Raider end zone fan one Sunday.

Before that, the Raiders had pooh-poohed their unflattering public image. It was all a figment of press imagination, they counseled.

By now, the country knew different. In incident after incident of rowdyism and hooliganism as far away as South Florida, culprits were seen to sport Raider jackets, Raider paraphernalia. They seemed to be the uniform of the scofflaw.

In some cases, communities sought to ban the sale of Raider memorabilia, perceived as it was an inciter to riot. It became almost synonymous with the swastika, a symbol for nihilism.

When the Raiders came to L.A., their attitude was reminiscent of that of the Dodgers when they first came abroad. They were doing the city a big favor. The Dodgers' crowd behaved with almost curl-lipped contempt as if they were city slickers ankle-deep in cow manure. Most of them were New York–born and bred and deeply suspicious of and superior to everything west of the Hudson.

It was a preposterous attitude. A healthy portion of the population out in L.A. had migrated earlier from New York but the Dodgers' hierarchy so alienated parts of the community with their high-handed attitude, they very nearly lost the election that permitted them to come there.

The difference between the Dodgers' and the Raiders' move to L.A. and the migrations of the Rams and the Lakers was simply that the Dodgers and Raiders had been wooed by the community, begged to come. The Rams had come, so to speak, with their hats in their hands. Not only was the community ambivalent but the colleges—who had the L.A. Coliseum all to themselves, to say nothing of the undivided attention of the area's football fans—had opposed the Rams' entry into the market. The Rams were made to feel like unwelcome guests in the house of the Trojans and Bruins.

The Raiders and the Dodgers were welcomed like rich uncles. They behaved, consequently, as if they expected, so to speak, their cigarettes to be lit for them, their car doors held and their favorite foods prepared. They were almost insufferable.

None of this ever bothered Al Davis. He never made a move that could be considered conciliatory or apologetic. His philosophy was Win and they fawn over you. Lose, and all the banquets in the world won't help.

Sub Davis, the Raiders were always hard for the media to "cover," to find out exactly who was in charge of what. Unlike other corporate sports entities, they had no established, clearly defined public relations person.

All power flowed from the top—Al. In fact, the Raiders resembled nothing so much as a Mafia family—and Al was the godfather. He was all-knowing, nothing got done in the organization without his OK.

He could be engaging if he chose but, with Al Davis, it was impossible to overlook the aura of intimidation: Not only did Davis put it forth himself but it extended down into the nether regions of the Raider family.

They were an obdurate bunch who made newsmen feel like unwelcome spies, an attitude that sometimes permeated the organization. They were just short of being rude—to the public and the media alike. If ever an institution was the lengthened shadow of one man, the Raider institution was it. Everybody, significantly, was known as an "administrative assistant." Here, "assistant" was the operative word. Nobody but the managing general partner got marquee billing on the Raiders. (An "administrative assistant," with indistinct authority, once threw CBS's Irv Cross off the field at a Super Bowl in Tampa. Davis surrounded himself with more irascible types than a Mafia don.)

The Raiders, who came to Los Angeles as winners of the Super Bowl twice in five years, were somewhat less than an artistic success their first L.A. season. But that was largely due to the players' strike, which truncated the season to nine games.

By contrast, 1983 was a triumphal march. The Raiders swept to a 12–4 record, toppled Pittsburgh and Seattle in playoff games at the Coliseum before over ninety-two thousand spectators. They annihilated Washington in the Super Bowl, 38–9.

Meanwhile, back at the fort, another firefight began to erupt. Al's reason for the move to Los Angeles was the renovation of the ancient, rotting Memorial Coliseum, with the construction of luxury boxes added. Davis soon found he was dealing with that hydra-headed monster—a politically appointed committee.

Davis found the changes in the coloration of the commission bewildering. He might have taken a leaf from Walter O'Malley's book when O'Malley, after repeated rebuffs from the city fathers and the commission, finally demanded in some exasperation, "Who's the man in charge here? It's anarchy!" Jack Kent Cooke found the same roadblocks put in his path. Both ended up constructing their own playing field and arena.

Davis couldn't do that. So, he did the next-best thing. He tried to get some *other* community to build one for him.

He first played coyly with a community known as Irwindale, a gas stop on the road between Pasadena and the San Gabriel Valley. This tiny municipality (a population under two thousand!) had delusions. It had a perfect site for a stadium—an old quarry pit—and not much more.

Not surprisingly, its bid came to naught—and Al Davis set out on a search for a new home for his migratory franchise. Have team, will travel.

He proceeded to try Sacramento. He even went back to Oakland!

For anyone else, the process would have been demeaning. Al Davis didn't care. Al Davis cares about one thing in this world—his football team.

What effect did all this have on his football team? Al Davis left his football team with one directive—"Just win, baby!" He would take care of the rest.

The Coliseum Commission, which had run Jack Kent Cooke out of town (to Inglewood), had lost the Rams, Lakers, Kings and UCLA Bruins and was no match for Al Davis. While he was running around the state offering his franchise to the highest bidder, the politicians finally relinquished their grip on the Coliseum. They agreed to turn it over to a private management firm, Spectacor, which immediately contacted Davis and lured him back with a promise that things would be different.

Davis, for his part, had always been reluctant to leave L.A., but he privately—and publicly—considered the Coliseum politicians a pack of ingrates, given that they had profited by $15 million in the lawsuit against the NFL that the Raiders and their legal staff had basically pioneered. (Davis's lawyers—who were spearheaded by the smarmy ex–San Francisco mayor Joe Alioto—got $10 million.)

Al stayed in Los Angeles. But it would never be possible to say the fandom took his team to its bosom. When they won, there were ninety thousand fans in the seats. When they lost, there were thirty thousand fewer.

And something happened to Al Davis that had never befallen him before. For the first time, he seemed unable to come up with that heart and soul of football success—a quarterback.

Davis had always been blessed with outstanding athletes in the pivotal position. Daryle Lamonica, slow but armed, who came to answer to the nickname "The Mad Bomber," Kenny Stabler, "The Snake," a lefthanded Joe Namath type, unflappable, cool in combat, as surehanded a passer as the game has ever seen. Then he lucked into Jim Plunkett, a power quarterback, a Heisman Trophy winner from Stanford whose career had been short-circuited by being tossed into mortal combat too soon by the New England Patriots.

Davis got Plunkett via the waiver route, as he was generally considered a washed-up football player. But Plunkett's confidence, which had become eroded behind New England's porous line, was suddenly rebuilt when he got behind a Raider line that included Gene Upshaw, Art Shell, Dave Dalby. He put the Raiders in two Super Bowls. He won them—big.

But with the departure of Plunkett, Al Davis seemed to lose the formula. He paid big bucks for Brigham Young quarterback Marc Wilson (Wilson was coveted by the U.S. Football League and Donald Trump), but Wilson proved to be the most indecisive player the league had seen. I was uncharitable enough to observe if you gave Marc Wilson a two-page menu he'd starve to death. In a playoff game against New England once, he burned up a timeout in the third quarter owing to his indecision, went to the bench, got a play, got back to the line of scrimmage, didn't like the defensive lineup, called a second timeout, went back to the bench, got a play—and went back in and threw an incompletion.

Davis let Wilson go in disgust. The Raiders without a quarterback were just another football team. They made it to the championship game in 1990—where they got beat, 51–3.

Al Davis doesn't suffer humiliations like that gladly. He tried to shore up the position by signing a USC kid, Todd Marinovich. From a football family, Marinovich had quit the SC campus in a row with his coach. An attitude problem. Then he managed to get arrested for cocaine and marijuana infractions.

It was the kind of scenario Davis liked best. It fitted the Raider image of the nonjudgmental, just-win-baby! big brother franchise that held society's laws in contempt. The Statue of Liberty calls, "Give us your tired, your poor, the wretched refuse of your teeming shore, your huddled masses yearning to breathe free." Davis's slogan was, "Give me your scorned, your troubled, your rejected, your helpless, your escapees from middle-class morality—we just play football here."

Davis and the Raiders have to hope Marinovich is another Matuszak, Alzado, Hendrick. And not another Wilson. Not even Davis can win without the field general. Al needs a quarterback more than he needs luxury boxes.

Which is just as well. Because Al never did get his luxury boxes, or renovation of the Coliseum, or any of the things he was promised to move south. The downturn in the economy, the cataclysmic riots, the cooling off of the TV networks conspired to make football a low community priority.

But it's a high Davis priority.

Al Davis has struck many positive postures with his Raiders. He hired the first black head coach in the NFL. He has been to four Super Bowls and won three of them.

But the image of his team as a pack of lowlifes who would mug their grandmothers if they came into their pass zones probably stems from Al's disinclination to remove or even change that image. Al is putting a football team together, not a monastery.

It isn't as if he encourages antisocial behavior on the part of his athletes. Al just thinks it's irrelevant. He judges players by what he sees on film Monday mornings. What they did Sunday night after the game is somebody else's concern.

It is an attitude that has won favor with a lot of football players, notably malcontents. They feel the Raiders have a light in the window for them.

They do.

The modern pro football franchise has a table of organization like General Motors. There is an executive in charge of each division of business. A pro football team historically has had a press relations officer for dealing with the media. The Raiders came into town without one as such. At the Raiders, the table of organization is one.

Davis is loyal if you are a friend. But the friendship has to be earned and is fragile and requires constant reaffirmation.

The Raiders have won championships with three different coaches, three different quarterbacks. No other team can make that statement. A multiple Super Bowl winner usually has one constant, either coach or QB.

On the Raiders, the constant was Al Davis.

Al Davis, in person, is scarcely intimidating. Until you know him. He has on his face what I would term a permanent expression of eagerness. He always looks as if he can't wait to see what happens next.

He is curious, a voracious reader. He is totally disinterested in adding the grace note to what he says. In conversation, he is apt to turn the conversation around. Which is to say, if you come to ask *him* questions, he goes on the attack. He asks *you* questions. I have seen him do this at a newspaper editors' luncheon. Newspaper editors being newspaper editors, they are, in a sense, fans, flattered to be in the presence of so distinguished a sports figure.

But when they answer a question about politics with a "Well, we don't know," Davis is almost offended. "But you're supposed to know. You write like you know," he will complain.

It is a tactic that has served him well. He has been the dog-in-the-manger at league meetings for over a decade now. He abstains from most votes, runs counter to the consensus on others. This is because he is on record as considering most of his co-owners "a bunch of dummies." He is so contemptuous of them, he threw his weight in with the old, disbanded USFL in its lawsuit against his own league. Al Davis sees the handwriting on the wall. And it doesn't bode well for the Establishment, he feels.

After he moved from Oakland to L.A., the league saw the Colts move from Baltimore to Indianapolis and the Cardinals move from St. Louis to Phoenix. This was not the first move for the Cardinals, who had moved from Chicago to St. Louis in the first place. Boston's Redskins had moved to Washington in antiquity. Al took the position he could move his franchise to Mars if he so chose.

There would seem to be a point at which a sports franchise bears a responsibility to a community. After all, it draws emotional support from that community. Its geographical identification is important to it. A football game is just a football game if you have no emotional stake. The "My-team-can-beat-your-team" is the linchpin of professional sports. If teams wore blank uniforms, who would care?

But the professional franchise counters that it, in turn, is only important to the community if it wins. Otherwise, it struggles to exist.

No one cared when the Boston Braves moved out of Boston, not even their fans, of whom they had not many. They were losing money, the town was apathetic.

But Al Davis moved a team that had had a decade of sellouts and, if Oakland is not Gotham City ("There is no 'there' there," Gertrude Stein is supposed to have said of it), neither was it Possum Hollow or Milano Junction. Nor was it even Green Bay.

But Al Davis apologizes to no one. "You don't want to get Al Davis pissed off at you," Gene Upshaw once warned.

He all but destroyed Pete Rozelle. Rozelle failed to copy a leaf from Baseball's notebook, which held that you never—*never!*—get your sport in a court of law. Professional sports is so far outside the parameters of the Constitution that every trip down

173

a courtroom aisle is like a trip into lion country. Rozelle and the league lost millions.

Davis is not universally liked. But he is universally feared. Which appeals more to him. He has left a trail of enemies.

He is not dislikable in person. But he is blunt in his opinions, quick to spot what he perceives as posturing. As one adversary grudgingly admitted, "You always know where you stand with Al Davis. You get no bullshit."

What he's about is winning football games. He has even invented a persona that fits that goal. The boy from President Street in Brooklyn, who spent two short years in South Carolina (at The Citadel) and a stint at Fort Belvoir, Virginia, sometimes sounds like Nathan Bedford Forrest. "I" comes out "ah," and other words come out as if he learned to speak through a mouthful of corn pone—instead of blintzes.

He is a world-class nailbiter at games. To sit under the Raider royal box at a game is to think periodically that an earthquake has struck. A fumble by his team, a mistake in play calling is apt to bring a hand, or a book, or a foot slamming down on the table or floor, followed by a stream of invective.

The Raiders are his life. Their take-no-prisoners philosophy is his philosophy. Like von Rundstedt, his hero, his goal is to surround his enemies—and destroy them piecemeal.

If he gets a quarterback, he'll probably do it.

14

· ·

Get the Other Eye, Louie!

B oxing is a moribund sport.
     It wasn't when I came into this business. It was one of the Big Three—Baseball, Boxing and Football.

Boxing was on network TV twice a week—the Pabst Blue Ribbon fights and the Gillette Friday Fights. Video staples.

Now, it's a sometimes cable thing.

There used to be weekly fights in every tank town arena in America. And in St. Nick's in New York and the Olympic in Los Angeles. Now, there're only fights when TV comes up with the money. Big title fights endure but only at the pay-per-view level. The sport has disappeared at the grass-roots level.

What has happened? Well, I think the realization that it is impossible to legislate out the cruel or hurtful aspects of a sport in which the hurtful aspect is the core of the sport. In football, you can protect the quarterback with rules of contact. In baseball, you outlaw the beanball. In basketball, you discourage aggression by awarding foul shots. What do you do in boxing—outlaw the right cross? The left jab?

Periodically, through its existence, attempts have been made to outlaw boxing. There's always some Englishwoman member of Parliament who wants to put it to death before it does it to its practitioners. Even politicos in this country have legislated against it. Remember, it was permitted in New York only as an "exhibition" sport up until the 1920s. Victors won unofficial "newspaper decisions." Before that, it was periodically outlawed everywhere.

But it survived on the barges, in secret locations, on islands off the coast. It was harder to kill than Rasputin.

That's because it's great theater. There is no moment in sports to rival the electric charge that goes through an audience in the moments just before the bell for a heavyweight championship fight. Nothing can touch that. No Super Bowl coin flip, no World Series introduction, no Final Four, Wimbledon or Stanley Cup can match it.

I have always been aware of the atavistic aspects of a sport whose symbol is the brain-wave machine and the "physician at ringside." But, as with auto racing, I felt it my duty (my right?) to cover it so long as society permitted it. I was always uncomfortable with the role of crusader anyway. I felt that, if you printed the truth, that was crusade enough. I was not Cotton Mather. I was not the type to march in parades even if I were not a journalist. Journalists are judgmental but not advocates.

What brought home the true nature of the sport to the everyday fan, though, I believe, was the Benny (Kid) Paret–Emile Griffith welterweight championship fight in 1962.

That was the first time a public execution was ever held on TV. And that's what it was. There should have been no doubt in the minds of any medical man looking on that that was exactly what he was watching from the tenth round on. Paret fell, mortally wounded, in the twelfth. He lingered in a coma for a week.

It shocked a nation. It triggered a worldwide call for the abolition of boxing. The game had to fight to survive. Sportswriters with a conscience questioned whether it should.

Emile Griffith was a strange character for a pugilist. He worked in a millinery shop, he had a lisp and a mischievous little-boy air about him that made it hard for one to think of him as a killer in the ring. Yet that is exactly what he turned out to be.

It happened that night he fought Benny Paret in the Garden. Benny Paret was your more traditional pug, a boy right out of the canebrakes of Cuba with a minimal, not to say nonexistent, education. He probably had no idea he was putting his life on the line. He came into the ring with a great left hook, a straight right—and not much more.

He had, unfortunately, an infinite capacity for absorbing punishment. And Griffith, that night, had an infinite capacity for dishing it out. I mean, how would you like to be known as "a fighter who can take it"? That was Benny Paret.

Benny invited his own demise. In the weigh-in the afternoon

of the title fight, he was incautious enough to refer sneeringly to Griffith as a *maricón*. This, apparently, was Spanish for homosexual.

Griffith was not amused. Although he was not ordinarily a knockout fighter, he went after Benny Paret that night with the ferocity of a jaguar leaping out of a tree. Paret was battered from ringpost to ringpost. He was bleeding, externally and internally. His brain was just a blood clot by the twelfth round when he finally sagged to the floor.

Referee Ruby Goldstein, an ex-fighter himself, had a reputation for squeamishness before that night. In short, he stopped fights before the bloodthirsty gallery wanted him to. This night, he waited too long.

The blows that killed Benny Paret almost killed boxing.

It's curious. But it seemed to have no effect on Emile. He fought, successfully, for fifteen more years after that night. He had 112 fights—81 of them after the Paret fight.

But, though the game survived, it was never exactly the same after that. Boxing crowds changed ever so subtly. You heard "Kill 'im!" and "Git the other eye, Louie!" less often. One night, actor Peter Falk sat behind a bloodthirsty fan who was screaming for his favorite, who was pummeling the other fellow. Finally, Falk tapped the fellow on the shoulder. "Your man is way ahead, why don't you let up?" he asked. "Because I get a hunnert if he wins but double if he knocks him out!" came the answer. Falk listened to "Don't let him get away!" a few more times and finally tapped the guy on the shoulder again. "How much do you get if he kills him?" he purred.

Muhammad Ali saved boxing in a very real sense. First of all, he was a stylist, not a homicidal maniac. He was fair of face and swift of foot. A fight was part ballet, part soliloquy.

The Rocky movies also helped. Although they were gore-ridden exercises in brutality (any one of those fights would have been stopped if they occurred in a real ring), they had the requisite happy endings. They were thinly disguised backlashes to the excesses of the Ali legend—Apollo Creed was, after all, Muhammad Ali. But even Ali liked them.

Hollywood always portrayed the world of boxing as a hoodlum

empire, replete with corruption, double-crossing, double-dealing, larceny and perjury, and maybe it was. The late Red Smith once told me when I was decrying the advent of Sonny Liston, an ex-convict, in the hierarchy of the game, "Jim, there are very few archbishops in boxing."

I always found the cast of characters in boxing more comic than sinister. The Mafia is not funny. But if that part of it which tried to run boxing is representative, the Republic is safe. This gang couldn't shoot straight either. Muhammad Ali put himself under the protection of an organized religion and I would have to say they were more frightening in their heyday than the broken noses ever were.

Like society as a whole, boxing got more and more violent. Dempsey was a hobo. But Tyson was a rapist. Liston assaulted cops. Doc Kearns was a con man. But Don King was a killer.

Was Don King funny? That depended on whether you were fighting for him—or just listening to him. He was a Shakespeare-spouting, hearty-acting, role-playing ham with a head of electric gray hair, a booming laugh. It would always be a good idea to cut the cards when dealing with this man. And when Don King got the first count, you had just made your first mistake.

But boxing had always had double-dealers, guys with fifty-one-card decks, dice that couldn't throw your point and rubber checks.

Tex Rickard, Dempsey's promoter, was a taciturn individual, a gold prospector and a gambler who would bet a million on the turn of a card in the days when a million was all the money in the world. He was crafty and without prejudice. He once gave Jack Johnson's white girlfriend a fur coat to ingratiate himself with the black champion at a time when the rest of the country wanted to lynch Jack for having a white girlfriend in the first place. Rickard, with the help of Damon Runyon, made pugilism as big a business as owning a railroad, and he was an up-front guy.

Don King was no Tex Rickard. He was a violent man who had killed not one but two men in the course of his career as a numbers runner in Cleveland. King was armed and dangerous throughout his life.

His father had been killed in a steel mill when he was a boy but Donald King had the restless energy of two men. History tells us he shined shoes at a country club, he worked two shifts at the steel mills and, finally, he hustled numbers in the black community. He hungered for an education but was too busy making money to get one. "Vice is a Negro's Wall Street," a wise black woman activist once told me. And vice was Don King's stock market.

Selling illegal lotteries to the people in the ghetto was big business and, in 1954, Don King shot and killed his first man, whom he accused of trying to muscle in on his business and steal his receipts. He was acquitted on a plea of self-defense.

A numbers war broke out. A bomb blew off the front of King's house. He was shot in the back. And then, in 1966, he beat a man to death with his fists and a pistol butt on the streets of Cleveland. Over a six-hundred-dollar payment. This time, he went to prison.

It was a university for Don King. He spent his time reading—everything from Schopenhauer to Balzac to Shakespeare to St. Thomas Aquinas. He came out of Marion Correctional Institute at least garrulous, if not educated. And apparently, Machiavelli had been one of his principal instructors.

I first caught up with Don King in, of all places, Kinshasa. He was promoting the Ali–George Foreman fight. He had been turned into a fight promoter by the simple expedient of picking up the phone one day and asking Muhammad Ali to consent to an exhibition fight for a hospital charity in Cleveland. Within a year, he was putting on the title fight in Zaire in conjunction with that country's strongman, Joseph Mobutu.

King was curiously subdued in that fight. The champ, George Foreman, didn't wholly trust him nor his relationship with the Ali camp.

That trip was, by all odds, one of the most extraordinary of my own career. Here we were, in darkest Africa, for a prizefight that was to take place at five o'clock in the morning (for a closed-circuit telecast back to the States).

We stayed at a compound—N'sele—that had been built for Mobutu by the Communist Chinese. It was Ali's camp and at night we played poker with the trainer, Angelo Dundee, and the sparring partners, and we ate in the camp commissary a mystery entree that tasted like mutton, which the natives gleefully told us was braised monkey head. And maybe it was. It quickly turned an entourage into vegetarians, whatever it was.

Don King was hardly his bombastic self on this trip. He seemed a little afraid Foreman would bolt the promotion, and maybe George wanted to, but the dictator had sealed off the airport.

Some scribes were of the opinion George Foreman "anxie-tyed" himself out of that fight before the bell ever rang, so sure he was that a plot was afoot against him. But it is the notion here that Ali could always beat those big slow guys. He needed no more plot than his rope-a-dope. They were made to order for him. Foreman's training was such in those days that he was ready to go only five rounds anyway. He had had only two fights in his entire career that went ten rounds. And thirty out of thirty-four fights had gone three rounds or fewer, most of them one round or less. Ali waited till George was out of breath, then cuffed him unmercifully.

We felt like spies the whole sojourn. There was only one phone line out of the country to the rest of the world when we arrived and I quickly staked it out to avoid possibility of censor-ship—or of being deported from the country for unfriendly prose. A Montreal sportswriter, fed up with eternal delays, harassment and frustration with the African bureaucracy, resorted to cussing them out volubly. In French. He forgot Zaire was the former Belgian Congo. French had been their national language. We spent the rest of the trip hiding him from the authorities, smug-gling him into the fight and looking dumb when the secret police came round looking for him.

Ali made the fight game global. He fought Liston in Lewiston, Maine. He fought in Kuala Lumpur, Manila, Kinshasa, Jakarta, Frankfurt, Munich, London and Tokyo.

He even survived his association with Don King. King pro-moted eight of Ali's fights and Ali sued him only over one of them. King settled out of court.

Otherwise, Don King got sued by nearly every fighter he represented. His business dealings were a miasma of interlocking contracts. It's well known that pugilists are hardly Harvard MBA candidates and Don King, in contravention of athletic commission rules, frequently ended up as the promoter of a fight while his son—or himself—managed both fighters.

When King formed a partnership with the television network ABC to promote a "United States Boxing Championship," the eligibility list proved to have a high content of Don King fighters with highly suspicious—not to say fictitious—"fights." The resultant scandal had ABC running for cover and the once-prestigious publication, *Ring* magazine, going out of business amidst rumors it published erroneous records at King's behest.

The government even took its shot at Don King. The United States of America indicted him—and his secretary, Connie Harper, on twenty-one counts of tax evasion from skimming receipts—nearly $1 million worth that never made the company books.

She was found guilty. King went free. The jurors came over and asked him for his autograph after the verdict. A disillusioned prosecution lawyer was heard to mutter sourly, "I think some of them already got one—on a check."

What makes Donnie run? Well, when you start out in life shining someone else's shoes or getting shot because you can't pay off the Mob, you can never get enough. Don King has a two-thousand-acre spread of land in central Ohio with a thirty-room mansion, his own tennis courts, lakes and training camp. He has a townhouse on the East Side in New York, a condo on an island off Florida, one in Vegas and one in Los Angeles, and he goes everywhere in a white limousine.

He plays the buffoon but he's far from it. It has been said patriotism is the last refuge of the scoundrel. Well, charges of racism are overtaking it. Whenever Don King is caught manipulating—and some thirty civil suits have been filed against him—it is, to hear him tell it, only white America trying to lynch the black man. The fact that many, if not most, of these suits were filed by other black men is irrelevant to King.

It was probably for all these reasons that even the fight mob groaned "Oh, no!" at the news Don King had moved in on Mike Tyson three years ago.

They had a lot in common. Mike Gerard Tyson was fatherless, a child of the streets, full of restless energy, no morals to speak of and living deep in the heart of violence in Brooklyn. He had an enormous head, a flat nose and a malevolent stare, like an animal surveying its dinner from the bushes.

But he was not the aggressive street criminal. He kept pigeons. The standard story is right out of Disney: He became a street fighter the day some bully stole one of his birds.

Everyone knows how he was picked out of a reform school by Constantine Cus D'Amato, the fight manager who had found his champion, Floyd Patterson, the same way.

I knew Cus D'Amato. A more paranoid individual never lived. Once, when his then challenger, Patterson, was fighting (Jimmy Slade) in Los Angeles, I drove to the Mayan Hotel to interview the fighter. As it neared fight time, D'Amato grew nervous. The limo from the promoter did not arrive. It grew later. I offered to transport Cus and the fighter. D'Amato's eyes grew wide. "How do I know you're not from the 20th century Boxing Club?! [his mortal enemy]?!" he demanded. I just looked at him. "For cryin' out loud, Cus! I'm from *Sports Illustrated*! I never hijacked a fighter in my life!"

I drove them to the Olympic Auditorium. Floyd just looked bemused. Cus was a nervous wreck. "Why are you driving down this street for?! This is not the way to the arena!"

Cus had to baby Patterson's career along. He tried to match him with every registered hemophiliac or short-armed fighter in the hemisphere. He didn't have to cosset Tyson. Mike was a match for the Red Army right from the start—crude but with the lust for combat of a hungry leopard.

I first met Mike Tyson as we rode from the airport to a television show together. My first impressions were favorable. He had a puckish sense of humor and an encyclopedic knowledge of the fight game and its history. So did I. We whiled away the noninterview time testing each other on boxing trivia. I caught him on Lou Brouillard, an obscure early thirties middleweight champ. He caught me on Peter Godfrey, an early black heavyweight.

I recall his answer when I asked him if he ever thought two years ago he'd ever be riding around L.A. in a stretch limousine on his way to star in a national TV show. "If I was in this car two years ago, I'd be stealing it!"

He inherited his zest for boxing history from his co-manager, Jimmy Jacobs. Jimmy was a strange study himself. A UCLA graduate, he had been the world handball champion when he lived in Los Angeles. He won the title from the ageless Vic Hershkowitz, a Brooklyn fireman, in a national championship tourney sponsored by the silent film comedian Harold Lloyd.

He was a celebrity in his own right but Jimmy Jacobs was an obsessed prizefighting buff. He had the most extensive collection of old fight films in the world. He prowled the world looking for obscure reels, like the Dempsey-Willard films and the Johnson-Willard, which had mysteriously disappeared from the archives decades before.

Jacobs often confided in us his life's ambition was to own and manage a legit heavyweight contender. But he had no luck until his film library brought him to New York where he wound up rooming with that other fight buff, Cus D'Amato. They were pugilism's odd couple, the suspicious seventy-year-old ex-manager and the avid, enthusiastic young Jacobs. Jimmy's film trove put him in touch with advertising exec Bill Cayton, whose own archival films had been part of a post-fight TV show in previous years.

This unlikely triumvirate, D'Amato, Jacobs and Cayton, ruled the early Tyson career. The arrangement was, Cayton would control the business, Jacobs would control the promotions and the hype—and D'Amato would control the fighter.

Unfortunately, D'Amato died after Tyson's eleventh fight. Jacobs contracted leukemia. And Tyson was tied to Cayton only by a contract.

There was a feeling at large, it may only have been a myth, that Mike Tyson would have been a good little boy, a model citizen, had either Cus or Jacobs lived. The fact of the matter was, Mike Tyson had exhibited some of his nastier traits in encounters even before he lost his "rudders." There were incidents with salesgirls in department stores, sexual harassment of meter maids. There is evidence Jacobs and Cayton had to cool more than one episode with the Catskill, New York, and even Albany police.

But this was child's play to what happened when Don King finally moved into the picture. This was as cataclysmic a union as the Axis. With Cus dead and Jimmy Jacobs dying, Tyson was out of control. There was the well-publicized million-dollar lawsuit by a young lady whose buttocks and breasts he fondled in a New York disco. There were the lewd suggestions he made to the legal secretary taking his deposition in another lawsuit. There was a lot of drinking—Tyson drank champagne.

It soon became apparent Tyson was in the grip of a lovesick octopus. Don King had long thirsted to get his tentacles on Tyson and, when Cayton and Jacobs incautiously opened the door a crack—they agreed to let him promote the Tyson–Larry Holmes fight—that was all the opening Don King needed.

I never interviewed Don King where I got an answer to any specific question. I got an illustrated lecture on the selected sayings of Pliny the Elder and Marcus Aurelius. He spouted more Shakespeare than the Old Vic and you got blinded with diamond jewelry, but you never found out anything you needed to know. Don was a master of obfuscation. He would rumble by the hour about what a great country America was. Two days later, he would be raging in a courtroom someplace about how America was frustrating him at every turn because he was black and this was a racist country.

King couldn't control Mike Tyson. He was in no position to moralize. He was hardly dealing from a position of moral superiority himself. King had assured the fighter he needed black management. Bill Cayton, he was to testify, was "satan."

Cayton and Jacobs had tried to rein in the fighter's excesses. Don King bought him new $175,000 Rolls-Royces. Tyson gave away a new Bentley to police after a wild, argument-filled ride through the Lincoln Tunnel with his bride, Robin Givens. Bill Cayton got it back for him.

The inevitable happened. Tyson got knocked out in Tokyo by journeyman heavyweight Buster Douglas. He had come to the fight overweight, undertrained, overconfident and overpaid.

The world cheered. Buster Douglas was Rocky I, II and III.

Don King became unglued. He got hysterical. He flew around the ring that night, collaring officials, demanding the knockout be ruled invalid. He all but grabbed his puppet, the World Boxing Council president, the pathetic Jose Sulaiman, by the scruff of the neck and demanded he "suspend recognition" of Douglas as champion because Tyson had "knocked him out" first. Unhappily, Sulaiman agreed. He damaged whatever credibility he had in the fight game irretrievably.

If the calamity in Tokyo had any real effect on Mike Tyson,

it didn't show. The next time I saw him, at a prefight press conference for his comeback fight against Henry Tillman, Mike was only mildly chastened. When someone wanted to know whether the loss made him "suicidal," Mike chortled. "I have a lot of money to spend yet and a lot of girls to love before I kill myself!"

Tyson was an accident on his way someplace to happen. He had his appointment in Samarra.

The accident happened in Indianapolis. The arrest and indictment on a charge of rape startled Mike Tyson. What he had done in Indianapolis, he had obviously done hundreds of times before. It wasn't always rape. He had dozens of pliant women wherever he showed up. On his way to Tokyo for the Douglas disaster, he had stopped at his condo in Los Angeles, where the doorman told a boxing writer that "there were so many women lined up in the lobby waiting to go upstairs to him they should have taken a number."

Tyson never felt guilty. Never thought he would be found guilty. After all, when the girl he'd fondled in the New York disco sued for a million dollars, the jury awarded her one hundred.

But Tyson had the most curious defense at Indianapolis any of us had ever seen. His lawyers set out to prove his behavior was so abysmal, not to say Neanderthal, that the young woman in question should have known she was accepting a date with King Kong. Sometimes, it was hard to tell which side was the prosecution.

Don King, once again, was busy at ringside trying to get the judges to overrule the decision. He had powerful allies—the Reverend Jesse Jackson and the heads of one of the most powerful black churches in the country.

Someone offered the family of the girl $2 million to drop the charges. Someone persuaded other girls in the beauty pageant that week to change their testimony.

Tyson had already lost a $30 million fight. If he went to prison, he would lose out on ten more. He would take an industry down with him.

The counterattack was not long in coming. Donald Trump leaped in almost before the verdict was read with a "suggestion" Tyson not go to jail but instead be permitted to fight for charity— a fund for rape victims would be nice, The Donald noted.

The fight mob fell down laughing. They knew how these "charities" worked. The principals, the promoters, pugilists, managers get millions, the casino operators get the "drop" (the money the crowd gambles on the tables fight week). The charity gets the part that goes over the fence last. The whole un-American idea was that, if you pay enough, you don't have to go to prison. The consensus was, that's true enough in chambers without confirming it publicly for everyone to see.

For all its seedy aspects, Tyson's trouble with the law didn't blacken boxing's eye as greatly as another event did—Muhammad Ali's sudden, inexplicable inability to function properly. His slurred speech and uncertain gait smacked in the public mind of the old boxer's nightmarish condition known to the public as "punchdrunk."

It used to be a common sight in the lobby of fight arenas. Oldtime contenders in dark glasses could be seen selling pencils to the fans as they went in to see a new generation of youngsters risking their eyes—and their brainpans—to provide entertainment for the masses. Former champs could sometimes be seen shadowboxing telephone poles. Red Skelton, the comic, had a whole routine about a punch-damaged fighter.

But Ali seemed exempt from the ordinary pitfalls of his profession. First of all, he was hardly the defense-be-damned brawler, the punch sponge. His skills were defensive, his style elusive, poetic. But he had fought in the most terrible fight I will ever see—the match against Joe Frazier in Manila. It is the notion here that neither one of the principals in that prehistoric encounter—like two woolly mammoths in a tar pit—really survived.

Ali's skills were verbal as well as pugilistic. To see him reduced to unintelligibility is as damning an indictment of the sport as it was to see Benny Paret crumpled dying in a corner.

But boxing is nothing if not resilient. It keeps Don King off the streets. It has been heralded as a way out of the ghetto for generations of young athletes.

There probably should be a better way. As one fight manager, Jack Hurley, once said, "It beats shining shoes." The only trouble is, a great champion, Beau Jack, ended up shining shoes (at the Augusta National Golf Club). He could have done that without the cauliflower ears and broken knuckles and ringing in his head.

15

· ·

He Didn't Have Fights, He Gave Recitals

I suppose Muhammad Ali, née Cassius Clay, was the most classically constructed athlete you will ever see this side of a Greek statue. He was glib, articulate and, when he first came up, possessed of a kind of appealing, roguish innocence. Everybody loved him. Kids adored him. He was a Frank Merriwell hero come true. He ennobled a brutish sport. He won his victories with flash and flurry. Not for him the plodding infighting, the methodical punishment of a boring foe. He fought at long range like the USS *Missouri*. He choreographed his fights. He danced, he skipped. He dared you to hit him.

He didn't have fights, he gave recitals. The opponent was just the piano, the backdrop. All eyes were on Ali. He loved it. It was his stage, his life. He was like Bob Hope with a troop audience, Olivier at the Old Vic.

I remember, one night, my wife, Gerry, who disliked fights, was balking at attending an Ali–Jerry Quarry bout in Las Vegas. Emmy Cosell, Howard's late wife, and I tried to persuade her to change her mind. "It will not be a brutal, bloody Ruben Olivares fight," we assured her. "Quarry will not know which way Ali went all night and Ali will not want to hurt him badly because, if the fight ends early, he will lose his audience."

We were right. What we saw was a clumsy, groping Quarry, stumbling around the ring like a guy looking for a door in the dark. It was vintage Ali. Half-bout, half-ballet. All art. Nijinsky in the ring. Tchaikovsky should have scored it.

I saw Ali on the finest night of his career. That was in 1964.

It was in an ugly, treeless quarter of Miami, a nondescript stucco house. It was known to the natives as Colored Town. It was a quiet place at three o'clock in the morning. In that pre–Cuban Revolution time, it was a work town, the place of the resort city's work force.

I remember a single bulb glowing behind the frosted glass at the bungalow at number 4610 Fifteenth Court, N.W., that long ago night.

In the front yard was the gaudy red-white-and-yellow bus with the lettering on the side, "Sonny Liston Will Fall in Eight—Cassius Clay the Next Heavyweight Champion of the World."

Liston had fallen in seven in one of the stunning upsets in pugilistic history that night as I approached the front door in the company of fellow journalists Brad Pye and Doc Young.

There was no clinking of glasses, no shouts of hangers-on coming from number 4610, and we thought the once and future heavyweight champ of the world was not at home.

He was. He lay on a sofa in white shorts and gray socks with an exhausted but mystical expression on his face. No crowds in mink, no loud music, no sounds of sycophants. The man who had just won his way into sport's richest vault was lying there just staring as if he couldn't believe what had happened.

Ali (then Cassius Clay) spoke like a man in a trance that night. He wept, whispered, marveled. I have kept my notes and my column from that remarkable night because it was an Ali the public was never to see—withdrawn, staring at something only he could see. ("I'm the champ now because God wants me to be champ. If it wasn't God, now who was it?")

Who, indeed?

The first time I saw Cassius Clay, I thought he was working the biggest con on the world since Barnum. It was hard to take him seriously. Everywhere he went you could almost hear the calliope playing.

It was impossible to think of this beautiful specimen as a heavyweight pug. He didn't have a mark on him. No broken nose. No scar tissue over the eyes. He could hear perfectly through his ears. He was almost fair. World-class good looks.

Oh, he had won the Olympics—but that was hardly to be equated with St. Nick's Arena on Saturday nights. College-boy boxing, we thought.

He talked. He bragged. ("It ain't braggin' if you can do it!" he was to tell us.) He was "on"—or so it seemed—twenty-four hours a day. He was a pitchman. He was selling.

But he was knocking over stiffs. Tunney Hunsaker was not to be mixed up with Jack Dempsey or any Rocky. Neither were Donnie Fleeman, Lamar Clark or Herb Siler. Duke Sabedong, who was a surfer, went the distance with him. A nobody named Sonny Banks knocked him down.

He fought a clumsy but respectable South American, Alejandro Lavorante. Alejandro could punch some. He was slow but persistent.

Cassius was not particularly impressive in knocking out Alejandro in the fifth round. We didn't know it that night but Cassius had left him for dead. Poor Lavorante was to die after a bout with a nonentity named Johnny Ringer later that year, but there was very little doubt the beatings he had taken at the hands of Clay and, earlier, Archie Moore had been the real murder weapons.

As Arthur Miller was to say, attention had to be paid. We were not dealing with a clown prince here. But were we dealing with the legend Cassius said he was?

Once, when he was in training for the Lavorante fight, promoter Aileen Eaton threw a press party for the participants. They came dressed in tuxedos with white dinner jackets and black tie.

Lavorante, it so happened, was as handsome a specimen as you could find in a ring. He looked like a tango teacher. Black, curly hair, big brown soulful eyes, the figure of a Greek statue. Cassius looked stunning.

My wife, Gerry, looked on in dismay. "My God!" she said. "Who in the world would put two such gorgeous specimens as you in a ring to bloody each other up?"

Cassius was overjoyed. It went right into the act. "I'm too pretty to be a fighter!" he would shout. "I'm too pretty to be fightin' these big old ugly bears!"

It was an evaluation the sporting press could fall right in with. Who could believe this pretty boy could ever be a pug? He was living a little boy's fantasy, we assured ourselves.

I don't think he ever crept into the national consciousness as anything but a burlesque act, comic relief, a hype job, till he fought Sonny Liston.

*   *   *

It's hard to recall now what a mountain of menace Charles (Sonny) Liston was in those days. A graduate of the Missouri State Penitentiary, a sullen, glowering bully who had once broken the leg of a cop trying to arrest him for a traffic violation, Liston made white America shudder. The president of the United States (John Kennedy), no less, had implored Floyd Patterson to beat him. He was considered a disastrous role model for the country's youth.

Liston knocked out Patterson twice in the first round. He was held to be unstoppable. He had fists like bowling balls, he was ill-tempered. He played the villainous titleholder to the hilt. He reveled in the title, he threw tantrums when waitresses or receptionists resisted his sexual advances.

What was a little bit less known was, he was a closet drinker. In his days in the Jefferson City slammer, he had managed a celibate, abstemious life—which he made up for once he got out and got the championship. He was, in the words of a Doc Young biography of him, "The Champ Nobody Wanted." The press deplored his successes. Fortunately, Sonny couldn't read.

Still, it was unthinkable that innocent little Cassius Clay could cope with this monster. It was the greatest mismatch since Little Red Riding Hood and the wolf. Liston was an eight-to-one favorite by ringtime.

Cassius had gone across the country in that painted bus with the gaudy lettering—"Cassius Clay the Next Heavyweight Champion of the World" and "Sonny Liston Will Fall in Eight" on its red-and-white side.

It was the master psych job in pugilistic history. Cassius parked the bus outside Liston's residence in Denver and then interrupted his sleep with a bullhorn and a night of long-distance but highly audible taunts. He irritated Liston. He also puzzled him. Liston feared no rational human being. But he was later to confide that, even when he was the prison bully of the cell block, he steered clear of the "crazies" in the prison yard. Liston was a superstitious, backward man. Graveyards made him tremble. Mania disturbed him. And he considered Cassius Clay crazy.

The weigh-in for the first Liston-Clay fight in Miami should have been painted by Hogarth. Clay came stamping in with a snake-headed cane, screaming and raging till he all but foamed at the mouth. His eyes popped, his veins stood out. His blood pressure soared above two hundred.

Those of us watching deemed it the ranting of the terrified sissy in the schoolyard. Noise is the classic defense against fear, it was written, and Cassius had fear written all over him.

This didn't jibe with his demeanor less than an hour before the fight, when he slipped quietly out of his dressing room to watch his brother, Rahaman, in a fight on the undercard. Cassius was as calm and collected as a contemplative monk. His performance at the weigh-in had all been for Liston's benefit.

When Cassius stopped Liston in seven that night, the world was shocked. But, in his living room, alone with his thoughts at three o'clock that morning, Cassius quietly explained his part. "Everybody say, 'Listen, he got no emotions. Cassius wastin' his time,' but do I? No. Liston is a man, you put too much pressure on him and he's not ready. He's not mentally ready for pressure. He can be spooked. I got my sources. I know he's having trouble sleeping. I know I'm spooking him, never mind what everybody says. You see, I'm a wise man. I can think and maneuver under pressure.

"That weigh-in won my fight. My temperature runs over one hundred and somethin', my heart's racin' but I know what I'm doin'. That man is spooked. I learnt that from fightin' Archie Moore. . . . Liston in the first round, I put it to him and he back off and get the fear in his eyes."

The Liston fight was a watershed for another reason. In the middle of the prefight hype, promoter Bill McDonald, the former Chicago doorman who had parlayed a fur hat into millions in oil and gas money, got some disturbing news: The contender, Clay, had fallen in with a religious sect known as the Black Muslims, an intransigent order of militant, antiwhite blacks calling themselves the "Nation of Islam." They were dedicated to separation of the races. They not only accepted segregation, they welcomed it, and they came into focus in white America as a dangerous, separatist movement, anathema to liberals as well as conservatives.

Malcolm X, the most strident of the followers of Elijah Muhammad, had been visible around Clay's training camp and another camp follower, Abdul Rahaman (née Sam Saxon) did the proselytizing for the Nation of Islam.

Cassius Clay became Muhammad Ali the night after the

Liston fight. He didn't choose the name. It was chosen for him several days later by the Honorable Elijah Muhammad in a radio broadcast from Chicago. In it, he confirmed his protégé's conversion and denounced his given name as "having no divine interpretation."

Ali rejected Malcolm X's offer to join a Muslim splinter group. He opted to stay with his mentor and guru, Elijah Muhammad. Within a year, Malcolm X was assassinated. No one was ever charged with the crime and Muhammad Ali would never comment on it.

For a while, the irate press refused to identify the heavyweight champ by his new name. They heaped scorn on him and it.

Gradually, the flimsiness of their position became manifest. A man can choose to be called whatever he wishes. A Mansberger can become Mason, a Norman Selby can become Kid McCoy. But in the fourth estate's defense, it must be remembered that Black Muslimism at that time had elements of demonology in its liturgy. White people were inferior, it taught. They were descended from a loathsome creature called the Big-Headed Yakub, who had been so disruptive a member of the black race that they kicked him out to form that terrible body of humanity, the white race.

It was difficult for a lot of people to separate this kind of racism from that of the Ku Klux Klan. If it wasn't all right to discriminate against an individual because his skin was black, why was it okay to discriminate against him because his eyes were blue? White men were "blue-eyed devils" in the early teachings of the Honorable Elijah Muhammad.

Gradually, the religion moved in the direction of the Moslem religion and conscience-stricken editors finally forbade their more combative sports columnists from addressing the champion by other than his chosen name.

None of this did wonders for the new Muhammad Ali's hold on the public, particularly when his newfound religion stuck in the way of his obeying an army draft order.

The once and future champ had been drafted on the eve of the Liston fight for service in Vietnam and had been found wanting. The army said he was physically sound but his IQ computed out at seventy-eight, which was well below the qualifying standard for army service.

The public view was that the champ was simply feigning stupidity to dodge the draft but this wasn't true. Ali just had trouble figuring out "If Farmer Jones had ten boxes of oranges and gave away one-third of them, how many would he have left?" Ali's academic career had stopped well short of algebra. In fact, it stopped well short of multiplication.

The army stuck by its guns, so to speak, until two years later when the war began heating up and the mental requirements were lowered.

This was when Ali dropped his most famous statement: "I ain't got nuthin' against no Viet Congs."

But, by now, instead of igniting the country and a torrent of abuse, the United States had half a population agreeing with Ali. He became a rallying point.

It had never been a prerequisite to military service in this country to hate the enemy, but Ali elevated the issue to a national debate. Then he declined to step forward for induction on grounds that his religious ministry excluded him.

He was sentenced to five years in prison but never served a day. His appeals were routinely denied all the way to the Supreme Court. He was stripped of his title and, for three years, he was out of the ring.

He whiled away his time giving lectures at college, where he stubbornly refused to fit his convictions to what came to be known on campuses as the politically correct. He was against integration, as opposed to racial intermarriage as the reddest neck in the peckerwoods of Georgia. He declined to pander to the currently popular stands. He abhorred homosexuality, he was scornful of pot use. He was, as usual, his own man. But he became enormously popular. There was an appealing, engaging side to Muhammad Ali, an almost purity it was hard to overlook.

Some were to say Ali lost the best years of his pugilistic life, but this is conjecture. He didn't drink, he didn't smoke, he didn't philander. His deportment, if not exemplary, was at least not destructive.

On June 28, 1971, the Supreme Court of the United States, that august body of antithetical attorneys-at-law which could be expected to vote 5–4 on the proposition that the world was round, voted 8–0 to absolve Muhammad Ali of criminal charges for refusing induction into the armed services.

Cynics could say this unparalleled unanimity stemmed from a political climate in which not even the highest court in the land cared to buck the rising political tide of black activism coupled with growing antiwar convictions.

To be sure, the decision wasn't as resolutely one-sided as it appeared. Earlier votes deadlocked the prestigious panel of judges but, in the end, Muhammad Ali had won a unanimous decision.

Selective recollection has it Ali's return to the ring was authorized by the Supreme Court ruling. Bets would be lost. Actually, Ali had returned to the ring almost a year (eight months) before and, in point of fact, had fought one of the most famous fights of his career (the first Joe Frazier fight) over three months before.

Ali had been relicensed in, of all places, that citadel of the Confederacy, Atlanta, Georgia, where he fought Jerry Quarry on a social night that, for high fashion, black society hadn't seen since the heyday of the Cotton Club in Harlem.

Ali's finest hour came, of all places, in the African Congo in 1974. He might have been at the peak of his powers but his opponent was six years younger, fifteen pounds heavier, undefeated and possessed of the most awesome punching power the division had seen since Louis. George Foreman was everything Sonny Liston had been thought to be, only much younger.

If the truth be known, Ali could always handle those big, slow guys. If nothing else, he could outthink them.

His strategy for Foreman was eye-opening. From the first bell, he appeared to want the champion to be able to hit him at will. In the body. He lay on the ropes and invited the burly champion to push punches into his sides, his arms, even his shoulders. He had correctly perceived that Foreman's forte was the three-round blowout of his opponent. George had not gone more than three rounds in a fight in almost three years. Only three of his forty-one fights had ever gone more than eight rounds. Ali knew Foreman was not mentally—and probably not physically—prepared to fight a long hard fight.

Typically, he called his strategem "rope-a-dope," which called for a conservation of energy on his part, a punched-out fatigue on his opponent's part.

When he saw Foreman's mouth fall open by the fourth round, Ali subtly went on the attack. Foreman kept lumbering after him but he could hardly get his hands up by the eighth round. Ali looked like a bouncer handling a drunk. Ali cuffed Foreman at will, finally spinning him on the ropes and hammering home a right hand that dropped the champion for the count.

We never again saw that Ali. Oh, there were a few flashes of his old brilliance. But that was against the likes of Joe Bugner, Chuck Wepner and Jean Pierre Coopmans, and in a comedy match with a wrestler in Tokyo, a contemptible exhibition unworthy of the heavyweight champion of the world.

Then, there was the "Thrilla in Manila." That was on October 1, 1975, and may have been the most terrible fight of all time. It's for sure Joe Frazier and Muhammad Ali dealt out more punishment that night to each other than either of them had ever sustained. When it was over, Joe Frazier's corner had thrown in the towel. Frazier was a pile of battered flesh with slits for eyes and blood coursing from his nose. He was hardly conscious. In the other, Ali collapsed in a heap. The fight embodied all that is worst about boxing. It had kidney damage, eye, ear, nose and throat damage and, probably, brain damage. The worst film fight sequence in any of the "Rocky" pictures was less brutal than this. Only it wasn't make believe. The blood wasn't ketchup, the falls weren't choreographed. It was the real, homicidal thing. Neither fighter ever was the same.

Boxing has a lot to answer for but the Ali-Frazier fight in Manila should be on its conscience forever.

What happened to Muhammad Ali is the shame of sport. The beautiful body became lumped and swollen but the face remained as prettily handsome as ever. But the speech, that once nonstop flow of high tenor prose, comes out haltingly, mumbling, almost inaudible. The athlete who once lectured in college auditoriums at the top of his voice without a microphone cannot be heard distinctly across a dinner table.

Punches to the head? Ali didn't take that many. He had perfected the dangerous but useful tactic of jerking his head back at the precise instant a punch arrived. It frustrated the opponent and left him open to the quick slashing counters that were the Ali trademark.

But it was a reflexive action that slowed as the years wore on and, ultimately, backfired. Joe Frazier was one opponent Ali could never quite get out of harm's way against. It was Frazier, after all, who gave him his first professional defeat and knocked him, shockingly, to the floor in the fifteenth round. Ali himself blamed his subsequent difficulties on the Manila bout, which ringsiders agreed was the most destructive fight seen in a title match in history. There were no winners in Manila that night in October 1975.

But what actually happened to Ali? What eventually flawed the once-magnificent specimen? Was he punchdrunk? ("Pugilistica Dementia," the doctors called it.) Probably not, medicine concluded. Ali's troubles were not cerebral, they were in his motor skills—speech, walk, coordination. His difficulties lie in communicating, not in cogitating.

"Parkinsonism" was the medical dignosis. This is a watered-down version of Parkinson's disease, controllable by medication but not exactly reassuring. Parkinsonism can be caused by the onset of Parkinson's disease. But it can also be caused—or at least aggravated—by blows to the head.

It can also be congenital. When Sugar Ray Robinson began to evince signs of senility in the early eighties, the medical profession was disinclined to single out pugilisim as the root cause. They opted for Alzheimer's disease, which Sugar Ray surely had. It is a disorder more commonly associated with excessive mental stimulation over the years and related stress than with strenuous physical demands.

Could two such proficient boxers—the best the profession had seen this side of Willie Pep—have fallen prey to too many blows to the brain stem?

It surely seemed a remarkable coincidence. And a tragedy. Sugar Ray Robinson, when he died, had regressed mentally to the status of an infant in a high chair.

Ali was a little more complicated. His condition puzzled me. His problem seemed mainly verbal. Although it was difficult to understand the words, the sense was there. Ali appeared to have total recall of incidents of our past relationship. He still had that sly little grin that was his trademark. He could think faster than he could talk, a fatal combination.

He was, in many ways, the most appealing figure in the new

Golden Age of Sport. It was impossible not to like Muhammad Ali even when you disagreed most violently with him.

He was the most palatable militant of his time. Unlike a lot of his contemporaries in the American Muslim movement, Muhammad Ali never hated whites. Ali never hated anybody. It was not his nature. It was incredible that a man who could be such a destroyer in the ring could exhibit such kindness out of it. Like every great fighter—Joe Louis included—for all his pious, self-deprecating statements, Ali had a mean streak in him. But it surfaced only when the bell rang. He administered cruel beatings to Floyd Patterson and Ernie Terrell, and he beat Joe Frazier to a pulp. He was capable of taunting his opponent in the ring (before the fight, it was all hype).

But Ali was a soft touch who would hand a thousand dollars to a street panhandler looking for a quarter. He was approachable, available. He used to round up key members of the press on the eve—or even the few hours before—a big fight and sit and banter with them.

He was a mystic. Given his druthers, I always felt, Muhammad Ali would rather have been a preacher dressed in a white costume with spangles and rhinestones on it, addressing this huge tent of the faithful. He would rather have healed than hurt.

There were two Alis. The public braggart, the arrogant, invincible champion—and the private Ali, who usually needed to find some dark corner to meditate and reflect. I remember once in Zaire two days before the Foreman fight, I went looking for him. His aides were adamant he couldn't be disturbed. A voice called out from a darkened room, "Let him come in." I was admitted to a darkened, windowless room where the man who had just been issuing one hour of bombast, hitting a cane on the floor for emphasis in a training ring, was lying with a hand over his eyes. He spoke in whispers, sane, rational evaluations of the upcoming fight ("I have him worried, I have messed up his mind, he will have to fall"). Suddenly, a door flew open and in marched a troupe bearing cameras, microphones, cassette recorders. Ali jumped up on the table, his voice rose six octaves, the air rang with top-of-the-voice boasting, slogans, the whole shtick.

How will history judge him? A bearer of light—or a counter-productive force?

He was probably the most recognizable athlete in the world. As such he symbolized America in parts of the world where they had no other clear view of it.

He was an embarrassment to America—and he wasn't. He called attention to injustices by spurning the institutions and even religion of his homeland. He made the world aware the United States wasn't living up to all its promises.

At the same time, the world couldn't help but see this quasi-representative black man getting into and out of stretch limousines, onto private planes, into hotel penthouse suites. They saw him owning property in Deer Lake, Pennsylvania, Berrien Springs, Michigan, Hancock Park, Los Angeles, mansions in Cherry Hill, New Jersey, and the Gold Coast of Chicago. They saw him tweaking Uncle Sam's nose—and getting absolved for dodging military conscription, 8–0.

The death of Elijah Muhammad was an enormous relief to his disciple. The intractable Messenger of Islam practiced his own version of fundamentalist antiwhite religion that frequently inhibited his pupil Ali and painted a picture of a world that didn't entirely square with the one Ali encountered. The Honorable Elijah Muhammad even disapproved of Ali's pugilism.

Ali walked a tightrope between the rigorous separatism advocated by Elijah Muhammad and his own inner drummer. I remember on the night after the first Liston fight as we sat listening to a chastened, quiet, even though victorious new heavyweight champ, the door flew open and the Muslim liaison man, Archie Robertson, burst into the room. He pointed with hate at me, the only white face in the room. "What's he doing here?" he snarled. Ali rose onto his elbow. "I invite who I want to my house. I'm the boss here. Don't you tell me what to do."

Archie Robertson, who was to be assassinated himself within a few months, stammered an apology—and our interview went on for a short time.

The death of Elijah Muhammad in 1975 brought his more moderate son Wallace Muhammad into power, and he put the movement more in touch with traditional Moslem religion, devoid of the demonology and reverse racism it had theretofore employed.

It was impossible not to notice the relief the cha
posture brought to Ali. He became, if anything, mo'
he was a tolerant human by nature and always appea.
under the constraints of a religion based on enmity.

Like all pugs (with the possible exception of Gene Tunney),
Ali was a terrible businessman. No one can compute how many
millions he was bilked out of, or freeloaded out of. He didn't
appear to really care. There was always money. And he could
always find a way to get more.

The press always had the same fascination for Ali as Ali had
for the press. Unlike a lot of athletes who only tolerated them,
Ali really liked the company of sportswriters. I recall once, as he
was coming into Los Angeles for a Ken Norton fight, he took the
press conference podium to denounce an unnamed sportswriter
who had written the offending words "muzzle the Muslim." His
remarks were clearly directed at me. I was indignant because I
was sure I had never written those words. I stormed up to his
room in the (Marriott) hotel. Ali was lying naked under a blanket,
a crooked grin playing around his mouth. He had summoned all
his entourage around the bed. I angrily bet him one hundred
dollars I had not written the offending words.

Alas! I had. I believe I was quoting somebody else but there
they were. Ali slowly pulled the clip (it was several years old) out
from under the blanket and threw it down to me. I was dumbfounded. (Before storming his room, I had called the paper's library and had them read the past dozen or so Ali columns I had
written. I had not gone back far enough.)

I was embarrassed. Ali was delighted. I sent him the one
hundred dollars. A few days later, I got the check back in the
mail (I still have it) along with the following handwritten letter:

Dear Jim
Your letter was very very good. I have nothing to say bad
about anything you write, because burning words rise from
a flaming heart. For life is a fair trade wherein all adjusts
itself in time, for all you take from it, you must pay the
price sooner or later. For some things you may pay in ad-
vance, for some you should pay on delivery, and for some
later on when the bill is presented. So, Jim, we should
never feel guilty for speaking our true feelings, because a
guilty conscience robs the will of its power.

I was really surprised to get such a letter from you. You have a good heart. Most people of white in your possission [sic] would not admit what you call a fault of your own. Because most people give way to their faults by being passive towards them. Jim, a writer must think twice before he writes, because a biting tongue goes deeper than the point of a bayonet and cutting words pierce keener than a sword. Jim, the way to overcome error is, first to admit my fault, such as you did to me, next to refrain from repeating it.

So, that's all I have to say for now, but we must always remember that forgiveness belongs to God. But it becomes the privilege of mortal man only when asked by another.

Thank you,
Oct. 5-19-73
Peace always
Muhammad
Ali.

An extraordinary man. A man forced by the world into a cruel profession where he excelled. There is a famous scene in the movie *On the Waterfront* where Brando, playing an unsuccessful pug, reproaches his brother for mismanaging him into crooked fights and says piteously, "I coulda been a contender!"

Muhammad Ali coulda been a tight end (Vince Lombardi himself said so). He coulda been a point guard.

And he coulda been a television evangelist. A man with a mission.

Dempsey had to be a fighter. So did Louis. Jake LaMotta couldn't be anything else but.

Muhammad Ali, even though he may have been the best of all time, was miscast as a fighter. He paid the price. He was right, he was too pretty to fight. His career was caked in tragedy. I don't know whether boxing is at fault. Or the rest of us.

16

On My Blindness, with Apologies
to Milton

1978 pretty much started out like any other year. The Open was in Denver, the World Series was in Yankee Stadium. Bad luck, as usual, was keeping its hand hidden, its cards at its vest.

You learn in this game of life that you can go along on a winning streak only so long. Slumps are inevitable.

But I don't remember any foreboding when I took off for the World Cup golf tournament in Hawaii that December. A week in the sun, ukeleles, drinks with umbrellas in them, Pacific sunsets, Bali'hai.

Paradise is a terrible place to get your life ruined. But that is what happened to me.

The World Cup is ordinarily one of my favorite golf tournaments of the year. This is because any country in the world can send a golfer. Now, I don't know about you, but I can get awfully sick of these slick, automated tour golfers tearing our golf courses apart with successive 63s and 64s, eagles, birdies, three-hundred-yard drives, the whole bit.

A golfer from Iceland at the World Cup hits the ball like you and I. Golfers from Pago-Pago have no more idea what a birdie is than you or I. A friend of mine, Jimmie Eagles, a Texan, came in one night and announced he had just become the new champion of Czechoslovakia. It seems he had played a pro-am with the reigning champ of Czechoslovakia that day and beat him 3-up and by seven shots medal play.

The United States used to send its reigning Open champion

and PGA champion to these things, which was kind of ridiculous because the only countries that could give them a match were South Africa and Canada.

Still, I like a golf tournament where the principals struggle to break 90, and it was with a light heart that I checked into the Princeville resort with my wife that December.

The knell of doom was a ringing phone at seven o'clock in the morning. A ringing phone at that hour of the morning is unsettling enough but, as I ran for the instrument in unfamiliar surroundings, I hit a throw rug on quarry tile and flew in the air. I came down on my foot hard.

I crawled to the phone. It was some idiot who wanted to invite me to a cigarette company's cocktail party that night, some manufacturer from Long Beach.

I had already been invited to that cocktail party a month before. So had everyone else at the tournament. My life had been changed forever by a completely useless and unnecessary telephone call.

I had broken my foot. It had to be put in a cast. I had to learn to navigate with crutches.

Don't ever try it. Crutches are the most diabolical prosthesis known to man. I tumbled heavily a few times.

I came home in a cast. I hardly noticed that my left eye was getting blurry. I ascribed it to tiredness. My right eye was already filling up with a dense cataract.

Six weeks later, I went to the Super Bowl in Miami. I dropped my wife off in Sarasota to visit her father and stepmother there. I proceeded to Super Bowl XIII. Dallas was playing a rematch with Pittsburgh.

As the week went by, I kept rubbing my eye, trying to eliminate the blurred sections. My good friend Dr. John Perry tried eye drops. "John," I told him prophetically, "I don't think this is anything eyedrops can cure."

It wasn't. The vision got worse. The street signs suddenly began to look as if they were in Sanskrit. "Washington Boulevard" came out "W-A-X-Q-*-H-V-S-P" or worse. Miami seemed to be in the grip of a perpetual sandstorm. I mentioned this in passing to Dallas football player Thomas "Hollywood" Henderson one afternoon. He looked at me funny. "There's no dust in the air here," he told me.

I went back to the hotel room. I looked out. For the first time, I realized the dust was not in Miami, it was in my eye.

By now, I was going through the hotel lobby by Braille. Trying to put a quarter in a Coke machine was brain surgery.

On the Saturday before the game, it was traditional for a few of us to go to the racetrack. Gulfstream was running.

I had skipped breakfast; so, when I got to the track, I ordered the closest thing, an egg salad sandwich. I looked at the sandwich. It looked as if it were growing red worms. Before I took it back to the counter to protest to the cook, I looked up at the television screen. There was a gray horse up there. He looked like the loser in a bullfight. He was bleeding to death.

He wasn't. My eye was.

I was taken to an emergency room doctor. I hope nobody else ever had to go to this guy. He told me my eye was all right. I think he was the guy who told the captain of the *Titanic* not to mind the ice. I not only hope they take his license away, I hope they take it away from the school that graduated him.

My friend John Perry found an eye doctor for me. Ironically, it was Dr. Dave Sime, an Olympic sprinter on whom I had done a *Sports Illustrated* story earlier in both our careers. I was rushed into surgery.

Because I had had breakfast before reporting to his office, I was ineligible for general anesthesia. I could only have local.

People tell me I missed the greatest Super Bowl in history in the Orange Bowl that day. Oh, no, I didn't. The greatest Super Bowl in history was being played out in the OR at Mercy Hospital in Miami that day. As I wrote, I won't say I was in deep trouble, but Jimmy the Greek said that if you took me that afternoon, you got forty points. I'll tell you one thing: It was the most thrilling four quarters of my life. I'm sure Roger Staubach had his problems that afternoon. But Mean Joe Greene couldn't have inspired more terror coming at him than that curved needle I saw coming at my eye. When my blood pressure hit three hundred, they must have felt they had uncovered a slow leak in the Red Sea.

I had a detached retina. Four tears, in fact.

Now, I had always thought detached retinas were something

that happened to four-round fighters. They came from having a thumb in your eye all night.

Was mine caused by the fall in Hawaii? The medical profession was divided. That part of it over the age of sixty remained positive retinal detachments were caused by trauma. That part of it under sixty opted for congenital weakness in the eye. Like an ambidextrous infielder, I could go either way.

The repair to the eye, something called a "scleral buckle," didn't hold. It worked perfectly long enough to lull me into a feeling that everything was going to be all right.

The retina peeled off again on Easter night. I was watching a movie, *Operation Cicero*, when suddenly, on-screen, James Mason started to melt. He flowed off the screen onto the floor. Panicked, I called to my wife. I went to bed that night, to all intents and purposes, blind. The cataract in my "good" eye got so dense— and the fact it was centered in the eye, not on the periphery—that I couldn't even see television. Reading was out of the question. A four-hour operation couldn't put the retina back on this time. I lost my left eye.

What followed was a one-year trip through a dark tunnel. Blindness, I am sure, is the worst of life's afflictions. It is way ahead of deafness and, I feel sure, even other catastrophic illnesses. It is like going through life locked in a dark room. Among other things, it is claustrophobia inducing.

As the cataract worsened, the medicos nevertheless counseled getting along with the minimal eyesight I had because to operate was to risk pulling the retina down in the good eye as well.

I went back to work in midsummer. Writing was impossible. I couldn't see to write. I had to dictate into a cassette, attach the cassette to a phone and dictate into it.

Now, writing and talking are two different things. What plays on the written page often does not play on stage. One romances the eyes, the other falls on the ears. Dictating in a well-defined writing style is not always possible. I struggled, tinkered, relooped and reworked. It was almost as if I were learning a new craft.

I can never emphasize enough my gratitude to my newspaper, the *Los Angeles Times*, and to my editors, for their support through this trying period. They were more than supportive, they were insistent I go back to work. I am not sure I would otherwise have done it.

Because I was in my fifties, my medical retirement benefits would have been—get this!—five hundred dollars a month. I would have been living in a carton on Pico and Sepulveda.

The paper assigned a lovely young man from the staff to assist me and chauffeur me. John Scheibe became my eyes. I went to a World Series (Baltimore-Pittsburgh) with him where I couldn't even tell when it was raining. I had to be careful I didn't interview Dave Parker thinking it was Wilver Stargell even though I knew Willie well.

I tried to carry on as before but there were pitfalls. Once, in the Rams' camp, I crashed into a jutting rusty pipe, which, Dr. Bob Woods later told me, very nearly cost me my leg, it got so infected. Fortunately, I couldn't see it; so I had no clue as to the extent of the wound. Friends told me the leg looked like the aurora borealis.

When the eye condition finally deteriorated to the extent where I couldn't tell whether a door was open or closed—I would even have to grope for the opening—I began to canvass my opportunities for surviving cataract surgery.

I had been making periodic trips to Massachusetts General and to the famous retinal surgeon Charles Schoeppens, a remarkable character who had been part of the Belgian underground fighting Hilter in World War II. I found through him the brilliant Otto Jungschaffer and Dr. Richard Kratz, one of the four top cataract surgeons in the world.

I would be blind today without them.

There was an operational procedure for cataract removal called the Kelman phacoemulsification technique. Basically, it called for the extraction of the cataract and lens with a small incision and a supersonic drill, which could liquify and pulverize the cataract and remove it with minimal trauma to the rest of the eye. Dr. Charles Kelman had gotten the idea from a dental drill.

It was uniquely suited to my case, as nondisturbance of the retina was critical. Many years later, I was covering the Bob Hope golf tournament in the desert when I noticed one of the pro-am players was a "Charles Kelman." I checked out of curiosity to see if he was *the* Charles Kelman. I was told by his partners they thought he was an owner of a number of frock shops. I desisted.

The next year, I noted in the pairings, here he was listed as "Dr." Charlie Kelman. This time, I went up to him. I felt like Stanley discovering Livingstone. It was, indeed, *the* Dr. Kelman, I presume. I wrote a column about him. He was an accomplished golfer, an accomplished musician and, thank Heaven, an accomplished ophthalmologist.

I will never forget the evening after my cataract surgery. I spent the day with patches over my eyes. When they took the patches off, I looked up at what I had taken to be a spotlight over the hospital room door the night before. It was a television set. The first sight I saw was a football player wearing number 7 in the uniform of the Denver Broncos. It was Craig Morton, the quarterback. It was *Monday Night Football*. I will never forget that sight. For some men, the most beautiful sight they will ever see in this world is a Canadian sunset or the changing of the leaves of autumn. Not me. For me, it was Craig Morton on Channel 7. I never look at Craig Morton without recalling that thrilling moment.

One of the things I learned in my (effectively) sightless period was that doctors thought I needed the acute eyesight to be able to dissect a game. They thought I needed to be able to see whether the guy was out at second or not, whether the runner had stepped out of bounds, whether the pitch was a curve or a slider or how long the putt was. They gave me glasses with binoculars built in, magnifying eyepieces for distance viewing.

I finally explained that I didn't need to *see* these things. I could ask the athlete later in the locker room. What I really needed, I explained, was to be able to look up what year Ty Cobb batted .424, what year Army beat Notre Dame 59–0, which tournaments Arnold Palmer won last year. I needed to *read*.

Things being what they are, some friends were moved to comment on my "courage" during this period. It had nothing to do with courage. When you're in this predicament, what else can you do? It's not "courage" that makes a cornered animal fight. It's necessity. Desperation.

Besides, I didn't suffer my fate philosophically. I am afraid I didn't say, well, these are the cards I was dealt, I gotta play them. I railed against my fate. I was an original "Why me, God?"

person. Tommy Bolt had nothing on me. He would have understood perfectly. I managed to conceal this craven side from public view but in my private thoughts, I did not go gently into that good night.

I could not have made it without Gerry, my lovely wife, one of the greatest people ever put on this earth. I shudder when I think what this must have put her through. But she never complained. Not once.

It took a year but the retina in the other eye finally began to tear. Again it was Super Bowl time, the day before we were to leave for Detroit. I walked out into the garage—and there in the L.A. skyline was an old familiar rain of terror, a storm of dust. This time, I was not fooled. I had already lost one eye to this devil storm. I knew what was happening.

Every morning of my life, I stare into a certain corner of my bathroom mirror. I am looking for what I call "new dogs on the block." You see, after cataract surgery you have these permanent "floaters" coursing back and forth in your eye. They are distracting. But you get used to them. They are the old dogs in the neighborhood. When you look into the mirror and their number has been swelled by newcomers, trouble is afoot.

That's what happened on the eve of Super Bowl XV. Instead of being on a plane on the way to Detroit, I was in the backseat of a car on the way to the hospital. It was the longest, most terror-filled ride of my life. I couldn't imagine being in a crashing plane would be any more terrifying.

But Otto Jungschaffer was again equal to the task. He chose a new "cryo" technique to freeze the retina back on the eye.

Again I went through that night-after terror of the removal of the bandages. I remember while I was lying there, the phone rang. It was Reggie Jackson. As usual, Reggie had thought rules were for other people. "He'll want to talk to me. I'll buck him up," he told the operators. He was right.

Dr. Jungschaffer's magic had worked. The retina held. It has held till now. Nine years later.

I still scan the mirror for new canines on the block every morning and, when the capsule behind the eye became opaque, Otto was ready with that new miracle beam, the laser.

I am the most fortunate of human beings. The march of medicine is a boon everyone should profit from. There is very little doubt in my mind that my right eye would have long since gone to join my left and I would be in a white-cane mode now if it were not for the strides made in eye surgery.

I had thought I would never again see a Marciano get up, a Willie Mays guessing fastball, a Marcus Allen thread-needling a sideline, a Jimmy Connors service ace. Tommy Lasorda in an ump's face, Magic Johnson at the line. I had seen my last title fight, playoff game, Wimbledon final, Olympic sprint or British Open. I was the luckiest man among men anywhere. My real heroes were not named the Babe, or Mickey, Willie, or even Magic or Michael or Larry. They were named Otto, Richard and Charlie. There should be more of them—an All-Star lineup to hang on my wall forever.

1.

· ·

It's a Nice Place to Visit, But . . .

I guess I have to address my reputation as a serial killer—of cities.

There's hardly a hamlet in these here United States that didn't at one time or another want to hang me from the highest yardarm.

I don't know why. I kept doing them a favor. Telling them to get the politicians to clean up their act—also their city.

It all began, I guess, with Cincinnati. I made a trip with the Dodgers in 1961, a trip on which they lost ten straight games, and, ultimately, lost the pennant to the Reds.

We had a rainout when we got to Cincinnati. Now, to a ballplayer, a rainout is a well-deserved rest. To a columnist, it's a disaster.

Pressed for a topic, I took on the town. There was a rationale behind this. You see, some years before, when not even President Eisenhower could go there, a colleague of mine went to Moscow to cover a track meet. He was the only one in the whole magazine empire who could be cleared to go there. It was the Forbidden City. I couldn't wait to read the copy.

And you know what came out? A track meet. For all the clues in the prose it might as well have taken place in Modesto.

I was never so disappointed in my life. I wanted to read about people in fur hats, queues in front of Lenin's tomb. I wanted to know what Brezhnev looked like close up. I wanted to know what the cabdrivers thought about America. I got nonwinning times, splits in the fifteen hundred. I heard all about Rafer Johnson, who was meeting the Russian Kuznetsov in the decathlon. I knew all

about Rafer Johnson. I wanted to know about Ivan the Terrible.
I had a vision of my friend coming back from Heaven and, being
asked what it was like, answering "Johnson rapped out at sixteen
feet two inches."

I resolved never to get so afflicted with press-box myopia myself
that I would not comment on events surrounding an event.

That day in Cincinnati, I noted the state of disrepair of the
city's freeways and speculated on the possibility that, if the
Russians ever attacked, they would bypass Cincinnati, as it looked
as if it had already been taken and destroyed. When I came back
a year later to find the freeway still unfinished, in fact not much
changed from what it had been twelve months previously, I suggested that maybe it had been Kentucky's turn to use the cement
mixer. I hinted that there wasn't much to do in Cincinnati but
go downtown and watch haircuts or see them wind the clocks in
Fountain Square.

The devil made me do it. I was off and running. I said New
York should have a big sign on it, "Out of Order." I said from
what I could see its principal purpose was to catch all the chewing
gum chewed in the world and line all the subway platforms with it.

I said Minneapolis and St. Paul didn't like each other and
from what I could see I didn't blame either one of them. I dubbed
the ballpark they had at that time "Early Erector Set." I wrote
they should evacuate Cincinnati and mark it "Closed for Repairs"
but that when they fixed it, nobody would go back.

I said you should bring a lunch if you went to St. Louis and
you should take your shoes off so as not to wake it up. I said
Philadelphia was closed on Sunday and should be the rest of the
week as well. I resurrected W. C. Fields's epitaph, "All things
considered, I'd rather be here than in Philadelphia."

I called the Kentucky Derby "a hard luck race in a hard luck
town." I said that My Old Kentucky Home was a rooming house
with a bath down the hall. I said the grass wasn't blue and neither
was the sky. I said Louisville—predictably, I called it "Lousy-
ville"—was America's still. At night, it smelled like an old bar
rag. It was settled by people who tried to beat life with a pair of
treys. The pickpockets were the only ones who went home winners on Derby Day. Unless you counted the concessionaires, who

put a nickel's worth of bourbon in a cheap plastic glass with
weeds and a lump of sugar and charged ten dollars for it.
the cabdrivers on Derby Day should wear masks. I reminded
that the writer of "My Old Kentucky Home" died in the hallway
of that flophouse with a losing place ticket in his pocket and a
pawn ticket where his watch used to be.

New Jersey didn't escape. I said that the Jersey Mead-
owlands' principal export was soot, that there wasn't a guy in the
state who drank from a glass and it was a great state if you were
a ball-bearing and if you didn't have a tattoo they knew you were
a tourist.

When a track meet went to Warsaw, I wondered out loud
how you could get there since nobody ever went to Warsaw except
on the back of a tank or the front of a bayonet. When I got to
Russia for the Olympics I said I would pass on the chance to go
to Lenin's tomb and that if I wanted to see dead people I would
go to Kabul, which the Red Army had just taken over. I questioned their hospitality. I said we were like Woody Hayes's Rose
Bowl teams, that we only got to see the country through a bus
window, that the last group of tourists able to move freely through
the country was the Wehrmacht. When they unfrocked Stalin they
took his name off the map, I noted that the cartographers of the
Kremlin could do what Hitler couldn't do—wipe out Stalingrad.
I suggested it was like renaming Gettysburg New Peoria.

Not even San Francisco could escape. I pointed out it was
the only city in the world that couldn't tell the difference between
an earthquake and a fire and that when the city got toppled by a
quake, they told the world it had burned to the ground and that,
next time, they would say it was a flood—if they could find somebody who had left a faucet on. I said it wasn't a city, it was a no-
host cocktail party. It has a nice even climate: It's always winter.
It was a place where a newspaper could run the line, "Yesterday
was the coldest day in San Francisco since last July sixth," with
a perfectly straight face. I said that only a place that calls an
earthquake a fire could call what was played in Candlestick Park
baseball. I wondered why they put it there when the Ketchikan
Peninsula was available.

When Pittsburgh and Baltimore got in the World Series, I
covered it by remote control. But I didn't want them to think I
wasn't there. So I said these weren't cities, just kind of compli-

cated truck stops, and that Baltimore, like every town across a bay from a great city (Brooklyn, Oakland, Tacoma), suffered from a massive inferiority complex. I said it was the team nobody knows in the town where nobody cared, that there were guys in the Russian secret police who had higher visibility than the Baltimore infield. I said Pittsburgh had three guys who were going to the Hall of Fame—and twenty who were going to the American Association.

Pittsburgh came in for some attention. I said it was America's Slag Heap. I called the local delicacy, kielbasa sausage, "botulism on a bun."

I saved some for Oakland. Oakland, I told the readers, was this kind of town: You had to pay fifty cents to go from Oakland to San Francisco. Coming to Oakland from San Francisco was free. And when you know that, I suggested, that's all you have to know about Oakland.

But I wasn't through with it. Oakland was the place of which Gertrude Stein said, "There's no *there* there!" When someone wanted to know "How would I get there from San Francisco?" the answer was, "If you get to San Francisco, you won't want to go to Oakland." It was a town where the count had been 3-and-2 for twenty-five years. It was like a fighter who needed a knockout to win.

When I went to New York, the first thing I did was get out all my old clothes, put on a cheap watch, and copy down all my credit card numbers so I could report their theft. I practiced screaming a lot and carefully listed my blood type on my wrist. I called my insurance man to make sure I was covered for all the kinds of wounds—knife, gunshot, blunt instrument, broken bottle, brass-knuckle, fist eye-gouge, burning, stomping, getting pushed off a subway platform, eaten, chained to death, lynched. I said I would carry a tape recording (in case I was knocked unconscious from behind) saying, "Please. My money is in my righthand pocket. In the event it is not enough, please revive me and I will write you a check." I said the amount of money you carried was critical. Too little and they would kill you for violating the mugger's minimum wage law. There is a floor in their industrial scale, too. Violate it and there's no arbitration.

After a certain hour, you were never to go out on the streets of New York without one or more companions, preferably ex-wrestlers. That hour is ten in the morning.

You are not to think you are safe in a church, taxi, elevator or lobby. The only safe place in New York City, I suggested, is Grant's Tomb. Which is to say Grant is safe, not you. I said, "Do not go down in the subway after dark. Do not go down in the subway before dark." I said to practice begging for your life a lot. "Carry an onion so you can cry readily. On second thought, the onion won't be necessary. You won't have any trouble crying." I said that only one thing bothered me: the fact that I had all this gold in my teeth. In fact, in New York, you might be sorry you have teeth.

I said Philadelphia was a town that would boo a cancer cure. Philadelphia was a place to park the truck and change your socks—or go unload a freighter. It was a place where sixty-three thousand fans showed up at Veterans Stadium fearing the worst. And getting it. Philadelphia was the kind of place that even the British gave up without a fight. And of which Robert E. Lee, on his retreat from Gettysburg, was said to have said, "Oh, well, this means we won't have to spend Sunday in Philadelphia."

You knew you were in Chicago, I wrote, when you picked up a paper and the headline said, "Quiz Five Detectives on Stolen Goods." It was a town where Al Capone didn't have a police record even though he kept the coroner's office on night shifts.

Alabama was a sitting duck. I didn't bother too much with the football game (Alabama–Georgia Tech). I zeroed in on the bigger game. "Birmingham, showplace of the Deep South, gateway to the Ku Klux Klan—a place where 'evening dress' means a bedsheet with eyeholes. Where bombed-out houses aren't the work of a foreign enemy—white, male Americans are the enemies of America here. The Constitution being torn in half by the people whose ancestors helped to write it."

You can see where these freewheeling travel tips didn't endear me to the local Chambers of Commerce. Nor the citizenry. You can take on the smallest community in the United States—and a few hundred people in L.A. will have come from there. They would promptly clip the offending columns—and mail them back to the mayors of their hometowns. Once, when I undertook to describe Iowans at a Rose Bowl as "thousands of people in

nd John Deere caps in their Winnebagos with their pace-
and potato salad looking around for Bob Hope," the gover-
less, got mad and denounced me on the floor of the state
ture. You'd think I was John Dillinger.

Usually, the aggrieved parties would write to say "How dare
you write such tripe about our town when you live in such a . . ."
and they would go on to say worse things about L.A. than I had
ever said about their hometowns.

But I didn't spare L.A. I said it was underpoliced and over-
sexed. Its architecture has been (accurately) described as "Early
Awful" or "Papier-Mâché Provincial" or "Moorish Nauseous." I
would add: "It's four hundred miles of slide area. One minute
you're spreading a picnic lunch on a table in the Palisades and
the next minute you're treading water in the Pacific. It's a place
that has a dry river but one hundred thousand swimming pools.
It's a place where you get one hundred days for murder but six
months for whipping your dog."

I ratted on Long Beach. I said that it was "the seaport of
Iowa," settled by a slow leak in Des Moines, and that it was
sinking under the skeletal work of millions of dollars' worth of oil
wells and that the only reason for going to Long Beach was to
see if it was still there. I predicted it would put to sea and said
they bought the *Queen Mary* because that would be the only part
of the city above water when the oil wells sank.

All good clean fun. Or what's a sports column for anyway?

City bashing for form and distance is hardly an Olympic
sport. I got into it by accident, but once in, it was like the Mafia
or the Book-of-the-Month Club. You couldn't get out. I was like
the old gunfighter who wanted to hang them up but the public
wouldn't let him. When I got to Spokane one time, they were in
tears at the notion I might go straight and the local sports editor,
Harry Missiledine, begged me, "Listen! You can say it's the biggest
collection of used brick in the world. They ought to knock it down
and ship it to North Hollywood for fireplaces. How's that?"

I always conceived my function to be to entertain the reader.
They could find the score elsewhere. Basically, I find, most people hate to be informed. Unless they're spies or rapacious business
types always looking for an edge. Information can be boring. Peo-

ple read to be amused, shocked, titillated or angered. But if you can amuse or shock or make them indignant enough, you can slip lots of information into your message. Sort of like putting castor oil in orange juice. Satire is the best weapon in a writer's arsenal to attack injustice. Frothing at the mouth turns the reader off. Angry voices are always assaulting us from all sides. The humorless we always have with us. And they always have their soapbox. The din of indignation gets deafening.

The identification of fans with athletes always baffled me. I would get ten- to twelve-page single-spaced, typed letters from fans on the subject of their aggrieved sports heroes, written in language that would make you think they were talking about a well-loved infant child. I would always marvel that an individual in this society could so blithely overlook inflation, joblessness, the environment and his own personal daily struggles to devote so much energy to an athlete who, after all, was a stranger to him. I would think, "My God! Don't these people have mortgages, children who stray from the paths they want them on, divorces, trouble with their girlfriends, their jobs, their health? How can they be so wrapped up in (leave blank for name of sports figure)?" I always wanted to write back, "Get a life!" but I never did. After all, these people were my bread and butter, too.

Cities I could understand. No one likes to be told their cities look as if they were in the midst of condemnation proceedings. Even if they do.

But I make no apologies. An old editor of mine once told me that was the worst thing you could do in this business. It's not too good an idea in any business.

Besides, Louisville *did* smell a little like an old bar rag when you got downwind of the distilleries. It did have more broken windows than any place this side of Berlin in 1945. And it did turn into a pumpkin the day after the Derby.

I always remember when the great Ring Lardner, for whatever reason, took on the city of Bridgeport, which, I think, he found stultifyingly bourgeois. (Never my trouble, I *liked* bourgeois.) The city finally lured him to its banquet table for a reconciliation feast. All went well till Ring was overserved (and overpatronized). When the mayor got up to say, "I just want you to know, Mr. Lardner, that you're welcome to Bridgeport," Lardner got up gravely, pushed his plate aside and started to leave. "No, Mr. Mayor," he corrected, *"you're* welcome to Bridgeport!"

18

The Baby of the Family

There hangs in my bedroom a picture some thirty-five years old, and it is the first thing I see when I get out of bed in the morning. And it hurts to look at it.

There is the family. Not my wife, Gerry, she was notoriously camera-shy, but the four kids. There are the two older boys, Teddy and Tony, one smiling with a discolored tooth damaged in a skating accident. There is the daughter. And, then, there is Rick.

Rick was the baby of the family. He looked like his mother, big brown eyes, dark skin, generous mouth. Usually he was smiling, but this day I believe he had a cold. Even in a picture you could sense his head was stuffed, his nose raw.

Gerry had dressed the kids up for the photo shot. Pammy had the little Mary Janes on and the ruffled dress. Rick had a neat little checked suit on and he was clutching some kind of stuffed toy and was staring straight ahead into the camera.

I can't look into that picture long without feeling smothered. Grief always is a smothering feeling for me. I can't breathe in it.

Rick was the light of his mother's life. She loved all her children but he was the baby, the last one, we knew, that we would have. Gerry had a hysterectomy shortly after he was born.

He was, like her, given to laughing a lot. He was, you might say, happy-go-lucky. As with a lot of families, he was overshadowed to some extent by his older brothers' powerful personalities. His sister pretty much took over his childhood activities. He relied on her. It was not uncommon for the two of them to lie on the floor watching television and to hear Rick repeatedly ask, "What are they going to do now, Pam?" He trusted her implicitly.

He trailed along happily in the caboose of the family. Rick was no trouble. His given names were Eric Patrick but no one ever called him anything but Rick or Ricky. He and his mother were pals. I don't remember his ever coming into that house but that he was already calling out, "Mom! Mom!" to share some experience of that day with her.

We moved to Malibu when he was three and Ricky was totally a product of that environment. That meant surfing, guitars, the beach life, a cutoff from the frantic pace of the city. Malibu of that day was an enclave of the movie rich in the "colony" (a stretch of desirable beach houses that had been the summer homes of the silent film stars but now was round-the-calendar living just north of the smog for the new film elite from stars to moguls). But mostly it was middle class and given over to the kind of people who wanted to run horses or just wanted to escape the bustle and toxicity of the city. It was a one-road community built along a twenty-seven-mile stretch of Pacific Coast Highway.

It looked like paradise. So, I think, did Gomorrah.

We had moved there in 1956. I was not yet a columnist.

I bought the acre-and-a-half property, which I was later to sell to Bob Dylan, simply because I had gotten tired of coming home to the urban Palisades residence and seeing the kids congregated around the back door, bored, restless. "Why don't they go climb some trees, play down by the creek like we used to when I was a kid?" I would ask, crossly. "What trees? What creek?" Gerry would demand. "This isn't Michigan or Connecticut."

So I bought a house overlooking the mightiest of oceans. On a headland called Point Dume where pirates once off-loaded their stolen gold. It was idyllic. I had an acre and a half with nothing between me and Japan but a few offshore islands crowded with seals.

I thought I had bought happiness in our time. The cove right next to our property, to give you an idea, was called—aptly, I thought—Paradise Cove.

Turned out to be where they landed the dope.

But we didn't know that in 1956 when we moved to our point. I don't think anyone foresaw the drug epidemic, the chemical plague that would all but destroy a generation then. We were afraid of earthquakes in California then. Earthquakes would have been benign compared to what hit us.

To this day, I don't quite know what happened. Several things: First, I became a columnist five years after we moved to Malibu. Second, Malibu was almost the eye of the storm in the drug hurricane that twisted across America. Like so many things in our culture, from supermarkets to drive-in banks, it seemed to start in California and move slowly East. Leaving devastation in its wake. And, third, we lost control and influence over our young, who turned instead for guidance and inspiration to wave after wave of wandering troubadours with manic group names and messages of rebellion, contempt for all authority and disdain for tradition. These were their role models. Where we might have looked up to an athlete, a writer, a statesman or a war hero, they looked up, generally, to some bare-chested Englishman with dirty hair playing an amplified guitar.

To this day, unreasonably, the sight of a guitar evokes the same emotional reaction in me that the sight of a swastika would in a rabbi. I associate it with terror in the night, years when you picked up a ringing phone or answered a knock on the door with a pounding heart.

I could not keep my feet in those changing, swirling times. I didn't know what was going on. The verities of my youth went right out from under me. Being Irish, I was somewhat prepared to deal with a drinking problem. But when it came to drugs, I believed, with Harry Ainslinger, that addiction to any drug, even marijuana, only led inevitably to ultimate addiction to heroin.

Drug use became endemic in Malibu. Family tragedies erupted left and right. Inevitably, it crept into ours.

Looking back on it, I did all the wrong things. Threats, cajolery, dire pictures of ruination. I didn't even know what the kids were talking about. I never heard of "acid." When they talked of taking "trips" I thought they meant to the valley, not the moon.

We get lessons in everything from sex to how to play golf. But we get no lessons in the most important function we will ever have to face in our lives—how to be parents. Gerry knew it by instinct. I didn't have a clue.

A measure of our desperation can be seen in a pamphlet I was preparing for distribution to other aggrieved parents, who included most of Malibu:

I make my living writing, not child psychiatry. I'm pretty well versed in the infield-fly rule but the generation gap I leave to Dr. Spock.

But it occurs to me that the most beleaguered minority on the earth today is as unorganized and disarrayed as any defeated army—the ununited parents of America.

We are fighting an invisible army. And we are fighting it alone, in dark places, on his terrain, without allies, without communication, without supply lines—without hope.

The enemy, we all know, is dope. Pot, smack, speed, acid—call it what you will, it has successfully competed with us for our young. It has a more powerful hold on them than we ever had. It is a bridge through puberty for some. It is a trestle to hell for others.

Parents are without weapons because they are shackled by shame. We are told by the shrill voices of those who revel in disruption because of God-knows-what neuroses of their own that it is our fault—and maybe it is.

It doesn't matter whose fault it is. It doesn't matter whose fault an earthquake is. The thing is, what do you do about it?

Parents today seem to cower in the dark, waiting for the sound of a car driving home, listening for the sound of a voice, hoping it's not slurred, looking into the pupils of the eyes of loved ones, hoping they're not dilated.

We are without resources because we try to fight it alone, in silence, in darkness. We are locked in a cellar with a leopard. A cry for help is unthinkable. I mean, *let-the-neighbors-know?* Heaven forbid!

The trouble is, the neighbors *do* know. They have the same problem. If they don't, they will.

People who face a common foe have always banded together—allied themselves against a common tyrant. The world has changed today—but not that much.

Fathers can't seem to give their sons chores today—"chores" were done in concert on the farm. Father and son went out together to battle nature. Father goes to an office in a skyscraper, movie studio, a missile think-tank today. He doesn't bring in alfalfa, he brings in money.

Girls don't churn butter, pull taffy or cook for threshers, either.

Part of the kids' trouble is, they're bored. It's not the Bomb, the war in Vietnam, the ecology altogether—it's boredom.

But I—you, we—do not quarrel with their political or diplomatic grievances. That's their birthright. It's when they use that birthright to destroy themselves mentally and morally that we have a crisis.

The authorities are helpless to meet that crisis. Their "get tough" policies have eroded. School lectures on the evils of narcotics only seem to have titillated some into trying them, have made cynics of others. Mom and Pop trying to scare them with that old bogeyman story again.

We are at bay. We are besieged by our young—and we pretend we aren't.

We take action only when the police call. "We have your boy on a felony possession-for-sale rap," says the desk sergeant. The cat is out of the bag. Your problem is on page five. The world now has its eye to the keyhole. You are afraid they're secretly gloating.

No, they're not. Not unless they'd gloat if they found out you had bubonic plague. Today, you, tomorrow, the world.

The kids are allied against you without meaning to. *You* are authority. *You* are the one who wouldn't let them eat all the candy they wanted. On some silly pretext it would ruin their teeth. You are the one who wouldn't let them see *Easy Rider* or *Midnight Cowboy*. On the silly notion that an impressionable youngster might think that, if Peter Fonda does it, it must be all right. You are a control freak. "No one was ever ruined by a movie," insists the anticensorship group. Then, they go out and lobby against stars smoking on-screen.

Parents are portrayed on TV as well-meaning bumblers hopelessly behind the times, wrongfully inhibiting their children. Outlaws have been glorified in films since the first camera was turned in Hollywood. No good to tell your kids the Sundance Kid—or Billy the Kid—was a moronic, uneducated slob with an IQ a little higher than a dog and morals that would shame a female jackal. He wasn't romantic. He was just a cretin with a gun.

We fight the whole weight of an unwitting propaganda machine that, without meaning to, gets a message that decency, morality, self-denial are unexciting, unrewarding. Who wants to pull weeds if he can get a gun and go be Robert Redford or get a motorbike and be Dennis Hopper?

So, what do we do? Well, the first thing we do is what any army on the run does: It exchanges intelligence. It tries to correlate its defenses. It gives ground stubbornly. It harasses the enemy. It fights for time. It tries not to turn a defeat into a rout.

We have to try to establish some kind of communal pressure. Not to make the kids conform politically or socially. But to conform *morally.* "Conscience" is a scorned word—for those who scorn the abstract itself. "Conscience" here is not theology, it is a built-in mechanism in the human organism *for its own protection.*

Conscience—and societal obligation—is the first casualty of pot or dope or opium. Or any other intoxicant. "Drop out" is the operative expression. Loss of conscience means loss of self-respect. Dirty feet, dirty hair, unkempt appearance, falling grades—you name it—personal hygienes are easy conquests once the main fortress of conscience has been breached. The rest is just a mop-up operation.

A Jesuitical argument? I don't think so. I'm not talking about the hereafter. I'm talking about *now.* I'm talking about kids destroyed in hellfire before they die. Before they've lived. I'm talking about parents in Purgatory before they've even sinned.

I don't have any pat answers. I just know I need help. We all do. People will band together proudly to save the environment. Well, aren't the kids part of the environment?"

I'm afraid my cry in the night didn't have much impact. I reprise it here only as an example of our desperation at the time of its writing. It didn't work. I don't remember why. You could get 'em marching in the streets to save the whales. It was just too hard to organize a march or committee against drug abuse. Nobody wants to look ridiculous.

The moral stance was hard to take. After all, we would rush home from work at night and, pulling off our ties, quickly build a double vodka martini. We looked hypocritical taking the high moral ground against pot.

Except that the illegal drugs accelerated the destruction. With the drug alcohol, overdosing took years, not minutes, to kill.

I don't know when our Rick joined the ranks of the damned, the chronic users. By the middle sixties one brother (Ted) was in the army in Germany, the other (Tony) was a student (and baseball player) at Berkeley.

Rick was an easy recruit. He was a musician. He had inherited his mother's uncanny ear and perfect pitch. He became a self-taught, marvelous guitar player. His idol was Jimi Hendrix. That should have told us something. We didn't know who Jimi Hendrix was. By the time we found out, it was too late.

It was the old, sad story. Classes skipped, grades falling.

There was a horrifying sidelight. On one of the calls from school, the counselor at Santa Monica High asked me to stay out of the picture. He had reason to think he had a better grasp of the problem.

I was happy to oblige. We were ready to try anything to save Rick.

But, then, a terrible event occurred. The counselor's own son, on an LSD trip, took a shotgun and shot and killed his younger sister as she was watching television one day. (The young man was later to immolate himself, climbing a telephone pole on Sunset Boulevard and setting a match to himself.)

Nobody had a grasp of the problem. Least of all, me.

It is an undeniable fact of life that being the offspring of a famous man is a hardship. But, for most of my family, notoriety came late. My oldest son was nearly fifteen before I became a columnist. And it took several years of writing before you could say I became an identifiable, permanent fixture in the L.A. celebrity scene.

Rick, of course, was only eight when I started the column. Pam was ten. You could say they grew up in its shadow. But, I can remember, my daughter had no clear idea of what I did for a living until, one day, when she was riding the school bus and listening to a local favorite disc jockey. The fellow, as disc jockeys are wont to do, took exception to something I had written. He let me have it.

Pam came home terribly upset. "Emperor Hull ranked on you on KMPC all morning, Dad! What did you do?!"

I used the kids in columns. Harmless stuff. Pam prancing through the house as she was trying out for Sergeantettes, Samohi's cheerleading corps, Little League stuff, a spoof column on returning from a vacation trip, usually titled "Mom Sez," and having myself put down for pomposities or ludicrousness on the trip.

It all went by too fast. One minute they were all in the back of the car, shiny-faced, on their way to Disneyland. In no time, they were growing moustaches, letting their hair grow, insisting on torn jeans to wear to school.

One minute, they're wanting to ride the Matterhorn or the Jungleland boat. The next, they're coming home on motorcycles.

I began to lose contact with my boys. I was bewildered, they were defiant.

But I don't think it dawned on us that Ricky was dabbling in the drug scene. Until the time we came home from a trip—which one is lost in the mists of time—and my wife found Rick mysteriously cultivating some plants out beyond the eucalyptus trees behind the house. Since Rick had always betrayed a minimal interest in horticulture, she was moved to investigate. Rick had, so to say, joined the Colombian cartel. Rick was growing marijuana.

Years of hell followed. We dreaded the sound of a phone ringing. It might be the police, a student counselor, a parent. Whoever it was, it was bad news.

I clung to the column like a life raft. I can't tell you the mornings I crept out to my office, which I had built with my Time, Inc., retirement money, to try to pen droll columns when my own life was a shambles.

But I had my column. Gerry had nothing. She had given her life to her children and now they were obliterating every dream she ever had for them—or her.

Because Ricky was a musician, his behavior seemed not only perfectly acceptable to him but even desirable. I mean, Jimi Hendrix did it, right? The Beatles' song "Lucy in the Sky with Diamonds" was code for "LSD" and their film *Yellow Submarine* was named for an LSD pill. Would the Beatles mislead you?

He was right in one respect. Our troubadours were the leaders of youth. What they said was important. Ricky yearned to join them. He wrote songs by the bushel, the organized and disbanded bands.

There was a lot of screaming. There was also a lot of crying. Rick was kicked out of the house. Then he was brought back. We tried reason, we tried threats. I took him to a psychiatrist, a Dr. Mack, recommended by my lawyer, Paul Caruso. Ricky thought it was a lark. The psychiatrist concluded my fears were not groundless but not that menacing. Ricky was "just a vagabond, a nomad," he told me.

Rick had a certain cachet with his peers. Remember, he was an accomplished guitarist in an era when every redblooded boy in the country wanted to be one, too. Rick was sure his future lay in the concert business.

I made halfhearted attempts to help him—an interview with the music *meister* and TV producer Pierre Cossette, an audition at MCA.

I should have been more supportive. I didn't understand the music business and didn't have any faith in it. I was a Beethoven man myself.

On one of his periods out of the house, we were driving along a road in West L.A. and we saw our son sitting on a traffic island in the middle of the street playing a harmonica and hitching a ride. We made a quick U-turn and picked him up just as he was getting into a pickup truck.

When he got home, he soon began laying plans to go to England. After all, Jimi Hendrix was there, Mick Jagger. That was where it was at.

He went to England for a year. I heard from him mainly through a colleague of mine, Dudley Doust, with whom I had worked on *Sports Illustrated*, and who had since become a journalist on a London paper.

Apparently, England was not very hospitable to young, cheerful American wannabee musicians. Rick found getting a job impossible and he existed by "busking" (that is, playing for the subway crowds and passing the hat), and he roomed by "squatting" (that is, living in abandoned buildings).

Rick was in London for a year. I got a call from England one night. Rick wanted to come home. But he had lost the return portion of his plane ticket. I phoned my longtime Pan Am representative, a colleague of mine, and we arranged for Ricky to leave Blighty.

He didn't want to return to California, he wanted to sample life in New York. When he came back, he domiciled in the roughest section of the city—Avenue C in the Lower East Side. He sent for his brothers.

When I went to see them, I found them living in such squalor, I couldn't believe boys raised in Malibu could stay in it overnight. The spiral downward got dizzying.

I can still taste the bile of those years. Rick finally shook free of New York and came home but it was to a miasma of drug arrests, petty thefts (a six-pack of beer!) and related scuffles with the law. A job at the newspaper didn't help. It was a low-paying pressroom job, owing to Rick's dropout status, but within a few months, maybe a year, the pressroom boss was phoning me apologetically. He had to let my son go. He had taken to sleeping on the rec room tables, among other things.

Rick finally hit rock bottom and was sent to the county honor farm—for what drug-related offense I've forgotten. But his mother was relieved. At least, she knew where he was at night.

It was a long, melancholy ride out to Saugus where I went to visit but Rick stood it good-humoredly. He would delightedly tell me stories of the inmates, whom he found endlessly funny.

When he got out, he came home and we had a period of a few months of comparative peace. Then, he met Laurie.

Laurie was another drifter through the hallucinogenic world of L.A. in the seventies. In a way, she was the quintessential Valley girl. Her conversation was sprinkled with "likes," as in, "She goes, like, 'What do you mean?' and he goes, like, 'Well, it's all settled,' and she goes, 'Well, like I'm supposed to know, right?' " She was a waitress in the restaurant where Rick got a job as a cook.

They decided to set up housekeeping together. We assisted with bedding and furniture. It was not exactly Ozzie and Harriet but she appeared to adore Rick, whom she called Eric.

It didn't work. We never found out what happened, but Ricky was soon back on the move again. He lived in the San Fernando Valley section of Los Angeles in a succession of apartments, with an assortment of roommates. Laurie was, like, one of them from time to time.

Looking back, it was the classic Southern California tragedy in the making. But it didn't seem so at the time. We still clung to the dream there would be a turning point. Rick clung to the dream his music would be discovered. On that basis, his lifestyle made perfect sense to him. That it made none to us seemed irrelevant.

The last time I saw my youngest son, he had been picked up for fighting. Someone had insulted his "lady"—Laurie, I suppose. He came home and we dressed him in one of my suits for a hearing at the city attorney's office. We did not want him in his Woodstock wardrobe. It was okay with Ricky. Everything was okay with Ricky.

It was a very minor fracas. It didn't take long to quell the beef. In fact, I remember protesting to the city attorney that it seemed to me the other person was the one who should have been arrested for disturbing the peace or whatever the charge was. And the city attorney—a woman—turned to me sharply and said, "Mr. Murray, if you want this reopened, we can do that," and Ricky was pulling on my arm and laughing and saying, "Come on, let's go!" and, as we walked to the car I remember admitting that I had always told my family, "When you get in court just be sure you don't talk too much." And here I had come within a verb of talking too much.

A small thing, but it was probably our last shared moment. Rick drove me to a doctor's appointment and that night, after dinner, we drove him back to his apartment. We had our two-year-old granddaughter with us and I remember she was most unhappy to see her uncle leave. She wanted him to stay. Ricky laughed and waved good-bye and trudged into his apartment. He was carrying a sack with his clothes in it. That was the last we would see of our youngest son. He's just a picture on the wall today. He was still wearing my suit that night. He was buried in that suit.

On a Sunday two weeks later, when we came home from Las Vegas—I had gone there for a City of Hope banquet and an interview with prizefighter Gerry Cooney, who was readying a fight with Larry Holmes—we drove in the driveway and, as we did so, for some reason I glanced over to the front door and saw a card stuck in the knob. "Oh, there's a card there," I remember saying to my wife. "Someone's been here."

I picked up that card and it was the most terrible moment of my life. It was from a city policeman. It told me to call the coroner's office.

I still have that awful card. "Please contact the LA county coroner at 226-8001 re: case # 82-7193."

I shake as I write this. I do not want to re-create that terrible scene that afternoon in my mind. I remember the voice on the phone saying, "We've got your son down here in the morgue." And I remember saying, "Which son?"

It was Rick. Case # 82-7193 was our Rick. He was twenty-nine years old.

It had been a party. Drums beating, guitars strumming, girls laughing. Rick had laced his drinks with codeine and some other arcane chemical substance—what the druggies call "a load." He drank too much of it, went to bed—and never woke up.

His mother was inconsolable. The dreams were gone. The sight is seared in my mind of her running blindly into the bedroom, where the picture of her child was, throwing herself on the floor and weeping uncontrollably and saying over and over, "My baby! My baby! Not my baby!" He was that little boy in the picture with the stuffed toy.

Did she blame me? No. But I did.

I noticed something many years later going through some old pictures after Gerry's death. Gerry's eyes never smiled again. There are earlier pictures where her smile is bright and her eyes dance. Never after her son's death. The mouth may smile. The eyes are dead.

What had really happened we were never to know. Our son's blood alcohol level was .1, which is legal intoxication, but just barely, and hardly lethal. The substance the drinks were laced with apparently did the damage. We had taken Rick to Dr. Bob Woods that winter, primarily in the hope he would throw a scare into him. Dr. Woods warned Rick that his liver was at peril with mixing drinks and drugs but, so far as we know, the liver at that point was not sufficiently damaged to be life-threatening.

We went to a rehab clinic twice that summer, the first time to get our second son to treatment and the second time when we finally got him there. The professionals convinced us we were a dysfunctional family.

It was not hard to fix the blame. I was the dysfunction. My

wife was, by code name in therapy, the one who had to ?
"Super Spouse."

They let you have it in rehab. They are ruthless, merciless.
They have the courage of their textbooks.

Part of the problem was the famous-father syndrome. But it
was part paternal neglect. I had gone chasing my career, and, in
so doing, had lateraled off the main work of raising the kids to
my wife while I went after "success."

I plead guilty.

As relentless as they are in these rehab sessions, they do
throw you a sop. If the sins of your sons are your fault, a result
of your legacy, they also encourage you to blame your shortcom-
ings on *your* parents—or even ancestors. They lay the sins of the
parents back to *their* parents. Go back far enough and you can lay
the whole matter on Adam. It's no comfort.

There is a predisposition to addiction, they tell you. It is in
the genes. The sins of the fathers *are* visited on the sons. They
tell you to accept it. Their position seems to be, Guilt is good
for you.

That was 1982. A little more than six months later, Gerry
returned from a trip to see her sister in Seattle, and no sooner
was she home than she began to notice her handwriting trailed
off badly and her speech on occasion slurred.

We didn't think too much about it. We thought it was an
inner-ear disorder.

And then, one night, as we lay sleeping, she awakened.
"Hold my hand," she asked me. We held hands. We had done
that a lot in our grief over Ricky. But this time, she said quietly,
"I know I'm dying." In that moment, I knew it, too.

We went to my doctor, Gary Sugarman. He was immediately
suspicious. His suspicions were correct. The Cat scans showed brain
tumor. Cancer. Maybe the most terrible word in the language.

It had started in the colon, metastasized to the liver and the
brain. Inoperable in the brain but advisable to remove it from the
colon.

Thus began the most bittersweet year of my life.

The doctors thought it best to break the news to Gerry. She
had a year to live, they estimated.

She was bitter, disillusioned, at first. But, being Gerry, she
came to terms with it.

The year is a blur, a kaleidoscope of images. Gerry had no pain. She briefly had phlebitis after the colon surgery. She lost her hair to the chemotherapy. She got a wig. I cry when I think of it.

I found some notes I made on my return from the hospital that sad night she got the news. She began bitterly. "It isn't as if I'm leaving nirvana. It's been five years of hell. My baby son is dead, my other son is gone. Ricky was the only one who truly loved me.

"I don't want to leave my little granddaughter. What makes me sad is I'll never see our [desert] condo again."

Then her mood changed. She became defiant. "Wait! I'm going to play my piano again! We'll have some fun. I'm going to get in my red Seville and go down to the desert again."

We did. It's where the end came, really, at our desert condo.

We had driven down for the Hope Classic golf tournament. Gerry actually had driven as far as Colton.

The year had not gone badly. She was up, around. We had gone to the desert for our thirty-eighth wedding anniversary. We had invited her brother and sisters to our condo for the event. They all flew out. It was not a sad time. We sang the old songs, relived the old times. It was a good-bye—but we didn't know it then.

But as we went down the following January to Palm Desert, one night, Gerry had gotten out of bed without awakening me in the middle of the night to go to the bathroom.

I was awakened by a loud thud—and Gerry cried out. She had slipped and fallen. She had struck her head.

With both of us weeping, we got her back to bed. We didn't know it then but that blow to the head was, in the end, fatal.

The next day, her head began to throb. She took a pan from the kitchen and kept it in her hand to spit up in periodically. I had returned from an interview with a golfer to find her in pain and fearful. We made plans to leave the next day for the 140-mile drive. I knew it would be to the hospital. I didn't know she would never leave it.

The drive home was the longest of my life. She began to slip in and out of consciousness.

We got her to the hospital and she lapsed into a coma. She was to stay in it for three months.

Before we had left for the desert, her brain surgeon, Dr. Carton, had advised us that the chemotherapy was no longer having an effect on the cancer. But he said he had one more procedure—called a "shunt"—that he might use to relieve pressure on the brain.

After she had been months in the coma, I asked the doctors if performing that shunt might have some effect in restoring her to consciousness. They were reluctant to do it. They were divided on it. They suggested it might have adverse effects. She might be paralyzed, she might not be sane, she might die.

I told Dr. Sugarman that I knew that if Gerry were paralyzed, she could handle it. If she could sit up and see her family again, it would be enough for her. If she were demented, I could handle it. It would be my fault, my miscalculation.

If she died? Well, what was three months in a coma? We were not prolonging life, we were prolonging death. A fastidious lady all her life, Gerry would have *hated* being in a coma, reliant on too-busy nurses for her personal toilette. Gerry was a person who put on a matching skirt and blouse to go to the supermarket. She would not even wear shorts in a public place. She had insisted to me—and her family—all her life that, when she died, she did *not* want an open casket. She did not want anyone looking at her when she was dead. Here she was, helpless, unable even to perform little tasks of personal hygiene.

Miraculously, the operation seemed to work. Gerry awoke from her months-long coma. I went to the hospital the next day and here she was out at the nurses' station—which would have been as far as the moon twenty-four hours earlier—sitting in a wheelchair. She sat up, she talked. She knew everybody. She had no recent memory—if you left the room and two minutes later someone came in to ask if you had been there, she would say in all sincerity "No."

But Dr. Sugarman was optimistic. We would put her in the Thalians' Clinic, a facility put up for that very purpose, which would, we hoped, restore memory banks—and blanks.

We spread the glad word. We phoned distant relatives. My daughter dressed our granddaughter in her finest little dress and shoes and we brought her in and stood her on a chair for her grandmother to fill her eyes with.

It was a miracle.

And then, it wasn't.

She began to slip again. After a couple of days, I've forgotten how many—too few—she went back into a coma.

She died in April. On the same day her mother had died twenty-one years before.

We would have been married thirty-nine years that October. All those happy days, all those years before when L.A. had been such a happy place for us and the future was so full of promise were gone and done with.

The world was instantly a poorer place. A neighbor put it best. "She always came into a room like a sunrise," she wrote.

We buried her up on the side of a hill next to her son.

19

· ·

Some of My Best Friends Are . . .

R ace was a factor we lived with every day of our careers. We thought we had done with it when Jackie Robinson broke the "color barrier," as it came to be known, and integrated the next to last bastion of organized discrimination in sports.

The fact that it came eighty-three years after the signing of the Emancipation Proclamation was disgrace enough. But, once the barriers were down, we thought—wrongly—that race as an issue would go away.

There was nowhere in baseball's charter where Jim Crow was in power. It was an "unwritten" law and like all unwritten laws, it was no law at all. Branch Rickey encountered only token resistance in his decision to strike it from the game.

Actually, Bill Veeck had planned to challenge it five years before. He proposed to buy the Philadelphia Phillies and stock them with star players from the Negro Leagues beginning with the legend-in-his-own-time Satchel Paige, Josh Gibson and others. Pearl Harbor thwarted that move.

It's unclear how much Veeck's planned maneuver had its effect on the Dodgers' general manager, Branch Rickey. Veeck went away to war and when he came back (ultimately minus a leg from it) Rickey had beaten him to the punch.

Rickey, known indulgently to the Manhattan press as "the Mahatma," was, after all, the creator of the farm system as a supplier to big league baseball. He had a big jump on his competitors in this regard but, by the mid-forties, the rest of the game had caught up to him.

He saw a way to steal another march. There was one big farm system out there, untapped, untouched, a pool of super-skilled players, probably superior, in lots of instances, to the existing big league players. Rickey reached in and helped himself to the cream of them.

How much Rickey was motivated by altruism and how much by an irresistible temptation to steal another march on his contemporaries, we will never know. It is an unalterable fact that, when he dipped into the Negro Leagues, he made the Dodgers the Yankees of the National League. The pennants—and the profits—piled up.

Baseball wasn't even Jackie Robinson's best sport. The greatest all-around athlete I have ever seen, he played baseball on the interest of his talent, so to speak. He was a better football player, basketball player, track-and-field star.

A staple myth of the grand old game is that Jackie, under the urgings of Branch Rickey, learned to turn the other cheek to the racial slurs, the on-field insults, the badgering he was to subject himself to.

Anyone who knew Jackie Robinson knew he was no good at turning the other cheek. Jackie fought for his rights. Jackie had been raised in Pasadena, not some Alabama cotton patch. You insulted Jackie Robinson at your peril.

Rickey picked him because he was visual. He had a name. He was proud, intelligent. And what a competitor! Robinson was the most ferocious competitor on the field since Ty Cobb, and his drive was probably fueled by the same energy source—smoldering hatred. Cobb hated society because his mother had shot his father. Robinson hated it because it had put up with a social injustice for centuries.

You can measure a ballplayer's worth two ways: You can tote up his personal accomplishments—or you can count the pennants. If you do pennants, Babe Ruth or Joe DiMaggio—or Jackie Robinson—get the nod as history's most effective.

Robinson forced people to respect him, not to like him. Jackie didn't care whether you liked him or not. He just wanted to hold America to its promises. And he did.

In the long run, Joe Louis probably did more to minister to

group esteem among black people. He literally knocked the white Establishment kicking. But Jackie probably did more to get his fellow blacks to shuck the "Yassuh, boss" image than anyone up to that time.

Willie Mays did, too. By being a lovable, eternal boy. Willie left the sociology to others. Willie just concentrated on hitting the curve.

In the decades since Robinson, baseball's integration is taken for granted. It is sometimes a nonissue. But it surfaces from time to time where you least expect it. An Al Campanis takes to the air to spout a lot of nonsense about black capabilities—managing or general-managing a baseball team is probably the easiest thing to do in our society next to being a guard at a railroad crossing where two trains a week come through.

But the integration, astonishingly, has never become total. You would have thought by now there would be fast, permanent interracial friendships. That players of different colors would become cronies after years of dressing and playing and showering alongside each other.

If so, I have never observed it. Back in the days when players slept two to a room on the road, some clubs endeavored to hasten the mix by rooming blacks with whites. The facts of the matter are that neither the blacks nor whites were happy with this arrangement.

There are still some clubhouses where there seems to be two teams, one white, one black. Sometimes, there's a third: Spanish-speaking. On occasion, when teammates get in a barroom fracas or otherwise on a police blotter, you scan the resultant story and find the miscreants are either all white—or all black.

To be fair, often not even white players fraternize with white players, nor blacks with blacks. It is a misconception of the public that star athletes in a sport enjoy going about in tandem, enjoy each other's company.

Nothing could be further from the truth. It's a nice, Pollyannaish notion but great athletes are rivals, in competition with each other. They may have to share the spotlight with each other in public. They don't want to do it as well in private. It was a conceit of hosts and hostesses that it would be a nice gesture to invite Jack Nicklaus and Arnold Palmer to the same parties. It was a nice way to make them both uncomfortable.

So locker rooms don't make bosom buddies of anybody. Ruth and Gehrig didn't speak. The Oakland A's used to punch each other out in the clubhouse. Mays never was buddy-buddy with McCovey. Don Drysdale and Sandy Koufax were never One and One-A. Sometimes the only thing teammates had in common was the city name across their jerseys.

But I can think of no solid instance where a black player and a white player of any note became inseparable pals—à la Whitey Ford and Mickey Mantle.

It could, of course, be the nature of the game. Cronyism was never a big part of baseball, white or black.

There were some black players you interviewed who made you conscious of a smoldering, deep-rooted hostility. The Dodgers had a first baseman who was that way, Eddie Murray. On the other hand, they had a white player who was just as inhospitable, Kirk Gibson. You never knew whether it was because you were white—or because you were a newspaperman.

There were other black players you could talk to—and five minutes into the interview you could forget color completely. Ernie Banks comes to mind. Maury Wills. I never thought of Maury Wills as anything but a great shortstop.

Sometimes you didn't know what was going through the athlete's mind. Henry Aaron gave no hint for years of the oppression he felt as he neared Ruth's record. When he made it known in his autobiography, a lot of people who had interviewed him over the years were surprised at the depth of his resentment.

I used to receive reproachful letters from supporters of his chiding me for using Babe Ruth as a symbol for home run power in my similes and metaphors. I tried, not always successfully, to explain that a writer, writing in a restricted structure like a daily column, frequently strives for an instant one-word image. "Babe Ruth" struck that image. In the same way "Cadillac" used to evoke exactly the kind of mental picture you were striving for in descriptive journalism. Once, when I was the owner of a Chrysler Imperial, the dealer would frequently complain that I wouldn't use the name of his car in that context. In vain, I tried to tell him that "Chrysler" did not evoke the kind of instant image I was striving for. Neither, alas, did "Henry Aaron."

But, given the fact that cronyism between blacks and whites did not manifest itself, it probably should not be surprising,

though it is deplorable, that, forty-five years after Jackie Ro
there should have been no major black migration into the
offices (or even coaching lines) of major league baseball
good-old-boy network was alive and at work in the game. You
had an opening, you hired your old roomie or your old bar-crawl
buddy. Al Campanis never thought of that when he undertook,
clumsily and shockingly, to explain the color scheme of the executive suites of his game.

There used to be a well-defined fear that a quota system was
in force. The black player, the suspicion was, had to be twice as
good as a competing white player. If two players were of equal,
marginal ability, the white player got chosen.

This was to prove to be next to impossible to detect. Given
the win-at-any-cost philosophy that had invaded American sports,
a manager or an owner, bent on a pennant, would certainly never
leave unsigned any player he thought might help him to that end.
In fact, the California Angels let a baby-faced young white player
with a fast bat and a big following go with a shrug while they
attempted to sign a player from Atlanta who was not only non-
white but was under suspension for drug abuse at the time and
would have had to sit out the first month of the season. Wally
Joyner left but Otis Nixon declined the Angel offer anyway.

There may have been teams on which an unwritten quota system
was in effect, but the California Angels were not one of them.

Actually, there were some sports where the opposite was true.
In basketball, it was widely considered to be a liability to be
white. Your attributes were suspect. A movie was made with the
provocative title *White Men Can't Jump*. In the NBA, an inability
to jumpshoot was known in the locker rooms as "White Man's
Disease." When Larry Bird came up, he was so white you could
see through him and the Boston Celtics were able to sign him
because other general managers were skeptical that a white-on-
white kid from Indiana could hold his own with the blacktop
players at that level. When Isiah Thomas of the Detroit Pistons
relieved himself of the opinion that, "If Larry Bird weren't white,
he'd be recognized as a journeyman player," his own black teammates hooted at him.

The NBA proved conclusively that the sporting public would
accept an all-black team. A white man on a starting lineup became
an increasing rarity.

*　　*　　*

It is unlikely that, given the option, a multisport black athlete would choose baseball, anyway. If a black player could excel in any sport, he would choose basketball first and football second.

Baseball was just not enough of a showcase. By and large, the black athlete likes to perform with style and verve. Baseball inhibits that. The idol of the ghettos in the nineties is Air Jordan, not Ozzie Smith, even though his feats were extraordinary as exhibitions of dexterity and coordination. Everyone wants to be Peter Pan. The young black athlete wanted to be above the rim, not down in the dirt. Marginal white players in the NBA got signed only if they were big enough and tough enough to act as enforcers, traffic cops, bullies.

Al Campanis to the contrary, there is almost no sport the black can't excel in and usually outperform the whites in. This is because most sports are speed sports, including boxing. And there can be no doubt the black athlete can outspeed the white one. It happens too often to be coincidence.

I overreached myself one day in attempting to explain this phenomenon. There is no more sound position for dealing with this than total ignorance. My anthropology credentials are faint to invisible but I took the plunge in response to an NBC show on the black athlete.

Rather than try to paraphrase what I said, I will reprint my ramblings, which, as I say, were delivered from an unassailable position—complete ignorance.

> A few days ago NBC, which should have known better, presented a one-hour seminar-type TV program that undertook to show that blacks are better athletes than whites. Next week, presumably, they're going to have one to show that the earth is round and water is wet.
>
> But it's when they got into the reasons for blacks being superior that they got into water they couldn't tread. They brought in grave scientists to give learned discourses. And when they traced it to physiological racial differences, they raised the hackles on large segments of the population.
>
> Any sportswriter could have told them that would happen.
>
> You see, none of us like to be told we're different.

Even if the differences are advantageous. With the exception of a few Anglo-Saxon eccentrics who despise the rest of mankind, we're a conformist lot.

If we're good at something, we don't like to be told it's because we have this twitch muscle not given to the rest of human beings. It's like being able to see better because you've got three eyes.

Great athletes, like great musicians, of course, have some gift the rest of mankind doesn't. Sam Snead, the great golfer, is double-jointed. Ted Williams, in his prime, had the eyesight of a circling hawk. But those were hardly group legacies.

Do black athletes have some edge that accounts for their preponderance of representation in all sports they undertake? Well, of course they do. There's an old saying that, when a thing occurs once, it can be an accident. Twice, it can be a coincidence. But if it keeps happening, it's a trend.

The poor doctors on the network, a physiologist and an anthropologist who stuck their test tubes into this liquid dynamite of an issue, appeared on television to be politically and sociologically naive.

They seemed startled their innocent research could arouse such vehement passions, as when the Berkeley sociologist, Dr. Harry Edwards, with whom few dare to cross adjectives and prepositions, thundered that their study was racist. You learn never to cross points-of-view with Harry. He's bigger than you are. Also louder.

The scientists were not only naive, they were a little unscientific. To understand why *American* blacks were succeeding in such boggling numbers, they studied *West Africans*. Figure that one out.

It didn't take Harry Edwards long to point out—correctly—that American blacks are a long way genetically from any African blacks. The American black, like the American anything, is a mixture of races, cultures and pigments. Sherman's army has descendants in every ghetto in America, you can bet me. Edwards himself reminded that panel that he had great, great grandparents who were Irish. So do I but I never had a good jump shot.

Harry likes to think racism and segregation drove blacks into the one avenue open to them in a closed society—sports. They got good at them because they were desperate.

I can buy that. Up to a point. Deprivation is a powerful motivating force. So is hatred.

But I would like to offer my own theory of athletic supremacy.

Unweighted by any scientific gobbledygook, not bogged down by any documented research, even cluttered by facts, Murray's Law of Athletic Supremacy is beautiful in its simplicity, based on a longtime nonbalancing of the issues, a resolute refusal to entertain any other points of view. Charles Darwin, I'm not. I base my findings on that most incontrovertible of stances—total ignorance. Compared to me, Darwin was equivocal.

First of all, I don't think it is twitch muscles or long tendons or larger lungs or even that old standby, rhythms, that contrives to make African-Americans superior athletes.

In the second place, I have never been able to understand the convoluted scientific efforts to explain away the darker pigments in some human beings. To me, it is a simple matter of geography. The closer you get to the equator, the darker the skin.

I mean, aren't southern Italians darker than Swedes? Skin coloring is a function of climate. I will cling to this notion until a blond, blue-eyed baby is born to natives in Zimbabwe or a black-skinned child emerges in Scandinavia.

I am absolutely positive that it you put a colony of Irishmen in the Sudan in, say, 5000 B.C. their descendants would be black today. If you had put a Sudanese population in Dublin in 5000 B.C., their descendants would have red hair.

Now we come to athletic prowess. Murray's Law is simple: Athletic prowess is bestowed on that part of the population that is closer to the soil, deals with a harshness of existence, asks no quarter of life and gets none.

Nothing in my business, journalism, makes me laugh louder than to pick up a paper and find some story marveling, wide-eyed, at how some deprived youngster from a tarpaper shack in Arkansas, one of twenty-six children, rose to become heavyweight champion of the world, or all-world center in the NBA, or home run champion or Super Bowl quarterback. Well, of course, he did. That's dog-bites-man stuff.

A much bigger, more astonishing story would be if a youngster came out of silk-sheets, chauffeur-to-school, governess-at-home atmosphere in the mansions of Long Island to become heavyweight champion of the world or even left fielder for the Yankees.

You always get great athletes from the bottom of the economic barrel. That goes back to the days of ancient

Rome, when the gladiators were all slaves (later, Christians, and we all know the early Christians were the poor).

In this country, the lineups of professional teams were always filled with the names of farm boys or the sons of the waves of immigrants who came over here from the farmlands of Ireland or Germany, or Italy or Poland. How do you think Shoeless Joe Jackson got his nickname? Why do you think he couldn't read or write?

The African-Americans are simply taking up where the Irish-Americans, German-Americans, Jewish-Americans, Italian-Americans and the homegrown farm boys left off. Like their predecessors, they come from a long line of people who worked long, hot hours in the sun, growing grapes, chopping cotton, cutting cane. This makes the belly hard, the muscles rippling, the will stubborn, but accustomed to hardship. This is the edge the black athlete has. The same edge the boys from the cornfield, the boys who came from a long line of Bavarian stump-clearers, had in another era.

And what happened to them may happen to the American black. Already, as blacks migrate from the levees and cotton fields of the Old South, and get more than one generation away from it to the metropolises of the North and East and live their lives by radiators and soft beds and eat junk food instead of soul food, they are losing their places, increasingly, to the hardy breeds from Central America and the Caribbean. That's the way it goes.

Don't ask me to explain any of this. Trust me. I'm fresh out of test tubes. Don't burden me with facts. Or twitch muscles. As Harry Edwards and I could tell you, Irishmen don't have twitch muscles.

Well, I got away with it. No one showed up with a net and a white coat. No one said, "Right on!" either, although I did get a call from the great Jim Brown to say he thought it was, or had a chance to be, right.

The black players get sick of the widespread "they-do-it-all-with-twitch-muscles-or-longer-heel-bones-or-jutting-hips." Snapped Isiah Thomas once, "When [a white man] makes a great play, they say it's due to his thinking and his work habits. It's not the case for blacks. All we do is run and jump. We never practice or give a thought to how we play. It's like I came dribbling out of my mother's womb. It's like we're animals, lions and tigers, who run around wild in a jungle. This white guy on the other team who is supposed to be very slow, with little coordination, who can't jump, all of a sudden out of nowhere, jumps in, grabs the ball, leaps up in the air as he's falling out of bounds, looks over the court in the space of two or three seconds, picks out a player cutting for the basket and hits him with a picture-perfect pass to win the game. You tell me this white guy did that with no God-given talent?!"

Golf, to its shame, was the last sport to be integrated.

In other sports, the discrimination was "unwritten," just tacitly understood. In golf, it was written. The game, believe it or not, had a "Caucasians only" clause in it.

When the Brentwood Country Club in Los Angeles, a club whose membership was almost exclusively Jewish, was awarded the prestigious PGA tournament (one of the four "majors") in 1962, the attorney general for the state of California, Stanley Mosk, was apprised of that offending clause in the membership statutes and demanded blacks be allowed to play or he would enjoin the tournament out of California. It not only violated the U.S. Constitution, it violated California's. Either blacks played, or no one played.

I wrote a column applauding Mosk's ultimatum. I found a black golfer, Bill Spiller, who had been good enough to lead the opening round of an L.A. Open one year (it was one of the few "Opens" that was truly open) but had since been reduced to caddying and hustling because there were so few avenues open to black players.

The PGA remained fixed in the Pleistocene Age. They jerked the tournament to Aronomink in Philadelphia where they had stronger stomachs. Ironically, a South African, Gary Player, won. You can imagine how this played at the NAACP convention.

Stanley Mosk had his victory anyway. The PGA struck down the offending clause. (You wonder how much longer they would have been able to keep a "Caucasians only" clause in the light of the soon-to-be-endemic Japanese sponsorship of PGA tour events.)

Golf was not completely enlightened. Tournaments found a new way to keep the color scheme. They designated their tournaments "invitational." This meant they were not excluding anybody, they were just not inviting them.

Some of us took off on the Masters. This was a tournament

that had, almost in spite of itself, been elevated to the rank of "major," but its field was as hard to get into as the House of Lords. It was an exclusive club with a field so limited the same people kept trading golf championships. First, it was Hogan-Snead, Snead-Hogan, then it was Palmer-Nicklaus, Nicklaus-Palmer. Some in the field were octogenarians, others amateur players out of the Hamptons clubs in Long Island.

The Masters did invite select foreigners. One of them who got in on a pass, so to speak, Gary Player, won it.

When some of us had urged the Masters to open its doors to blacks, the operators of this prestigious event, Bobby Jones and Cliff Roberts, argued that blacks were not *specifically* barred. There were ways to get invited.

The ways were unrealistic for blacks. For instance, the first twenty-four places went to the players who had finished twenty-fourth or better in last year's Masters. How could you make that when you hadn't been eligible to play in last year's Masters? Former Masters champions had lifetime invitations. So did former British Open champions. U.S. Amateur champions. The Walker Cup team. Rich kids' tournaments. The first eight players in last year's PGA championship could make it. But before 1963, this could not be, by law, a black.

You had, really, only one shot. You could finish sixteenth or better in the U.S. Open. Jack Nicklaus in his prime was never a cinch to do that.

But when Gary Player won it, we pointed out he had been invited despite meeting none of the criteria. The unfairness of a South African winning it when native Americans couldn't get invited came in for a lot of my attention.

I had a suggestion. At the time, the crack American black golfer, Charlie Sifford, had won two tournaments. So it wasn't as if they would be inviting some passer-by or weekend player out of Cucamonga.

I thought it would be a nice gesture if the former champions, who met in a private dinner on the eve of the Masters every year, could vote and invite one player of their choosing. Any player they wished.

Why not Charlie Sifford, I wondered? It would serve to make

up to him and every black golfer for the years of unfair exclusion. Besides, he deserved it.

The suggestion fell on deaf ears. The former champions continued to do what they had always done—invite a crony who could not be expected to break 80.

But the campaign finally did have an effect. Too late to help Charlie Sifford, the Masters masters decreed that any golfer who won a tournament on the tour got into the Masters.

I like to think I had a part in that forward move. And a few years later, my friend Lee Elder became the first black to play in the Masters. He missed the cut—but that was to be expected. He had cameras stuck in his face from the day he arrived. He had no more chance to concentrate on golf than a guy going to the electric chair.

Golf has never completely joined this century, anyway. There are country clubs where not only are blacks not allowed, neither are Catholics nor Jews. It's too bad such a great game has to be played in such a stultifying atmosphere but it has been ever thus. Until comparatively recently in British history, not even golf professionals were allowed in the front doors of the clubs. They had to take the tradesmen's entrance along with everybody else who worked for a living.

Recently, men of good will thought they had found a way to drag golf clubs into the twentieth century. It came about as the PGA was about to stage its annual tournament at the club in Shoal Creek, Alabama. This time, it wasn't Stanley Mosk taking the tournament to task; it was a group that threatened to boycott the products advertised in the PGA telecast because the tournament was being played at a country club that excluded blacks.

This time, they couldn't move it to Aronomink. A crisis emerged as potential sponsors threatened to pull out rather than be perceived as lending their support to a bastion of bigotry.

The club hastily enrolled a black. The boycott was avoided. Men of good will exulted. They thought they had uncovered a formula to bring the rest of golf in line.

They hadn't. At the old Crosby tournament, the haughty Cypress Point Club extracted its course from the rota of courses where the Crosby successor, the AT&T, is played. They were glad of an excuse to get out.

The boycott threat was supposed to have whipped golf

courses in line from coast to coast. The thinking is t/
ancient, venerable golf courses are panting to have PG/
and even regular tour tournaments. They're not. The stu....
club, the less it wants them. Los Angeles Country Club, one of
the haughtiest this side of the Royal & Ancient in Scotland, could
have the U.S. Open anytime it wanted it. It won't have it. The
club actually had the U.S. Amateur some years ago and—in a
kind of trial run—it staged a U.S. Junior. They were horrified
when the public showed up in (ugh!) shorts and no shirts, smoked
cigars, which they littered the course with, and, in general,
showed little respect for the musty old place, actually looking in
the windows and disturbing the members dozing in front of their
cribbage games.

L.A. Country Club turned back the Amateur with a shudder.
This is the club that once not only blackballed Franklin Roosevelt's
son but kicked out the member who had proposed him! They
had a rule against actors' belonging, which ruled out Bing Crosby
even though he had an ancestor who came over on the *Mayflower*.
Victor Mature tried to get around it by saying he wasn't an actor—
and offered to bring in prints of his three latest films to prove it.

Sports reflects the society it's a part of. It can't heal generations of wrong by itself. Football never was overtly guilty of discrimination. Fritz Pollard played pro football in the dawn of the
sport. Few if any succeeded him but that was not by league fiat;
that was because, to play pro football, first you had to play college
football. When blacks made colleges in those days, their parents
didn't want them to waste time playing football.

Now, it seems, they don't want them to waste their time
studying.

Are blacks being exploited by football? There are two ways
to look at it. First of all, this is the only way some of them would
ever get to look at the inside of a book. Or the outside, maybe,
for that matter. They have a chance to get an education. Not a
good chance. But a better chance than they'd have back in the
'hood dealing.

20

· ·

Television—the Red Light District

W hen I first took my seat on the fifty-yard-line all those (forty) years ago, the Giants were in the Polo Grounds, the Dodgers were in Brooklyn and if the Japanese made cars no one knew about it. The Lakers were in Minneapolis, and if anyone had told you a major league baseball team in Oakland would have a payroll of $39 million a season, you would have looked around for his keepers.

Sports exploded before our very eyes. A new royalty sprang up in our midst. A new ruling class formed. As a people, we were supposed to abhor an aristocracy. Ours was to be the Century of the Common Man. No earls and archdukes and baronesses for us. We didn't even wear old school ties. We were a nation of working stiffs and proud of it.

Sports changed all that. Television changed all that. We became addicted to the little glass box. It became reality for us.

The nation went sports mad. The new upper class went directly from peasant to penthouse not only in the same generation but overnight.

The new peerage were dunk shot artists, home run hitters, quarterbacks, putters, tennists. Cities vied to build them palatial places to play in at costs whole cities used to be built for including bridges and subways, outlays that would have once built railroads from sea to sea.

We had to have it. Woe to the politician who could be perceived as denying us our daily rations, our fixes of sports. The electorate wanted home teams, not hospitals, pennants, not policemen. They wanted to bask in the reflected esteem of a home team. By 1990, there were only three major league baseball parks left that had been there in 1960.

Television fueled the trend till it became orgiastic. Sports were the last—the only—spontaneous entertainment on the air. Everything else came out of a cassette. Everything else was scripted. Sporting events were the last melodramas. Even national elections were predictable on the basis of early returns. You had a winner in the first inning, so to speak—hell! at the kickoff. Only wars, floods—and ballgames—had any suspense left.

Sports stars became mythic. They occupied the place the knights errant did in Arthurian England. They were larger than life, richer than Croesus. They drew the adulation movie stars did a generation before. No czar, no Caesar, king or president ever commanded the obeisance from the public they did.

How big did they get? Well, Michael Jordan, a guard for a professional basketball team, the Chicago Bulls, passed up an invitation to the White House in 1991 because he was too busy with more important things—like making a few million more dollars selling shoes, soft drinks, cars or fast-food menus. Actually, he also wanted to play golf. If the president of the United States wanted to see him, let him buy a ticket.

Television, the yawning maw that chewed up talent, novelty, news, history like a mindless, grazing shark, gobbled sports whole. The ante went up—and up and up. Television seemed to be shoveling money at the gamesmen off the back of full trucks.

The numbers boggled the mind. They insulted the senses. It became hard to believe Babe Ruth only made $80,000 a year in his heyday, Joe DiMaggio only $100,000, Lou Gehrig, less than $50,000. Pete Rose, after piling up his first two thousand hits, publicly expressed the hope he might become the first $100,000 "singles hitter." Within a decade, he was making $3.5 million for hitting singles.

When a basketball player becomes bigger than the president of the United States, something is dangerously out of whack. The marriage of television and sports might have been a match made in hell. It may have distorted an age. It may have distorted a country.

Only a small percentage of any sports-playing community hit the big time, the big money. That didn't deter the rest from dreaming—the 99 percent who didn't make it into nirvana. Not every kid could run the hundred in 9.3, not every kid could swish in a three-point basket, hit a home run off Dwight Gooden, star in the Notre Dame backfield, win a heavyweight, or even welter-weight, championship.

But they all thought they could. What was worse, some coaches thought they could. It's impossible to assess the number of wannabees who got as far as being offered a scholarship, which signified to them their future was assured. Ahead were the new Mercedes, condos in Florida, golf in the Bahamas. Their development stopped. Without a ball in their hands, they had no idea how to go about life.

For the ones who made it, the senses reeled. Pugilists brought up in tarpaper shacks with dirt floors, south-of-the-border pitchers, suddenly lived in bigger houses than George Washington ever slept in.

A lot of it was madness. A heavyweight fighter was the only athlete who commanded exactly what he got paid. He sold tickets for his cut. He bled and suffered for the gate receipts. Everything else was subsidized by the Great God Television to one extent or another. No one could really measure the right worth of a right fielder or a right guard. They got a million because the whole succeeded and the parts were thus deemed indispensable.

Baseball as an industry seemed particularly manic. The Pittsburgh Pirates, blaming what it totted up as $13 million in losses in two years, uncoupled two of its biggest stars, Bobby Bonilla and John Smiley, in order to cut $7 million from its payroll.

The Mets promptly signed Bobby Bonilla for $30 million. Minnesota grabbed Smiley for not much less.

Television laid out $1.5 billion for national broadcasting rights (unlike pro football teams, baseball teams retained local broadcast and telecast rights). Then they complained they lost $500 million on the deal.

It was estimated over half the teams operating in baseball lost money in 1991. A Japanese company had to bail out the franchise in Seattle. They paid $125 million for a franchise that had last sold for $57 million.

When expansion put two new franchises on the market for $91 million apiece (batteries or players not included), Baseball had no trouble finding investors.

Baseball owners cried poverty. Yet, when they went at selling their teams, they reaped inflated millions. The mania for collecting slopped over into teams. Financiers who should have known better bought teams at such high prices that they could not hope to recoup their investment in their lifetimes. They could have bought shipping lines, railroads, Manhattan real estate for what they paid for lineups of .230 hitters.

The union claimed the owners' projected losses were more the result of creative bookkeeping than honest deficits. But unions always claim that. The buggy whip makers union probably thought the owners were lying to them, too.

Anyway, the eager rich who kept buying teams played into the union's hands and supported the image of an industry that was crying "Wolf!" while licking its chops.

Not that baseball was the Sick Man of Sport anymore. Attendance topped out at a record 57 million in 1991 and the Toronto Blue Jays became the first baseball team ever to draw 4 million fans in a year. The Dodgers had become the first team in baseball history to draw more than 3 million fans and they did it regularly.

But the Dodgers were as cannily run as a poker hand by a riverboat gambler. Before the Dodgers, 2-million-fan seasons had been enjoyed only by the Yankees and the Cleveland Indians and Milwaukee Braves. Cleveland did it one year when Bill Veeck owned them and not only did he put on a promotion a night at the ballpark, but the team won its first pennant in twenty-eight years and only their second ever. The Milwaukee Braves in the height of their honeymoon after moving over from Boston hit 2 million for a while. But both Cleveland and Milwaukee soon turned back into pumpkins and the Braves even had to move to Atlanta to save their franchise. Their attendance slipped down into the low seven hundred thousands. The Dodgers could have drawn that many to batting practice.

Will sanity return to the grand old game? Not so long as there are bored rich people, tycoons who hanker for the recognition ownership of a sports franchise brings you. That is conspicuous consumption, which carries with it the cachet of belonging to a glamor world of headlines, sound bites, talk shows—the importance of being a Player, upper case, a part of the drama.

249

Tycoons used to be cut from a different cloth. J. Pierpont Morgan shunned the spotlight. He didn't want his neighbors to know what he did for a living, he didn't want the public to know what he looked like. Bankers used to communicate in code or under aliases. Not your modern financier. He wants to make the gossip columns, parade on the sidelines with his team carrying a parasol and doing the turkey trot. He wants to be, God help him, a Celebrity.

This has complicated the picture. Quite apart from what the franchise brings in, owners dip into the family coffers and come out with the cash for their ego trips. They like owning something there's only twenty-eight of in the world, never mind the cash flow, the projected accounts receivable or even the return on investment. They have certain perks. They can depreciate ballplayers faster than they could drill presses. But, most of all, they can write it off as the cost of fame.

Henry Huntington used to say, "The ownership of a fine library is the best and surest way to immortality." Well, the ownership of even a mediocre ballclub is the best and surest way to celebrity. George Steinbrenner used to make a very good living running ore boats on the Great Lakes. But that wouldn't put him in Liz Smith's column, get him the best table at Le Pavillon, that wouldn't get his picture in the better magazines. But ownership of the Yankees would.

Television, of course, underwrote the madness. At first, the networks ran the show. But gradually, a new word crept into the lexicon of show business and sports business: cable.

Broadcasting had been set on its path as an advertising medium early in the game. Shortly after its invention and application, some early entrepreneurs wanted to market the medium direct to the public. In other words, charge a fee for radio broadcasts.

The historians tell us it was General David Sarnoff himself, who had made his reputation as the operator of the telegraph system that relayed the plight of the *Titanic* to the world and who had risen in the Marconi company till it merged with Radio Corporation of America, who vetoed pay radio.

Sarnoff effectively blocked it and convinced the country the greatest good radio could do would be to move goods, to restrict its revenues to the advertising budgets of America's manufactories.

To a degree, Sarnoff was right. Radio sold toothpaste, miracle washday powders, soap, breakfast cereal, coffee, cars and cheese, to say nothing of cigars and cigarettes and razor blades.

When television came in, it started out as the same game. The networks and the advertisers were in charge. Sarnoff's legacy seemed in full flower. The national advertising budget rose to $3 billion in the sixties. But, while TV got a lion's share of that, it occurred to lots of people it was a piddling amount compared to what the medium could gross on direct sale to the public.

It began simply enough. The head of Zenith Television came out with a simplified system called Phonevision in which the viewer phoned the television source and put the programming on his phone bill.

Hollywood producers from C. B. DeMille to Darryl Zanuck hailed its existence. While they already sold their product directly to the customer via theaters, they could see the enormous potential of increasing their audience tenfold, of recouping the negative costs of a picture overnight with minimal distribution costs. You only had to bicycle a print over to a TV studio.

An ambitious program to install pay TV in California, called Subscription Television, was in place and ready to begin operations in the early sixties. The promoters had spent millions. Suddenly, a group was on the streets soliciting an initiative petition to put on the ballot a proposition banning the new form of TV.

In California, you can get anything put on the ballot if you have the funds to collect signatures. And there are firms that will guarantee you the signatures for a fee. They will put on the ballot any outrageous proposition from banning redheads from park concerts to licensing squirrels. An initiative banning pay television was child's play.

The ban-subscription-TV initiative got on the ballot and it won in a landslide. The money behind the kill came from movie exhibitors who feared pay TV would kill movie houses.

STV disbanded, took a grievous financial loss, wiped out a few sponsors. A year or so later, the state supreme court ruled the initiative ballot was unconstitutional, a restraint of trade and free enterprise. It was like licensing Buick to make motor cars only to give them away for Wheaties boxtops.

But the supreme court decision came too late to save the investors in STV. It was a shameful misuse of the democratic system but there was no one the burned investors could sue.

t was actually prizefighting that gave impetus to pay TV. The fight promoters bypassed the existing airways and managed to pipe their product directly onto theater screens. They charged as much as twenty dollars a head for selected fights—Rocky Marciano versus Archie Moore, for instance.

Their revenues made Dempsey-Carpentier, the first million-dollar gate, and Dempsey-Tunney, the first million-dollar payoff to a fighter (Tunney), look like giveaways.

It wasn't long before pay TV—or cable TV as it came to be known—proliferated. Heavyweight champions began to earn $30 million a fight. Giving $30 million to some of these thugs was like giving a machine gun to a baby, but that's another story.

The prizefighting experience sent a message to sports promoters, owners, general managers. They were virtually giving away their product by tying it to what advertisers could pay. The Dodgers' Walter O'Malley was an early and vociferous patron of pay TV.

Baseball decided early in the game to restrict its World Series to "free" TV. It, of course, wasn't "free" at all. Every time you bought a razor, you were paying for the World Series.

But Baseball's notion was, their World Series was a kind of public trust. To send it out with a price tag was to break faith with the Knothole Gangs or something. This didn't stop them from extracting the high dollar from sponsors, who, in turn, passed on the cost to the Knothole Gangs, but Baseball managed to feel good about itself and its public image.

There is little doubt that the event was selling itself short. In the earlier days, the Gillette razor blade company secured the rights to the games for one hundred thousand dollars, which was ridiculous.

But teams individually began to sign contracts with local cable outlets.

Cable was a factor. General Sarnoff's idea of the airwaves being used solely to move goods fell by the wayside. The government removed restriction on TV commercials (there used to be a law restricting them to a percentage of each half-hour of television). Deregulation brought the networks revenue but lost them customers. You had some fifty other dial settings for cable TV where in most cases (but not all) you could escape the all-pervasive commercials.

The effect of all this on the athlete was all too predictable. Overpaid, overadulated, athletes, like rock stars, began to think of themselves as the new high priests of our civilization. The incomprehensibility of someone getting paid $8 million a year for bouncing a ball up and down a hardwood court or standing in right field popping bubblegum all night never dawned on them. They must be worth it, else why would the man pay it to them? Everywhere they went, they were in demand. Lionized, even.

They certainly didn't need us anymore. We inkstained wretches—and our predecessors—had built these sports into the melodramatic happenings they were today. But the ballplayer of today (with some exceptions) felt no shard of responsibility to the past. Where a ballplayer of yesterday, making twenty thousand a year, might cultivate publicity in the notion that someday he would be out of baseball and about to open a restaurant or an insurance agency and could use the notoriety, the average successful ballplayer of today feels he has all the money he will ever need.

He doesn't, of course. But he totally fails to acknowledge the symbiotic relationship of the press and sports. TV, he tolerates—because he likes having his picture flashed back to the old hometown. But the papers he often doesn't read. Sometimes, he can't.

Where will it end? Or will it? Owners, periodically, try to put a check on their own rapacity. Basketball put a salary cap in. Why a union would ever agree to a salary cap boggles my mind. But there it is. Like the absence of pure free agency, it's meant to keep the rich from getting richer and keeping a league together. It's also to keep someone from offering Michael Jordan Rhode Island to play for him.

Baseball used to have a law that, wherever they paid a bonus of more than four thousand dollars, the recipient had to stay on the major league roster. The Dodgers could never option Sandy Koufax out to a minor league and it probably inhibited his maturity because they had paid him fourteen thousand dollars coming out of the University of Cincinnati.

This was meant to discourage outrageous bonus payments because no general manager wanted to sign a prospective young star and let him atrophy on the bench. The ploy never worked because no owner paid very much attention to it. They paid bonuses under the table, through a third party or out of secret funds. They turned into liars and cheaters and turned the athletes they signed into the same. Like some football coaches, they corrupted. They made cynics out of high school heroes. Then they made hypocrites out of them.

The sidebar to all this is—the fan doesn't care. Oh, he says he does. He deplores the massive doses of money settled on twenty-year-old athletes. He grumbles, protests. But he doesn't do the one thing that could right the situation tomorrow—stay home from the ballpark, turn off the TV (or turn it on to *Masterpiece Theatre*) when the ballgame comes on.

He goes to the ballpark. He can't wait to get in front of his TV. He has the veto power on this insanity but he doesn't exercise it. Without him, sports as we have come to know it couldn't exist. Somebody has to pay the freight. Somebody has to buy the cars, pay the cable, purchase seats.

He can't point a finger at George Steinbrenner. He can't boo Bobby Bonilla. He's responsible for them. He has the remote control right in his hands. He's paying for it ultimately, whether he knows it or not.

Doesn't matter. Like owners, coaches, managers, concessionaires, he wants a winner.

Of course, we knights of the keyboard bear some responsibility, too. We hold these guys up for public adoration. To be sure, we make them larger than life, more interesting than they sometimes are. We have a vested interest. We make these people interesting because the public will then want to read about them—to say nothing of wanting to go and watch them play.

Which came first, the chicken or the egg? Did the game make the writer? Or did the writer make the game? Would there be baseball as we know it without Ring Lardner, football without Grantland Rice, boxing without Damon Runyon? Would they have prospered without "The Manassa Mauler," "The Four Horseman," "The Sultan of Swat," "The Iron Horse," "The Yankee Clipper," "Stan the Man" or the other alliterations and apothegms of the press box? I don't think so. But I'm prejudiced.

Consider this: Television did its level best to make soccer (or international football) a popular sport. It couldn't. Why? Because you couldn't pick up the paper in the morning and see what the inside-right had for breakfast, find out whom he's dating or what his taste is in cars or check up on his escapades on Broadway.

There are other reasons for soccer's incapacity. For one thing, the suspense doesn't build. In football you have "And the Giants have the ball on the forty-yard-line, there are two minutes to play, it's first and ten and they need a touchdown to win! And Simms goes back to pass—it's complete on the thirty-three! Now, it's second and three and there is a minute and thirty-eight seconds to get in the end zone . . . !" And so on. There is dramatic progression.

In soccer, the ball is on the fifty-yard-line. Bang! It's down to the ten. Bang! It's back to the fifty-yard-line. Goals are infrequent and unanticipatable.

Another major drawback to the game—for Americans—is its absence of controversy. In American sports, arguments rage into the off-season. "Why dint he walk 'im?" "Why dint they try a field goal?" "Why dint they pass?" "Why dint he take the pitcher out?" "Why *did* he take the pitcher out?" "Why dint he bunt?" And so on. What do you say in soccer? "Why dint they kick a goal?"

Even so, I think the game's principal defect is the absence of urgent day-to-day coverage every other sport gets.

Pro basketball piddled around this country without noticeably electrifying anybody for years—until a new generation of sportswriters came on the scene fully briefed on the sport. The old-line sports editors scoffed at it as "round ball," "whistle ball" or an otherwise inferior athletic endeavor. They didn't deign to cover it. They really didn't know how. I remember the last story I did for *Sports Illustrated* was a diarylike trip with the Laker basketball team, "Ten Tall Men Take a Trip." So, when I took over the column, I was fully briefed on basketball as a sport. And I had it all to myself. No other columnist in town gave it so much as a look at the time. Papers didn't even staff it. Pro basketball was an orphan.

I helped it. It helped me. I remember once, as I was preparing to leave on a twelve-day trip with the Lakers, a colleague expostulated, "You can't write basketball for twelve days!" My response was, "I'm not going to write about basketball for twelve days. I'm going to write about people." And some of the most colorful characters in sports came in basketball trunks. Some named Magic, some named Wilt, Kareem and even Larry. Some we named "Mr. Clutch."

We embroidered sports. We expanded its dimensions. We made it, in some respects, a transcendental experience. Rare indeed was the person who said, "I don't follow sports." For many, it was all of life.

Does it get out of hand? To be sure. The silliness reached its apogee one day in June of 1992 in the *Charlotte Observer* where the following ad was placed:

"A three-trillion-dollar deficit.

"New holes in the ozone layer.

"Unemployment at an all-time high.

"The Hornets draft Alonzo Mourning.

"On balance, it's been a pretty good year."

On the bottom, the ad continued: "Congratulations to the Charlotte Hornets on drafting Alonzo Mourning."

The ad was the work of the Nike shoe company but it seemed to sum up the idiocy sports—and sportswriting and telecasting—spawned.

The late Art Rooney, the splendid owner of the Pittsburgh Steelers, used to ask his players, "What are you going to do when the red light goes out?" Meaning, "What do you do when television is no longer interested in you or your sport?"

The red light is not apt to go out now nor in the near future. Television is capable of saturating the market and cloying the viewer. But not even the all-sports network appears to have dulled the appetite of the All-American sports fan, for whom a new term has been invented—couch potato.

Will sports ever return to what it was? Not so long as that red light is on. Not so long as that long-running morality play— Us Against Them—is played out on camera with instant replay, pay-per-view, network and film-at-eleven. Sports is just corporate America in cleats. It should be listed on the Big Board. And it's the real opiate of the people.

21

. . . .

A *Final Word*

Well, it's been a grand ride. Fifty years on the 50-yard line. Ringside at The Greatest Show on Earth. American Sports. Barnum would be jealous.

It was Hamlet. It was East Lynne. It was a morality play. It was life in microcosm. It was a religion. There was no cult in the world like a busload of fans on their way to a home game. God was a 49er for a day. Or a Ram. Or a Met. The players were mythic. The fans were manic. They adored people they saw only through binoculars. Instead of saints, they hung pictures of ballplayers on the wall.

It was madness. But it was also fun. An athletic contest was The Great Escape for thousands. Millions. The mortgage is due? The job is in jeopardy? Forget it! We won in the ninth. Magic threw in a three at the buzzer! The Pack Is Back! Arnie eagled! Let's hear it for those Dogs! Hail to the Victors Valiant! Boola Boola! Sis boom bah!

The home team wins, the world's gonna be all right. Food tastes better. Wives look prettier. Works gets easier. Winning is the cure for everything.

You had to love the fans. They brought caring to a new dimension. The non-fan would look on disdainfully and mutter, "Get a life!" But they had a life. They not only had their heroes, they were their heroes. The athlete as surrogate could not be overestimated.

It was heady stuff writing for them. They were the ultimate captive audience. You could write a column starting "Sandy Koufax yesterday . . ." and two million readers would swear it was the greatest column ever written if you never wrote another word. If you wrote a column about whales in the Pacific, you'd better be good. If you wrote a column about Arnold Palmer, you didn't even need verbs in all the sentences.

The athletes needed the fans, the game needed the fans. And we needed the fans. They were as taken for granted as chlorophyll. But just as necessary.

I met many great men. Joe Louis comes to mind. I also met some buffoons—pick any tennis player. Well, not *any* tennis player. Just anyone whose name began with John or Ilie.

I never really figured out what made tennists such spoiled brats. I guess it's because of that—they *were* spoiled. Although they were not always themselves sons of riches, they were in a sport manned by them. Tennis was a sport invented by and for royalty. It was a monocle-and-diamond-tiara sport from its inception. It is a game best played by children. So it should not be surprising that it leads to cases of arrested development. All I know for sure is, if you write about it for two weeks in a row, the truck drivers stop reading you. They can take only so much of a sport where a shutout is called "love."

But, having said that, I must hasten to add that Rod Laver might be one of the four best athletes I have ever known in any sport.

Tennis is a funny sport. More than any other it is one in which you count on the opponent beating himself. They even have a word for it, "unforced error."

Laver didn't need it. Laver beat you anyway. You could play a perfect game and, in his prime, Laver would beat you.

You often feel any given tennis match can go either way. A nuance here, a mental lapse there, and the tide could turn. When Laver was "on," it didn't turn. There was an inevitability to it that could be produced by no other player I've seen, with the exception of Jack Kramer. Hitting a lob to Laver was like throwing a pork chop to a lion. You'd better cover up immediately.

Laver used to hit the ball so hard into the concrete over at the old L.A. Tennis Club that the ball would bounce clear over the second deck. You not only couldn't return it, you couldn't find it. It's where he got his nickname, "The Rocket."

Tennis was great theater, but it was a grueling sport to spectate. I always had the sense it was like pushing a rock up a hill with your nose. You couldn't rush it. It was draining if you rooted. Particularly in the days before the tie-breaker, when a Bobby Riggs or Bitsy Grant might make you go to 22–20. Your neck got sore watching—40 games just to win a set.

I liked all sports. But hockey was an enigma to me. I liked watching it, but I never knew what to ask those guys afterward. The usual stock questions—"What kind of pitch did you hit, Slugs?" "When did you think you could get open?"—didn't work on ice. What could you say—"Why didn't you put the puck in the net?"

Liking hockey was like liking caviar—an acquired taste. But hockey fans were as devoted as any. More defensive than many. They expected you to say "Hockey?!" when they confessed to a zest for the game as if you had caught them expressing a fondness for turnips.

It was hard to believe goaltenders had once (into the sixties!) played this game barefaced, without masks. A hockey puck is a misguided missile about the weight and density of a blackjack. It's no wonder goalies were among the more nervous elements of the population, given to bouts of depression, schizophrenia, and paranoia. It's a lonely life in the crease. There were no breathers for goaltenders. Their teammates changed "lines" and were only on the ice for a minute and a half at a time, but goalies were out there for the duration. They were the athletic equivalent of guys who defused bombs or put out oil-well fires for a living. I emphathized with them. I loved them.

Speaking of ice skating, I always admired the beauty of figure skating. When I came into the sport, it was scored 60 percent on "school figures," these precise scratchings of figure eights on the surface like a guy cutting diamonds. The freestyle portion used to count for only 40 percent of the total. It was boring. Joyless. The freestyle, on the other hand, was part Busby Berkeley and part speed skating. It was like keeping score on Swan Lake. It became the prettiest and most aesthetic of all sports.

The first time I ever covered the sport, the Nationals were at the old Polar Palace in Los Angeles. I was frustrated trying to find someone who would spell out the details of this esoteric endeavor. Everyone was too busy to help out. They hurried away from me till I finally found this pretty young lady standing by the rink and smiling. She was only too happy to help out, and we sat talking for an hour and a half about the sport. She explained it all in the minutest detail. As I left the building, I turned to a guard. "Who was that?" I asked him. "Tenley Albright," he told me.

She was only the world champion. She later became a renowned surgeon, I'm told. She was a great lady. I learned right then, the bigger they are, the harder they try to help you.

Every sport had something to recommend it. Football changed by the hour. Baseball changed by the century.

Most of the changes were built in to speed up play. Golfers were the biggest offenders in this regard, notorious for slow motion (although football came a close second). Golfers would hunch over a shot as if they were trying to get a long-distance call telling them to pack up and forget it.

I was less tolerant of efforts to speed up baseball. I don't know about the next guy, but I never went to a ball game in a hurry in my life. Baseball was to be savored. You allotted an afternoon or an evening to it. In fact, when we were young, we tried for doubleheaders.

Doubleheaders today are a lost art. They are scheduled only as makeups for rainouts or early-season weather postponements. The July 4th doubleheader used to be as big a part of America as Thanksgiving turkey (or pizza with everything). Seven hours at the ballpark was as close to Nirvana as a kid could get. You hated to see the final out.

I don't know when we got in such a hurry that everything had to be speeded up like one of those early jerky silent movies where the sprocket slipped.

In L.A., the citizenry took to going home in the seventh inning. Now, in lots of places the fans go home in the seventh inning of an 11–0 game, but Dodger Stadium would empty out at 1–1. We had a pool going that some night they might walk out on a no-hitter. Of course, they kept their radios turned to Vin Scully all the way home. Baseball is the last of radio sports—just as good on radio as on TV. Well, almost.

As for hurrying home? Well, what are the words to the game's anthem? "Buy me some peanuts and Cracker Jack/I don't care if I never get back"? Amen. If you're in a hurry, go to an airport.

Our predecessors spoke of the twenties as "The Golden Age

of Sport." Well, ours was at least platinum. We saw Ruth's reco
broken. Cobb's. We saw Nolan Ryan racking up *seven* no-hitte
I saw the wildest football game I have ever seen in 1974. Notre
Dame was ahead of USC, 24–0, with thirty seconds to play in the
half. They lost that game, 55–24, and there were twelve minutes
left to play when SC scored its fifty-fifth point. I have seen lots
of teams behind 24–0 at the half come back to win. But usually
by 27–24, or 31–27. Never by 55–24. I didn't think a team could
score that many points in a half even if the other team didn't
show up.

I never got bored. But I never rooted. If you root, you'll be in
a straitjacket by Mother's Day. But if I had a lead for a column
going in my mind and it required, say, Tommy John or Fernando
Valenzuela to do well that day, I rooted. I am a big fan of leads.

My profession underwent a sea change in the seventies. Watergate, of course, did it. Everyone hankered to be a Woodward or
Bernstein. Investigative reporters. It became fashionable to doubt
everybody's word, to find fault with everything that went on in
our country or our game. Everything was a cover-up.

It got way out of hand. You were up to your hips in negativism.
Everyone had the attitude, "They're not pulling the wool over
my eyes!" even when there was no wool there.

Sport had its corruption. But it wasn't that bad. It wasn't the
Savings and Loan business. Or Watergate.

I suppose its worst possible moment since the Black Sox scandal
of 1919 was the collusion episode. The arbitrator found the game's
owners had colluded in agreement not to sign any free agents.

They sure had. It was such a transparent ploy that it was, on
the face of it, evident skullduggery. All the same, I never felt it
could have been proven in a true court of law. That it took place,
there is no doubt. But lots of things take place in American juris-
prudence which can be obfuscated by clever-enough storefront
lawyers. I never felt there was a smoking gun (or a White House
tape) in the collusion caper. Baseball just threw its hand in and
took its punishment (over $200 million at last count). Baseball
never wanted to go into court for anything. It might lose its precious antitrust exemption.

Sport was a social wheel, a worldwide common denominator. It
was a nice, safe subject for conversation. You didn't have to reveal

much of yourself if you confined dialogue to whether Joe Montana (or Jack Nicklaus or Bjorn Borg or Michael Jordan) was the best ever, or how you thought the Cubs might do this year.

Baseball, in particular, was a generational thing. Fathers handed a love of baseball to sons who handed it to sons. It was the ultimate heirloom sport. A shared love. An inheritance.

More kids learned decimals and compound fractions computing batting averages, earned-run averages, or magic numbers in pennant races than they ever did out of a book.

Has sport served society well? I think so. The ancient Romans described the secret of successful rule as "Bread and Circuses."

I covered the Circus. I felt privileged to have done so. Some of the happiest hours of my life were spent in a press box. Sure, I helped keep the hype going, the calliope playing. I can live with that. It's what I am.

I would have made a lousy president.

Index